A HISTORY OF BRITAIN VOLUME THREE
PART 1: THE FATE OF EMPIRE

A HISTORY OF
BRITAIN

VOLUME 3 PART 1

THE FATE OF EMPIRE
1776–2000

Simon Schama

BBC
LARGE
PRINT

First published 2002
by
BBC Worldwide Limited
This Large Print edition published 2004
by
BBC Audiobooks Ltd
a subsidiary of BBC Worldwide Limited

ISBN 0 7540 5671 6

British Library Cataloguing in Publication Data available

Printed and bound in Great Britain by
Antony Rowe Ltd., Chippenham, Wiltshire

CONTENTS

And out you come at last with the sun behind you into the eastern sea. You speed up and tear the oily water louder and faster, sirroo, sirroo–swish–sirroo, and the hills of Kent—over which I once fled from the Christian teachings of Nicodemus Frapp—fall away on the right hand and Essex on the left. They fall away and vanish into blue haze; and the tall slow ships behind the tugs, scarce moving ships and wallowing sturdy tugs are all wrought of wet gold as one goes frothing by. They stand out bound on strange missions of life and death, to the killing of men in unfamiliar lands. And now behind us is blue mystery and the phantom flash of unseen lights, and presently even these are gone and I and my destroyer tear out to the unknown across a great grey space. We tear into the great spaces of the future and the turbines fall to talking in unfamiliar tongues. Out to the open we go, to windy freedom and trackless ways. Light after light goes down. England and the Kingdom, Britain and the Empire, the old prides and the old devotions, glide abeam, astern, sink down upon the horizon, pass—pass. The river passes—London passes, England passes …

H.G. WELLS, Tono-Bungay (1908)

the country houses will be turned into holiday camps, the Eton and Harrow match will be forgotten, but England will still be England, an everlasting animal stretching into the future and the past and, like all living things, having the power to change out of recognition and yet remain the same . . .

GEORGE ORWELL, *England Your England* (1941)

PREFACE

Readers in search of an exhaustive account of the careers of Sir Robert Peel or Reginald Maudling should put this book down right now. For, with this last volume of *A History of Britain*, it will be more than ever obvious that the cautionary indefinite article in the title is truly warranted, both in terms of the frankly interpretative reading of modern British history offered, and in the necessarily subjective judgements I have made about which themes to explore in most detail. As with the BBC2 television programmes, I have opted to concentrate on a smaller number of stories and arguments, but to treat them in detail rather than give equally cursory attention to everything bearing on the transformation of Britain into an industrial empire. As with the two previous volumes, this book gives space to many themes which could not be accommodated within the iron narrative discipline of the television hour. But even this does not mean there is any pretence at all to comprehensiveness. No one will be in any danger of confusing *The Fate of Empire* with a text book.

The last half of the 20th century is deliberately treated with essay-like breadth and looseness—partly, at least, because I have trouble treating any period contemporary with my own life as history at all (an illusion, no doubt, of the passing of years).As the title of this volume suggests, however, I have tried to do something not always ventured in histories of 19th- and 20th-century Britain: to bring together imperial and domestic history, trying at all times to look at the importance that India, in particular, had for Britain's expansive prosperity and power, and at the responsibility that the Raj had for India's and Ireland's plight.

New York, 2002

ACKNOWLEDGEMENTS

As the project *A History of Britain* entered its fourth year, I incurred even more debts to all the many colleagues, collaborators and friends. At BBC Worldwide it's been a pleasure to work with Sally Potter, Belinda Wilkinson and Claire Scott; many thanks also to Linda Blakemore and Esther Jagger, and to Olive Pearson, Vanessa Fletcher and John Parker.

At BBC Television I have been extraordinarily lucky to have been a member of a brilliant team dedicated to making *A History of Britain* something special in broadcasting as it has been in the lives of all of us who have been part of it: in particular Martin Davidson, Liz Hartford and Clare Beavan, without whom none of this would have happened in quite the way it did, or for that matter at all; the directors of the Victorian programmes, Jamie Muir and Martina Hall; our indestructible, imperturbable, incomparable genius behind the camera, Luke Cardiff, and our regulars on the crew, Patrick Acum, Patrick Lewis and Mike Sarah; thanks also to our Assistant Producers Helen Nixon, Ben Ledden and Adam Warner, and to Venita Singh Warner, Mark Walden-Mills, Georgia Moseley and Dani Barry for helping me get through the ups and downs of the shoot. Susan Harvey of BBC Factual invested her friendly genius in promoting the series. Laurence Rees, Glenwyn Benson and Jane Root have been such passionate champions of the project that I hope both the programmes and the book repay some of the debt owed to their enthusiasm and faith. Alan Yentob has, from beginning to end, been a warm-hearted supporter, accomplice and advocate. Greg Dyke's son (so he says) and Janice Hadlow both liked it, which is all that matters really. John Harle, our composer, has been a wonderful friend and gifted colleague without whose music the programmes would have lost an entire dimension.

I am grateful to those who read drafts of the chapters and made suggestions, helpful criticisms and/or encouraging noises on command, especially John Brewer, Jill Slotover, P. J. Marshall and John Styles; thanks also to Peter Davison, David Haycock, Suzanne Fagence Cooper and Peter Claus. My agents and dear friends, Michael Sissons and Rosemary Scoular, as well as James Gill and Sophie Laurimore, have had to put up with a lot, namely myself, in various states of hysteria, decomposition and tantrum, and have not only never flinched from the ugly job of getting me back on the rails, but have given every impression that it seemed worth it. I hope it still does. Terry Picucci kept me, literally, from getting bent out of shape and Alicia Hall has triumphed heroically over the day-after-tornado hell that was my office. Many friends have contributed to what cool I have managed to keep, especially Andrew Arends (through whom I became an hon. Crescit), Lily Brett, Tina Brown, David Rankin, Mindy Engel Friedman, Eliot Friedman, Jonathan and Phyllida Gili, Alison Dominitz, Geraldine Johnson, Nick Jose, Claire Roberts, Janet Maslin, Stella Tillyard and Leon Wieseltier. Augustus T. Box Sunshine has always been there.

Nearests and dearests always get the ritual dose

of gratitude for forbearance and support, but no family which has not endured a husband and father in two sets of simultaneous delirium—television and literary—quite knows the meaning of the term 'long-suffering'. For Ginny, Chloe and Gabriel, who have borne with all this and still given me unreasonable love, I return it with interest and with all my heart.

There is one old friend, Roy Porter, who, unhappily, will not be reading this book and giving it the benefit of his great-hearted, inordinately generous judgement. But if there was anyone to whose storytelling skills and human insight this volume owes any of its qualities it was Roy, to whose absence I will never quite be reconciled, and to whose memory it is dedicated.

In memoriam
Roy Porter (1946–2002)

CHAPTER 1

FORCES OF NATURE:
THE ROAD TO REVOLUTION?

While Britain was losing an empire it was finding itself. As redcoats were facing angry crowds and hostile militiamen in Massachusetts, Thomas Pennant, a Flintshire gentleman and naturalist, set off on his travels in rough Albion in search of that almost extinct species: the authentic natural-born Briton. Amidst the upland crags and chilly tarns of Merionedd, he thought he had discovered them: Britain's very own home-grown noble savages, the descendants of the earliest tribes, whose simplicity had survived, somehow, the onslaught of modern 'civilization'. At Llyn Irdinn he walked round two circles of standing stones, which he believed were undoubtedly the remains of 'druidical antiquities'. Nearby, he discovered the human equivalent, at the house of Evan Llwd, where Pennant was treated to hospitality 'in the style of an antient Briton' with 'potent beer to wash down the Coch yr Wdre or hung goat and the cheese compounded of the milk of cow and sheep. He likewise showed us the antient family cup made of a bull's scrotum in which large libation had been made in days of yore . . . Here they have lived for generations without bettering or lessening their income, without noisy fame, but without any of its embittering attendants.'

The harsh, rain-soaked countryside was full of such old British marvels, human and topographical.

1

At Penllyn lake Pennant found the hut of the nonagenarian Margaret Uch Evans, although its locally famous resident was off somewhere, perhaps shooting foxes. This was a bitter disappointment, for Margaret, he had heard, was a Welsh Diana, a Celtic Amazon: a prodigious huntress and fisher who, even in her 90s, 'rowed stoutly, was queen of the lake, fiddled excellently and knew all the old music, did not neglect the mechanic arts for she was a very good joiner'. She was also blacksmith, shoemaker, boat-builder, harp-maker, and well into her 70s had been 'the best wrestler in the country'.

Pennant became the specialist in documenting the remnants of ancient, outlandish, unpolished Britain: the wildcat and the ptarmigan; the mysterious, lichen-flecked megalith and the poor, tough people who lived among them. A few years after his 'excursion' into north Wales—and a year before James Boswell and Dr Johnson—he sailed through the Hebrides, taking with him Moses Griffith, his Welsh manservant and illustrator. There he beheld scenes that filled him, alternately, with melancholy and elation. The island people, like the shepherds of the Merionedd hills, were primitives, often dwelling in windowless hovels and surviving on oatmeal, milk and a little fish. Tens of thousands of them had been forced off their little farms in the 1760s and 1770s to make way for profitable herds of Blackface and Cheviot sheep. In desperation, many had made the Atlantic crossing as emigrants to the New World. Yet there were also little epiphanies: the sight of the herring boats at Barrisdale, 'a busy haunt of men and ships in this wild and romantic tract'; or the view from the top of Beinn-an-oir, the Golden Mountain, one of the (disconcertingly, three) Paps of Jura, which laid out for Pennant's exhilarated inspection the scattered pieces of outland Britain—the highland peaks all the way to Ben Lomond in the northeast; the isles of Colonsay and Oronsay in the western ocean; and, to the south, Islay and the distant hills of Antrim in Northern Ireland.

The result of all this clambering and trotting and sketching and jotting made Thomas Pennant the first great tour guide of a Britain still waiting to be fully explored by the domestic tourist. Five editions of his *A Tour in Scotland* (1772) appeared before 1790. But he was not the only author making a modest fame and fortune from the rediscovery, the redefinition, of the nation. In 1778, while His Majesty's forces were evacuating Philadelphia, and after Pennant's description of Wales had been published, it was joined by one of the first guides to the Lake District, written by Thomas West, a Scottish Jesuit living in Ulverston. West, like Pennant, was a scholar, much travelled through Europe. Tired of dragging bored milords through the beggar-infested Forum on their obligatory Grand Tour, he had returned and developed a second career, taking parties of intrepid and interested gentlemen and ladies through the lakes, cliffs and dales. Whether in person or through his guidebook, West would steer tourists to a successsion of visual stations, perfect for drinking in the British sublime.

The message that both Pennant and West had to deliver was simple, but revolutionary: come home. The British had wandered too much, too promiscuously, too greedily, from Mysore to

Naples. In forcing their native scenery to resemble Italy, tricked out with temples and statues and God knows what—or, just as bad, engineering it to resemble foreign paintings, so that they could stroll from the picture gallery to the picnic and not notice the difference—they had somehow lost touch with what made Britain Britain: its own unprettified landscape. By some miracle it had remained unspoiled in the remoter places of the islands, places thought too far, too ugly and too rude for polite excursions. But now the new turnpike roads had cut travel time to Chester or Edinburgh by half, so that the adventurous traveller could be whisked to the verge of sublime Britain—after which, it is true, simpler, rougher modes of transport such as the pony or the small ferryboat might have to suffice. And it was an unpleasant fact that exposure to the sublime meant being rained on a lot and being blown about by winds.

But it would all be worth it, Pennant and West implied, because a trip to the true Britain was not just a holiday; it was a tutorial in the recovery of national virtue. The British needed roughness because they had wallowed too long in vicious softness. Inspecting all those Roman ruins, they had doomed themselves to follow the notorious example of that empire's decay. Long before they had lost America, the Jeremiahs said, Britons had lost themselves. Old British virtues had surrendered to modern British vices. Liberty had been perverted by patronage; justice blinded by the unforgiving glare of money; country innocence contaminated by city fashion. The 'Ancient Constitution' that had kept the British free had degenerated into what its critics called 'Old

Corruption' or, more bestially, 'The Thing'. The triumphalists of empire had supposed that commercial robustness and Protestant plainness would immunize Britain from the usual laws of imperial decadence. But trade had become a euphemism for the crude gouging of revenue, enforced by British redcoats, or for the brutal traffic in African bodies. And God and history had inflicted their punishment at Saratoga and Yorktown.

The antidote to rot was horror. 'Horrid' was—along with 'bristling', 'shaggy' and 'precipitous'—one of the terms of choice in the promotional literature of Romantic British travel. At Falcon-Crag in Lakeland, West promised, 'an immense rock hangs over your head and upwards, a forest of broken pointed rocks, in a semicircular sweep towering inward, form[ing] the most horrid amphitheatre that ever eye beheld in the wild forms of convulsed nature.' At the Falls of Clyde, an obligatory stop on the itinerary of the British sublime, according to another gentleman travel writer, Thomas Newte, 'the great body of water, rushing with horrid fury seems to threaten destruction to the solid rocks that enrage it by their resistance. It boils up from the caverns which itself has formed as if it were vomited out of the lower region.' But these frightening experiences were not just perversely organized as holidays in hell; they were a spa for the sensations. The agitation of the senses was meant to shock the visitor out of the jaded appetite and torpor that was eating away the national fibre. The crystal waters of Cumbria, Cymru and Caledonia would be the cure for the diseases, moral as well as metabolical, of empire. In

5

the uplands, away from the noxious filth and polluted air of the metropolis, Britons would be able to breathe again. They would start a new life.

Everything was to be stood on its head. The forces of 'progress'—Romans, Plantagenets—were now to be thought of as the bringers of greed and brutish power. Contemplating the archaeology of defeat brought the traveller into communion with lost worlds of old British virtue, an antiquity that might actually serve as a template for the future. The stone circles and Iron Age terraces that bore the footprints of a Britain flattened by the Romans; the shattered Welsh forts blitzed by Edward I; the ruined abbeys dispossessed by Thomas Cromwell and then burned by Oliver Cromwell—all became invested with tragic eloquence. As early as 1740 the antiquarian William Stukeley's *Stonehenge: A Temple Restor'd to the British Druids* had argued that far from being the bloodthirsty barbarians described by Caesar, the Druids had actually been the descendants of one of the lost tribes of Israel, transplanted to Britain to create a new Promised Land, and had survived as the priestly guardians of an ancient and sophisticated culture. Their Celtic tongue was not just the original British language but the fountainhead of all non-Latin European languages.

Suddenly, being British was not the same as being English. Dolbadarn Castle, in the north Welsh fastness of Gwynedd, where Owain Goch, the son of the last independent Welsh prince, Llewellyn ab Gruffydd, took on the juggernaut army of Edward I, became a place of pilgrimage. Initially those who found their way there were Welsh antiquarians like Pennant, eager to reclaim

6

their patrimony as the 'original Britons', but soon enough Romantic English sympathizers followed. The shattered piles of masonry silhouetted against the dark sky were seen (and painted) as incomparably more 'feeling' than the brutally intact Plantagenet castles like Conwy and Harlech, called 'the magnificent badges of our subjection' by Pennant. Carrying their copies of Thomas Gray's epic poem, 'The Bard' (1757), reciting the last curses hurled at the oncoming king by the last blind poet to survive the Plantagenet extermination, Snowdonian thrill-seekers would peer into the ravines and shudder as they imagined the bard hurling himself headlong in a gesture of suicidal defiance. If they were very lucky they might be invited by the likes of Sir Watkin Williams Wynn to an eisteddfod, one of the gatherings at his country seat of Wynnstay in Denbighshire, featuring choirs and old, preferably blind, harpists like John Parry who would sing the tunes and lyrics of his forebears. From the mid-1750s a group of London Welsh calling themselves the Cymmrodorion met in taverns, and between rounds of strong ale, committed themselves to rescuing those epics and ballads from oblivion by writing them down and publishing them.

Wherever they looked, the Romantic enthusiasts of rough Britain believed, there were lessons to be learned that confounded the equation of cultivation with nobility. It was in the places furthest from corrupting fashion, in the heart of Britain's oldest landscapes—the landscapes which gave 'Capability' Brown nightmares—that truly modern marvels were to be beheld. In 1746 a builder called William Edwards had attempted to throw a single 140-foot stone bridge across the river Taff. After two collapses, by 1755 he had succeeded—no one quite knew how—and the bridge was still standing. By the late 1760s and 1770s, the Pontypridd was being compared in prose and verse eulogies to the Rialto in Venice as a 'monument of the strong, natural past and bold attempts of Antient Britain'.

William Edwards was an exemplar of this old-new Britain: a survivor from a rude world, but also a native *genius*. For now, that word was being used in both its ancient and modern sense, to mean someone who was rooted in a particular place *and* someone who was sublimely inspired. It followed, then, that a voyage of British discovery would have to happen as close as possible to the landscape that had protected and sheltered the true nature of Britain. And to do that Britons would first have to get off their high horse. It was only by direct contact with the earth of Britain that romantic tourists could expect to register, through their boots and in their bones, the deep, organic meaning of native allegiance. To be a patriot meant being a pedestrian.

Of course, the fashionable landscaped park had encouraged the estate-owner and his family to take a stroll along the rambling path, beside a serpentine pond or towards an Italianate pavilion, with the prospect of arriving at a poetic meditation, courtesy of Horace, Ovid or Pope. But the new walking was not just physically strenuous but morally, even politically, self-conscious. Picking up a stick, exiting the park, was a statement. In 1783 when John 'Walking' Stewart, the most prodigious of all the Romantic trampers, left India—where, in a 20-year career, he had served successively as East India Company writer, soldier and a minister of native princes—he was bidding farewell to empire in more than the territorial sense. He seems to have become a kind of Indo-Scottish *saddhu*, a holy walker, making his way through the sub-continent, across the Arabian desert and finally home via France and Spain. Before he set off again for Vienna and then the United States and Canada, 'Walking' Stewart became a minor celebrity—a fixture at Romantic suppers, and pointed out in St James's Park. The writer Thomas De Quincey, who knew him, was also in no doubt of the levelling implications of walking. When he calculated (a little dubiously) that William Wordsworth must have walked 185,000 miles, the figure was meant to advertise the poet's moral credentials—his down-to-earth understanding of ordinary people and places. At the height of the revolutionary crisis in France in 1793, during the reign of Terror, John Thelwall, the son of an impoverished silk mercer, who had become a radical lecturer and orator, would publish his eccentric verse and prose narrative of a walk around London and Kent, entitled *The Peripatetic* (1793)—a footsore glimpse of the lowly and the mighty.

Not everyone was ready for the sight of 'men of taste' taking to the roads. The first guide expressly written for the 'rambler' in the Lakes, complete with information on footpaths, and carrying the revolutionary implication that the landscape across which they tracked was a common patrimony (and not just the resort of beggars and footpads), would not appear until 1792. Some 10 years earlier, when the German pastor Karl Moritz walked through

9

southern England and the Midlands, he was constantly greeted with suspicion and disbelief. His host at Richmond 'could not sufficiently express his surprise' at Moritz's determination to walk to Oxford 'and still further' and when, on a June day, he became tired and sat down in the shade of a hedgerow to read his Milton, 'those who rode, or drove, past me, stared at me with astonishment, and made many significant gestures, as if they thought my head deranged'. The landlord of the Mitre at Oxford and his family made sure he had the clean linen that befitted a gentleman, but were bemused by his determination to walk. Had he not arrived in polite company, they admitted, he would never have been allowed across the threshold since 'any person undertaking so long a journey on foot, is sure to be looked upon . . . as either a beggar, or a vagabond, or . . . a rogue'.

Moritz presented himself as an innocent foreigner in a country evidently mad for speed, its citizens hurtling along the turnpike roads in carriages and on horses. Yet he also knew that walking made him, if not a democrat, then someone who openly and perversely rejoiced in his indifference to rank. It brought him into direct contact with the salt of the earth: a female chimney sweep and a philosophical saddler who recites Homer: the academy of the road. And it showed off the pedestrian as a new kind of man, a Man of Feeling. In that same year, 1782, he would finally have been able to get his hands on the work that rapidly became the Bible of thoughtful pedestrians, the *Confessions* (1782) of the French political philosopher Jean-Jacques Rousseau, and, as an appendix, the *Reveries of the Solitary Walker,* 10 disquisitions each in the form of a walk.

For Rousseau, a walk had always been away from, as much as towards, something. The *Confessions*—made available to the public through the good offices of an English friend and devotee, Brooke Boothby—recorded his first decisive illumination as he walked from Paris to Vincennes to see his then friend, the writer and philosopher Denis Diderot. Somewhere along that road it dawned on Rousseau, as he walked away from the city, that the entire values of the polite world were upside down. He had been taught to assume that progress consisted of a journey from nature to civilization, when that transformation had, in fact, been a terrible fall. Nature decreed equality; culture manufactured inequality. So liberty and happiness consisted not in replacing nature by culture, but in precisely the reverse. Towns, which imposed an obligation to conduct one's life according to the dictates of fashion, commerce and wit, were a web of vicious hypocrites and predators. Towns enslaved; the countryside—provided it too had not been infected with urban evils—liberated. Towns contaminated and sickened their inhabitants; the country cleansed and invigorated them. Rather than education assuming its mission to be the taming of children's natural instincts within the pen of cultivated arts and manners it ought to do precisely the opposite—preserving, for as long as possible, the innocence, artlessness, frankness and simplicity of those instincts. No books, then, before 12 at least; instead, romps in the fields, stories beneath the trees and lots of nature walks.

All of which made Rousseau's brief, dizzy stay

11

in London, in the winter of 1766, disconcerting to guest and host alike. He had come to England, on the warm invitation of the Scottish philosopher David Hume, because he had run out of asylums and because he had been reliably informed that the country was the sanctuary of liberty. In absolutist, Catholic France his writings had been burned by the public hangman. In his Calvinist native city of Geneva he had not fared much better, falling foul of the local oligarchy when he had rashly and publicly sided with challenges to their monopoly of power. For a brief period he had found an idyllic refuge, together with his mistress, Thérèse Levasseur, on the islet of St Pierre, near Bienne, where he went for botanizing walks or rowed a little boat. His last shelter was the estate of an English-naturalized Swiss, Rodolphe Vautravers, but the long arm of authority, in the shape of the Bishop of Berne's proscription for irreligion, caught up with him. Finally, he accepted Hume's invitation and travelled with him across the Channel.

It was not a pleasure trip. Rousseau arrived at Dover seasick, wet, tearful and cold. In London, where Hume attempted to introduce him to like-minded friends including the actor David Garrick, Prospective Men and Women of Feeling lined up to offer gushing admiration, tearfully sympathetic consolation, discreet applause. But although he came out of his shell enough to drink in the appreciation, and began to appear in his pseudo-'Armenian' peasant's costume of fur cap and tunic, it took no time at all before Rousseau's unique gift for alienating his well-wishers surfaced. When David Hume attempted to recommend him to

George III for a royal pension, it was perversely interpreted by Rousseau as a conspiracy. It probably didn't help when, to pre-empt Rousseau's excuse that babysitting his dog, Sultan, prevented him from going to the theatre in Drury Lane to meet the king, Hume locked the dog on the inside of the apartment, and, with Rousseau on the outside, insisted on taking him to the show. What Hume thought was a good-natured attempt to bring Rousseau a harmless degree of benign public attention was perceived by its intended beneficiary as a plot to subject him to 'enslavement' and ridicule. Rousseau even believed that Hume was the author of a hoax invitation from Frederick the Great urging him to come to Prussia. (The writer was actually Horace Walpole.) An ugly public row ensued. Hume himself began to realize, depressingly, that his guest was perhaps a little mad.

Escape to the country, in Rousseau's fevered mind, became virtually a matter of life or death. A house was found for him—where else?—in Wales. But there were delays in getting it ready, which of course further heated the philosopher's already seething suspicions about his hosts. Instead, he accepted the offer of a philanthropist, Richard Davenport, to vacate his country house at Wootton in Staffordshire, on the Derbyshire border and thus close to some of the loveliest scenery in England. Rousseau walked through Dovedale in his strange 'Armenian' costume where locals later remembered 'owd Ross Hall coming and going in his comical cap and ploddy gown and gathering his yerbs'. Occasionally, too, he would let himself be taken to Calwich Abbey where he met a group of local admirers and disciples, including Brooke Boothby, who were already committed to remaking themselves as Men and Women of Feeling (a novel by Henry Mackenzie, entitled *A Man of Feeling*, would be the best-seller of 1771).

Needless to say, it was not long before paranoia once again got the upper hand. With scant understanding of English, much less the kind spoken by the local servants, Rousseau became convinced they were saying wicked things about Thérèse and were putting cinders in their food. By the spring of 1767 he was back in France. But his cult of sensibility had put down deep roots among the sobbing and sighing classes of provincial England. Just 10 years later, the craziness had been forgotten and Rousseau's sojourn was remembered with the kind of veneration accorded to an apostolic mission. Something like a Derbyshire Enlightenment had come into being in which radical politics kept company with the cultivation of Feeling. A botanical society had been founded in the little cathedral town of Lichfield by Brooke Boothby and the polymath Erasmus Darwin, both of them luminaries of the circle centring on Anna Seward, the poet and essayist who held a salon at her residence in the Bishop's Palace. Unlike Rousseau himself, moreover, the Lichfield circle had no difficulty in reconciling the exhilaration of science with the cult of Nature. In Derbyshire they seemed to have the best of both, with the Peaks offering the breathtaking upland walks and deep caverns, as well as supplying the coal and iron to be mined from beneath the hills. The county's reputation as a place of exhilaration and mystery was such that in 1779 a play was staged at Drury

Lane called, without a trace of embarrassment, *The Wonders of Derbyshire*. It featured 21 sets painted by the scenic artist Philippe de Loutherbourg, depicting waterfalls, Marn and Matlock Tors, the Castleton caverns (both inside and out) and a 'Genius of the Peaks' who rose, mechanically, from 'haunts profound' to bestow his bounty on the locals.

Likewise the most successful Derbyshire artist, Joseph Wright, was equally at home painting the cliffs and gorges of the Peaks around Matlock or Richard Arkwright's mill at Cromford as if it were a romantically lit palace. It was Wright who supplied the definitive image of an English country gentleman, Brooke Boothby, made over into a Man of Feeling, not, as in a Gainsborough portrait, the imperious master of a landed estate, but folded into the greenery in the pensive, heavy-lidded attitude of a Jacobean poet. Boothby's dress is a studied advertisement for the new informality: the double-breasted frock coat and short waistcoat, left unbuttoned the better to expose the transparent sincerity of his heart; a silk cravat replaced by simple muslin. And where an earlier generation of gentlemen might have demonstrated their virtue by holding a copy of the Bible or volumes of the classics, Boothby holds the gospel of *his* generation with the single word 'Rousseau' just legible on the spine. Painted in 1781, the picture is not just a portrait but an advertisement of Boothby's role as the St Peter of the cult. For the book is surely *Rousseau, Juge de Jean-Jacques*, the confessionary autobiographical dialogue on which Rousseau had worked while he stayed in England. Five years earlier, in 1776, Boothby had travelled to Paris and

15

received the manuscript from the great man's own hands. Two years later Rousseau was dead, and the park at Ermenonville (inspired by Rousseau's ideas and where the philosopher spent his final days) was turned into a place of pilgrimage and memory for his cult. No wonder Boothby burned to spread the word.

The self-appointed task of all these disciples of the church of sensibility was not just to transform *themselves*, through pensive walks, into new Britons sympathetic to the sufferings of their fellows and ingenious in devising ways to relieve them. They were also resolved, through literature, education, philanthropy and their own personal example, to raise an entirely new generation reclaimed from the cruelty and corruption of fashionable society. In the midst of modern Albion, they would re-create the kind of ancient British innocence they had seen hanging on (although reduced to poverty-stricken subsistence) in the remote rocky north and west. In fact, what seemed to the cultivated man of the town to be the most miserable aspect of those societies—their weather-beaten coarseness—was precisely the kind of life that had to be instilled into coming generations if Britain were to be saved from degeneracy. The goal—however impossibly paradoxical on the face of it—was to preserve the instinctive freedom, playfulness and sincerity of the natural child into adulthood. The child, as Wordsworth would put it, would be 'father to the man'. If they succeeded, they would make the first generation of truly free compatriots: natural-born *and raised* Britons.

This, at any rate, was the task that another of the Lichfield Rousseau-ites, Thomas Day, set

16

himself. His mission would be as a father–teacher to a purer generation of Britons, who would respect nature—all of it, for Day had become an ecologist *avant la lettre,* who believed in the inter-connectedness of all created life and was therefore a vegetarian and an ardent foe of the then popular sports of cock-fighting and bull-baiting. Animals, he believed, just as much as humans, could be conditioned by kindness towards a life of gentle happiness. Would he want to treat all creatures with the same consideration, asked a sardonic lawyer friend, even spiders? Would he not want to kill *them*? 'No,' answered Day, 'I don't know that I have a right. Suppose that a superior being said to a companion—"Kill that lawyer." How should you like it? And a lawyer is more noxious to most people than a spider.'

Day set about making the perfect family for himself when, in 1769, he hand-picked, rather as if choosing puppies from a litter, two young girls as candidates for eventual wife and mother. His commitment was to raise them in line with Rousseau's principles, then to marry whichever turned out to be most suitable, and to provide the wherewithal for the other to be apprenticed. A 12-year-old blonde was taken from Shrewsbury orphanage and renamed Sabrina, a brunette from the London Foundling Hospital and given the name of the virtuous wife of Roman antiquity, Lucretia (overlooking that heroine's suicidal end). Not surprisingly to anyone except Thomas Day, the experiment did not turn out as planned. Whisked off to France to avoid the scandal of a grown man playing dubious godfather to two girls, Lucretia and Sabrina fought like hellcats with each other and with their mentor, even while he nursed them through smallpox and saved them from drowning in a boating accident on the Rhône. Brought back to England, Lucretia, condemned by her adoptive father as 'invincibly stupid', was apprenticed, as Day had promised, to a milliner, while Sabrina was taken to Lichfield where she suffered Day's often inhuman experiments—hot wax was poured on her arm to test her pain threshold, and guns loaded with blanks were fired near her head. Only when Day finally despaired of ever being able to turn her into his dream spouse did he pack her off to boarding school, an escape for which she was deeply grateful. She ended up married to a barrister.

Day, who awarded Jean-Jacques the title of 'the first of humankind', believed he knew exactly how Jean-Jacques felt, for he too had suffered from the spite of the fashionable. His origins were, like those of his spiritual mentor, undistinguished—he was the son of a well-to-do customs collector. But his heart had been smitten in 1770 by the daughter of an army major, on whom he had struggled to make any kind of impression. To improve his chances, Day had taken himself off to France for a drastic makeover: dancing masters, fencing teachers, tailors, fine wigs, even subjecting himself to the torture of a painful mechanical contraption designed to straighten out knock-knees. It was all to no avail. The object of all these efforts at personal enhancement took one look at the new Day and laughed even harder than she had at the old Day. Stung by his rejection, Day turned his back on the Quality. What did they know of sincerity, of the burning, beating heart? He eventually found an heiress to marry but salved his social conscience by inflicting a Jean-Jacques regime on her: no servants and no harpsichord, for he deemed it wicked to wallow in such luxuries 'while the poor want bread'.

None of these follies and disasters inhibited Thomas Day from imparting his wisdom about childhood in a three-volume novel, *The History of Sandford and Merton* (1783), which, as an extended parable of 'natural instruction' was almost as important in Britain as Rousseau's *Emile*. The book recounted the clash between the spoiled bully Tommy Merton and the quieter epitome of rustic virtue, Harry Sandford, who cries when he realizes he has inflicted pain on a cockchafer. Now deservedly forgotten except in university seminars on the sentimental novel, *Sandford and Merton* was a huge publishing success in its day. Reprinted 45 times after the initial appearance of the first volume in 1783, it was *the* book young parents read when they wanted to savour the victory of natural over unnatural childhood. As for Day himself, his peculiar life ended abruptly in September 1789 in his 42nd year, during an experiment to test his pet theories about taming horses with gentleness rather than breaking them. An unbroken colt he was riding failed to respond to the tender touch, and threw Day on his head.

The problem with Day's experiment, some of his friends might have told him, was that virtuous conditioning could only go so far. Perhaps the damage to Sabrina's and Lucretia's natures had already been done by the time that Day got to them, beginning with the contamination of their mother's milk. For it was another of Rousseau's

19

axioms that virtue began at the nursing nipple, from which moral as well as physical sustenance was imparted. Nothing was more harmful to the prospects of raising true children of nature than the habitual practice of farming babies out to wet-nurses who had no interest in their charges except that of commerce. Not surprisingly, babies from more ordinary families packed off to country women died in thousands. But if fashionable mothers could afford to see their infants better cared for, they had no means of knowing what kind of sustenance was being fed along with the breast milk. Who knew how many innocents had been poisoned and corrupted out of their true nature, from their nurseling months, by women whose milk was already tainted with drunkenness and sexual disease? Breast-feeding began to play a conspicuous role in sentimental novels, especially those where both men and women could be redeemed by recognizing the simple power of natural instinct. Men for whom the tantalizing glimpse of nipple was an invitation to lechery could be converted by watching the act of nursing. Women who had flaunted their decolletage, like the wicked wife in Samuel Richardson's novel *Sir Charles Grandison*, could advertise their conversion to virtue by making a spectacle of the same act. 'Never was a man in greater Rapture! . . .' the wife narrates: 'He threw himself at my feet, clasping me and the little varlet together in his arms. "Brute!" said I, "will you smother my Harriet? . . ." "Dear-est, dear-est, dear-est Lady G . . . Never, never, never saw I so delightful a sight!"'

Assuming newborns had been given the healthiest possible start to their lives through the gift of their mother's milk, the next task of parents of sensibility was to ensure that natural instincts were not prematurely crushed by too heavy a dose of either parental discipline or rote learning. In the older morality books animal spirit was by definition a sign of unchristian diabolical beastliness, Satan frolicking in his favourite playground: the soft and receptive bodies of the young. The first duty of parents wanting to save the souls of their offspring was to thrash this devilry, if necessary literally, out of their bodies. But if the connection between animals and humans was now regarded by the likes of Thomas Day as benevolent and not malevolent, and the resemblance to puppyish or kittenish animal play the sign, not of innate wickedness but of innocence, then it was important to preserve and nurture playfulness as the gentlest route to learning, even if the consequences might sometimes seem, to an older generation, shockingly anti-social.

A generation of frantically attentive and slap-shy parents was the result. Erasmus Darwin urged parents to follow his example and 'never contradict children but to leave them their own master', and was notorious for doing just that (with his own children). Even so flinty a father as Henry Fox, Lord Holland, paymaster-general in Whig governments, capitulated (after hearing endless Rousseau sermons from his wife, Lady Caroline Lennox) to the cult of play. The Foxes were a byword for indulging, not to say grovelling before, the sensibilities of their children. When his son, the future Whig leader Charles James, hurled a brand-new watch to the floor, his helpless papa merely managed a pained smile and muttered, 'If you must, I suppose you must.' On that topic of perennial inter-generational conflict, the length of hair, Fox virtually petitioned his older boy, Stephen: 'You gave me hopes that if I desired it you would cut it . . . I will dear Stephen be *obliged* if you will.'

Although there were plenty of books which still insisted on the strictly enforced moral policing of the young, rather than simply laying down the law to them, a new literature expressly written to be read *by* as well as *to* the young, and vividly illustrated, aimed to show through exemplary and cautionary stories what would befall those who took the right or wrong path. John Newbery, the entrepreneurial genius of children's books who published the tale of Dame Margery (otherwise known as Goody) Two-Shoes in this genre, also specialized in the sixpenny illustrated books that emphasized playful and practical learning. His bestseller, the first popular science book for children, *Tom Telescope* (1761), was the ancestor of all the 'do your own experiment' books, and aimed to make all kinds of knowledge, historical, geographical and mechanical, exciting as well as 'useful'.

One of Newbery's army of illustrators was someone who had himself, without any benefit of exposure to Rousseau, experienced precisely the kind of natural schooling supposed to make virtuous British patriots. Born in 1753 at Cherryburn House in the parish of Oringham in Northumberland, Thomas Bewick was the son of a farmer who also worked a colliery on his land. His family was, then, solid north country yeomanry, neither very rich nor very poor, but in any event many leagues away from the Derbyshire gentry who panted after Rousseau. Even so, he remembered in the lovely memoir written in the 1820s for his daughter, Bewick was spoiled rotten by his aunt Hannah who 'made me a great "pet". I was not to be "snubbed" (as it was called), do what I would; and, in consequence of my being thus suffered to have my own way, I was often scalded and burned.' At Mickley School, close by the colliery at Mickley Bank, Thomas was entrusted to the none too tender mercies of a local schoolmaster who, to judge by his enthusiasm with the switch, evidently had little time for the New Schooling. His punishment of choice was 'hugging' in which the little offender was mounted on the back of a 'stout boy'—rather like a mating frog—with his bottom bared for the flogging. When subjected to the ordeal, Thomas's reaction was to bite his mount in the neck, and when grabbed by the master, 'I rebelled, and broke his shins with my iron-hooped clogs, and ran off.'

Instead of being made to suffer for his revolt, Bewick compounded matters by playing truant 'every day, and amused myself making dams and swimming boats, in a small burn', joining his 'more obedient school-fellows' on their way home. The school of nature, then, became his real tutor— much like the childhood of William Wordsworth 20 years later on the other side of the Pennines. Even when Bewick was eventually obliged to learn fractions, decimals and Latin, he escaped from the dreary chores by filling every surface he could find—slates, books, and then, when he ran out of space, the flagstones of the floor at home, gravestones and even the floor of the church porch—with chalk drawings. His eye feasted greedily on images wherever he could find them, especially inn signs where the birds and beasts of Britain—bulls, horses, salmon—were gaudily displayed. To anyone with half an eye, it was obvious that Thomas had a precocious gift and—after he had chalked his way through every floor in the village—a friend finally supplied him with pen, ink, blackberry juice, a camel-hair brush and colours. His career as the first and greatest of all Britain's naturalist–illustrators, the British Audubon with a difference, had already begun. He painted scenes of the local woods and moors, and the beasts and birds that inhabited them, and got paid, though not very much, for hunting scenes—every hound 'faithfully delineated' on the walls of his neighbours' houses.

Two moments from his childhood years stood out in Bewick's memory as converting him from a rough and ready likely lad of the north into someone already feeling the pangs of sympathy for the rest of God's creation. The first was when he happened to catch a hare that was being coursed, and although he wrote that it had never crossed his mind for a minute that there was anything wrong or cruel about hunting, when he stood there with the warm, palpitating animal in his arms, and when 'the poor, terrified creature screamed out so piteously —like a child . . . I would have given anything to have saved its life.' Told to hand it over by a farmer, he did so—only to see the hare have one of its legs broken for fun and then made to set off again, limping, in order for the dogs to have theirs; 'from that day forward, I have ever wished that this poor, persecuted, innocent creature might escape with its life'. Bewick was too much a son of the British countryside to be against all hunting, especially where he considered the animals had a fair chance of giving the dogs and men a run for their money—badgers, for example, could fight back ferociously. But he hated gratuitous cruelty. When he knocked a bullfinch off its perch with a rock he took the bird in his hand, where it 'looked me piteously in the face; and, as I thought, could it have spoken, it would have asked me why I had taken away its life', and suffered another terrible pang of conscience, turning the dead bird over and over as he looked at its feathers. 'This was the last bird I killed,' he wrote, although he added, perhaps referring to all the stuffed birds he would use as models for his spectacular illustrations, many 'indeed, have been killed since on my account'.

Bewick was emphatically not a sentimentalist. He inspected the habits and habitats of the animal kingdom, and especially the combative, bustling universe of insects. Two centuries before the American sociobiologist Edmund O. Wilson, Bewick had already noticed that the colony of ants on Boat Hill, near Eltringham, formed a coherent social community 'as busily crowded as any among men leading to or from a great fair' and were so well organized that, when disturbed by a stick, they would quickly regroup and continue their business.

The social curiosity and compassion that, all through his long life, would remain one of Bewick's strongest qualities also drew him, when he was still young, towards ordinary people who had their own common, often awesomely encyclopedic knowledge of the world and its ways. One of them was an old pitman from the Bewicks' mine who had once rescued a fellow worker from a colliery accident; sitting on a stone bench, he showed Thomas the constellations in the sky. Another neighbour, Anthony Liddell, was remembered by Bewick as the 'village Hampden', the epitome of the no-nonsense free man of the village. He had memorized the works of the first-century Jewish historian Josephus and a lot of other history besides, and dressed as if he were some sort of feral person in old buckskin breeches and a doublet 'of the skin of some animal'. Liddell was articulate, stubborn and hot-tempered when it came to the subject of liberty and property, especially birds and fish, which, he insisted, God had provided for everyone, giving him the right to poach as freely as he wanted; for him, 'gaol had no terrors for he lived better there than he did at home'. But it was another of his father's pitmen, Johnny Chapman, who 'thought it no hardship' to work standing up to his waist in freezing cold, filthy water, who stayed in Bewick's mind as something like the ideal working-class stoical hero. He lived on milk, bread, potatoes and oatmeal; rambled, when he felt like it, in the open country or went off to Newcastle for some ale; and paid for his lodging by singing and telling jokes and stories in his broad Geordie dialect. When he got sick and old, Chapman, the innocent, was turned away from one parish after another as each attempted to offload its responsibility for poor relief. Living hand to mouth from odd jobs, 'he was found dead on the road between Morpeth and Newcastle'.

These, along with his open-air Northumbrian playground, were the scenes that lodged in Bewick's mind when he recollected his childhood;

26

and which in their gritty, black, sharply defined detail were translated into the extraordinary wood-engraved vignettes that punctuate the beginnings and ends of his bird and animal books. Between the plover and the waxwing, and in the guise of little morality tales, he smuggled in a portrait of an entire rural world—one a long way removed from the prettified illusions of ploughmen, shepherds and woodsmen who populated the Gainsboroughs on the walls of Palladian country houses. Bewick's country people do not pose in fetchingly ragged pastoral dress, nor are their babes in arms all apple-cheeked and dimpled. At the end of the Preface to Volume I of the *History of British Birds* (1804) a smartly dressed country gentleman, armed with a gun, points adamantly down the road to an old wanderer huddling against a stone wall for some shelter from the Northumbrian wind. The gentleman is not giving helpful directions. Between the black grouse and the red grouse a circle of men huddle strangely together, their backs to the beholder. They are watching cocks tear each other to pieces. Between the spoonbill and the crane, an old soldier with a wooden leg gnaws at a bone, watched by an equally hungry dog. Above him, just visible, is a grand country house. Bewick's country people break rocks by the side of the road; slurp gruel in a wretched garret; or hang themselves by the wayside. They are documents of a new kind of British politics: the politics of what contemporaries called 'social affection' and we would call sympathy: the assumption expressed in the novelist Laurence Sterne's sermon on philanthropy (based on the Good Samaritan) that 'there is something in our nature which engages us to take part in every accident to which man is subject'. Bewick carried *his* sympathy for the many 'accidents' befalling the poor of 18th-century Britain wherever he went. When, for example, he walked through the Highlands, unlike more sentimental tourists he saw immediately that the sweeping vistas and empty uplands that so delighted Romantic ramblers were actually the result of the mass clearance of crofters: the conversion of a country which had once supported families to a country supporting sheep.

Although there is nothing in the canon of illustrated natural history quite like Bewick's vignettes (Thomas Pennant's zoology, for example, was scrupulously confined to animal and bird classification), every so often an image of shocking clarity registers an exception to the visual platitudes of Happy Britannia: the country gentleman and family posed on a walk, or resting before their richly improved property. In 1769, for example, a retired officer with a restless moral conscience, Philip Thicknesse, wrote a horrifying account, accompanied with an equally horrifying print, of *Four Persons Found Starved to Death, at Datchworth*. Such things were not supposed to happen in Hertfordshire, in what were called the Home Circuits surrounding the capital.

But there were probably as many wretched people like the Datchworth victims in the south (especially the impoverished southwest of England) than in Bewick's Northumbria. For it was in southern England that the social results of 'rural improvement'—for good as well as for ill—were most dramatically apparent, especially in the lean years of the 1760s, when a succession of wheat harvest failures sent prices soaring and unleashed

28

food riots in the towns and cities all the way from London to Derbyshire. The oat-eating northern counties were for the moment in less distress. To the boosters of a rapidly modernizing countryside economy, like Arthur Young, whose *Six Weeks Tour through the Southern Counties of England and Wales* was published in 1769, after some of the worst harvests of the century, there was absolutely nothing to apologize for: 'Move your eyes whichever side you will and you will behold nothing but great riches and yet greater resources.' England's *truly* Glorious Revolution (he often used the word) had been achieved not with speeches and acts of parliament (unless they happened to be enclosures) but with turnips, seed drills and sainfoin. Manure moved him to rapture, to the point where he made a verb out of the noun 'dung'. Much as he appreciated the 'extensive views' engineered by the Marquis of Rockingham at his 2000-acre estate in Yorkshire, the very highest compliment he could bestow was to declare it 'amply dunged'. Drooling with excitement at 'one compost of which manure mixed with dung . . . was in so complete a state of corruption that it cut like butter and must undoubtedly be the richest manure in the world'. Let idle Romantics ruminate on the Druids as they crossed Salisbury Plain. All Young could think about was the criminal waste of so much good unenclosed land that might be fenced, divided and ploughed into profit.

To Young, sentimental hand-wringing about enclosures only betrayed ignorance of the basic facts of rural history and economy. Enclosures— taking the common land, or what was left of the open fields, previously worked cooperatively or in

29

divided strips—were a necessary condition of realizing the full productivity of farmland. And those strips and fields that the poets pined for had been incapable of supporting a peasantry that lacked the capital and—how Young bitterly regretted this—the knowledge to understand even the rudiments of modern farming: proper manuring, letting land lie fallow between crops, the use of seed drills and the like. Besides, although the process had admittedly speeded up in the 1760s, enclosures had been going on for centuries. Moreover, the tool employed to launch the new wave of enclosures, the private act of parliament, required the consent of four-fifths of landowners in any parish.

But not, the critics pointed out, with the consent of, or even consultation with the hundreds of thousands of smallholders and copyholders who had clung to little lots and patches of land on which they could eke out a living so long as they also had access to common grazing land for their animals. Now they were reduced to wage labourers. Young insisted that the booming market actually generated more, not less, work for the rural poor; that in their new circumstances they were much better off than when they had been attempting to make a living from inherently unviable scraps of land. Many of them did find work in local, rural manufactures, shopkeeping, or newly learned work like shoemaking. But newcomers to these trades would be competing with the already established, and some were reduced to finding casual, seasonal labour as ditch-diggers. Young complained bitterly that in Yorkshire such men earning as much as three or four shillings a day 'scarce ever work above three days a week but drink out the rest' and that the price of their labour was pushing up wages so much that 'labourers in winter [are] so saucy that they are forced to be almost bribed to thresh'.

It was not, in any case, enclosures that most distressed and angered the critics of Improvement. That dubious honour went to what was called 'engrossment': the replacement of many tenants by few, often the result of the incursion of 'new' commercial money into the high-price, high-rent land market. The economies of scale were said by Young and others to be another necessary condition for making the kind of investment that would bring about improved crop yields and better livestock, and thus enable the burgeoning population of Britain's cities to be fed. And they were probably right. But the casualty of the estate manager's relentless drive towards maximizing rents and profits was, so those same critics insisted, not just the countless numbers who now swelled the migrations to the towns—of America as well as Britain—but the collapse of an older, communally based way of life. In one of the great best-sellers of the 1760s (six editions in 10 years) Frances Brooke's *The History of Lady Julia Mandeville,* a 'Lord T' is upbraided for:

> pursuing a plan, which has drawn on him the curse of thousands, and made his estate a scene of desolation: his farms are in the hands of a few men, to whom the sons of the old tenants are either forced to be servants, or to leave the country to get their bread elsewhere. The village, large and once populous, is reduced to about eight families; a dreary silence reigns

over their deserted fields; the farm houses, once the seats of cheerful smiling industry, now useless, are falling in ruins around him; his tenants are merchants and engrossers, proud, lazy, luxurious, insolent, and spurning the hand which feeds them.

The complaints and laments were, of course, unrealistically nostalgic for a bucolic utopia of caring parsons, avuncular squires and humane magistrates that had never existed except as an imaginary counter-example to the iron laws of country property. But the wishful quality of this fantasy rural past did not prevent those who wept for its passing in verse and prose from rising to the most extraordinary eloquence in their protest, and from exercising an almost hypnotic influence on a generation yearning to respond to the call for social affection. The most powerful of all those verse polemics came from the prolific pen of Oliver Goldsmith, born in County Longford, Ireland, much travelled, often ruinously hard up, but finally in the 1760s arrived at metropolitan fame and fortune, and admitted to the select company of the Literary Club, along with Sir Joshua Reynolds, Dr Johnson and James Boswell. Goldsmith's earlier poem 'The Traveller' had already put in a poetic nutshell his retort to those who justified what was being done in the country by the fact that it was all perfectly legal and above board:

Each wanton judge new penal statutes draw
Laws grind the poor and rich men rule the law.

In 1769, a year before Thicknesse produced his

32

shocking image of starvation in Hertfordshire, Goldsmith published his long poem *The Deserted Village*, one of the greatest of all verse laments for the death of a dream hamlet—'sweet Auburn'.

> loveliest of the lawn,
>   Thy sports are fled and all thy charms withdrawn;
>   Amidst thy bowers, the tyrant's hand is seen,
>   And desolation saddens all thy green:
>   One only master grasps the whole domain,
>   And half a tillage stints thy smiling plain.

Goldsmith's couplets wander around the scenery of the dream, stopping at all the places and people that had made it a community. He visits the 'village preacher's modest mansion':

> The long-remember'd beggar was his guest,
>   Whose beard descending swept his aged breast;
>   The ruined spendthrift, now no longer proud,
>   Claimed kindred there and had his claims allowed;
>   The broken soldier, kindly bade to stay . . .

the schoolmaster and, not least, the inn where 'nut-brown draughts' were served, but which was much more than just an alehouse:

> Thither no more the peasant shall repair
>   To sweet oblivion of his daily care;
>   No more the farmer's news, the barber's tale,
>   No more the woodman's ballad shall prevail,
>   No more the smith his dusky brow shall clear,
>   Relax his ponderous strength and lean to hear;

The host himself no longer shall be found
Careful to see the mantling bliss go round;
Nor the coy maid, half willing to be pressed,
Shall kiss the cup to pass it to the rest.

Departing from his forlorn tour of the ghost world of 'Auburn', Goldsmith then turns to face the contemporary, commercial England that has engineered this desolation:

Ye friends to truth, ye statesmen, who survey
The rich man's joys increase, the poor's decay,
'Tis yours to judge, how wide the limits stand
Between a *splendid* and a *happy* land.
Proud swells the tide with loads of freighted ore,
And shouting Folly hails them from her shore;

. . . the man of wealth and pride
Takes up a space that many poor supplied;
Space for his lake, his park's extended bounds,
Space for his horses, equipage and hounds;
The robe that wraps his limbs in silken sloth
Has robbed the neighbouring fields of half their growth.

Justified or not, there is no question that Goldsmith's rhymed accusation had an immense influence on late 18th-century public opinion. It affected moralizing critics like Bewick and nostalgic Tories like Dr Johnson, both of whom mistrusted the concentration of economic and political power in the hands of the landowning oligarchs of England. The country came out of the fiery years of food riots, troop mobilizations and

34

hangings with its institutions intact but with its faith in the paternalism and even the moral legitimacy of the aristocracy, the judiciary, shaken. Only King George III himself, the first farmer of the country and manifestly a walking embodiment of the touted virtues of simplicity, honesty and sincerity, escaped the increasingly vocal criticism. The 1770s and 1780s saw the launching of any number of social crusades mobilized by determined, articulate pamphlet-writers, petitioners and sanctimonious trouble-makers. They took aim at particular evils, invariably and significantly described as 'unnatural': prison sentences for unmarried mothers (often made pregnant by debauched young and not-so-young gentlemen); the state of the prisons to which they, as well as debtors and common criminals, were sent; the indiscriminate application of the death penalty for trivial felonies. The plight of children—so often at the core of all the heart-tugging causes of the Romantic generation—was guaranteed to inspire pathos and fury from the growing constituency of social virtue, whether they were poor newborn infants given the virtual death sentence of being dispatched to one of the London wet nurses in the slums of St Giles's or St Clement Danes; African children torn from their families and villages, and herded on to the slave ships; or the 'climbing boys' sent up filthy, soot-caked chimneys to contract cancer of the scrotum and respiratory diseases before being got rid of at 12 or 14 as too big to do the job.

Common to all these crusades was their intense religious fervour. Most of the evangelists who burned to correct the evils of their age believed that the established Church had become too rich, too complacent, too aristocratic, to fulfil its Christian pastoral mission, and was part of the problem rather than an instrument for solving it. In response, the 1770s and 1780s saw the most extraordinary spiritual rebirth in Britain since the 17th century; a great flowering of dissenting faiths and Churches in which the Bible was read (as it had been by the radical sects of Oliver Cromwell's Commonwealth) as a proclamation of the doctrine of common humanity, and the gospel of compassion for the poor and downtrodden.

Not all of those Nonconformist Churches were necessarily radical. After all, true evangelicals, with their emphasis on mystical revelation, required surrender to its power. And John Wesley, the founder of Methodism, detested Unitarians and their rejection of the divinity of Christ, calling it 'poison'. But the intensity of his tirades was a backhanded compliment to the attraction of what could for the first time be called, without uttering an oxymoron, 'rational Christianity'. It was, in fact, hard to find a Unitarian preacher in the 1770s and 1780s who was *not* also a sharp critic of the social and political status quo. For men such as Joseph Priestley (better known to posterity as a scientist, one of the discoverers of oxygen) and the Welsh Dr Richard Price, Jesus was no longer to be thought of as the son of God but as the first of the reformers, an all round good egg and socially concerned citizen who, more than any other, had preached the indissoluble bonds of obligation tying the more fortunate to those less so.

'Am I not a Man and a Brother?' read the inscription on the famous anti-slavery ceramic medallion produced by Josiah Wedgwood's factory at Etruria in Staffordshire. And the new Churches of brotherhood under Christ preached their spiritualized civics using every means at their command: hymns; anthems; charismatic meetings at which the spirit of righteousness burst from their lungs; series of lectures; pamphlets and petitions to parliament; and, not least, the powerful medium of images, designed by artists who included William Blake and printed on every available surface—drinking goblets as well as paper. Each cause had its own particular story of infamy, repeated over and over as a rallying cry. The scandal of the slave ship *Zong*, when over 100 sick Africans were thrown overboard so that the master could collect on insurance, was used time and again to mobilize indignation against the so-called triangular trade—cheap manufactured goods from Britain to West Africa, that cargo then exchanged for slaves to the West Indies, in turn replaced by sugar and rum for the third leg back to Britain. The fresh converts thus recruited came from almost every class of society: reform-minded aristocrats as well as preachers, country gentlemen, lawyers, physicians and tradesmen—the same kind of broad church of the righteous, in fact, that had made the revolution of the 1640s. But this time it also conspicuously included men from the world of science and industry; very often they were the second generation of famous names, like Thomas Wedgwood, who felt they had to earn or even atone for their good fortune, and who wanted to distinguish it from money made from the trade in black humans. And among the congregations of the indignant were now counted completely new constituencies: well-read women, both genteel and middle class, and even domestic servants who were said to sit in the back rows of Dr Richard Price's meeting house on Newington Green in London.

That parliament needed reform was obvious. The electorate was actually 3 per cent smaller than it had been before the Civil War; there were rotten boroughs, like Old Sarum with an electorate of seven, which still returned a member. 'Placemen' bought their seats on the understanding that they would vote with the government; and the newly populous towns were grossly under-represented. But was the unreformed parliament beyond redemption? The first and most intensely felt complaint was the narrowness with which the Act of Toleration enacted in 1689 had been construed. The Dissenters wanted more than just to be allowed to worship; they wanted full civil equality —the abolition of the Test Acts, which denied them access to public office. (The Tory view was that Toleration had only been granted in the first place on condition that that was all that would be given.) But the reformers were forced to concede that there were occasions when 'Old Corruption' could be moved to act on their urgent appeals, especially when the issue was moral rather than political. In response to the campaign for climbing boys (which inspired Blake's poem 'The Chimney Sweeper', 1789), an act was passed in 1788 prohibiting the employment of children under the age of eight and sending them up a lit chimney. It also stipulated that they should be washed at least once a week. But the Act was largely unenforced, and for those people who were most concerned about the fate of the poor, it was not nearly enough. Attempts to reform poor relief based on the system adopted by the Berkshire parish of Speenhamland, which, in an effort to keep paupers from the workhouse, linked a wage supplement, funded from the parish rates, to the price of bread, depended entirely on the goodwill of local communities. To the critics, this was just sending the problem back to the consideration of those most likely to ignore it.

When Thomas Bewick began work as an engraver's apprentice in Newcastle, he smoked pipes and drank ale with well-read, articulate young men who had no hesitation in sounding off about the wicked indifference of the high and mighty. The most radical of all was the diminutive, pugnacious school-teacher Thomas Spence, whom Bewick described as 'one of the warmest philanthropists in the world. The happiness of mankind seemed with him to absorb every other consideration. He was of a cheerful disposition, warm in his attachment to his friends, and in his patriotism to his country; but he was violent against people whom he considered of an opposite character.' In the spirit of the Diggers of the 1650s, Spence had become convinced that all modern ills emanated from the original evil of ownership of land. He declaimed his communism at a debating society (one of thousands formed all around the provinces in this period, including some in London, expressly for women) that held its sessions in Spence's schoolroom on the Broad Garth. Although he evidently warmed to Spence's enthusiasm and to his 'sincere and honest' concern for the unfortunate, Bewick believed his ideas dangerously utopian, fit for some 'uninhabited country' but shockingly wrong in presuming to 'take from people what is their own'. On one day the argument got over-heated and the two moved from angry words to cudgels. 'He did not know that I was a proficient in cudgel playing, and I soon found that he was very defective. After I had blackened the insides of his thighs and arms, he became quite outrageous and acted very unfairly, which obliged me to give him a severe beating.'

But while property for Bewick remained very definitely sacred, there was much else about the self-satisfaction of the ruling order that angered him. For those meeting and debating the present and several ills of the country at Swarley's Club in the Black Boy in Newcastle, or listening to the reverends John Horne Tooke, Richard Price or Joseph Priestley denounce 'Old Corruption', it was less the facts of the unreformed parliament that stuck in their craw than the fantastic and self-serving mythology by which this state of affairs was defended. Much as the modern fantasy of the well-ordered, benevolent country estate, with all its tenants and labourers toiling and tilling in the land of plenty, hid the ugly realities of rural poverty, so the endless recitation of how very fortunate Britons were to be living in the free-est, most wisely managed, just and prosperous of all states came to grate on the nerves of the manifestly unfortunate and unrepresented.

The window-dressing of power came in two versions: Tory and Whig. The Tory version categorically laid down as a divinely ordained truism that the 'people' had no claim whatsoever to determine the ordering of their government; and that their natural and proper state was obedience and submission to a benevolent monarch, the

40

Church and a parliament elected by those who, through their property and interest, had a right to be included in the electorate. The Whig version was that the Glorious Revolution of 1688 had been all that would ever be needed to secure the 'ancient constitution' against the threat of monarchical tyranny, and that the 'Revolution Settlement', with its enactment of toleration and its guarantee of parliaments (elected only every seven years), was enough of a shield for the liberties of the free-born Englishman.

But the centenary of that revolution—approaching in 1788—was an unavoidable occasion for looking long and hard at both those justifications of the status quo. Such a critical re-examination was made to seem more urgent by the failure of William Pitt the Younger, first in 1782 as a 22-year-old MP and then in 1785 as a 25-year-old prime minister, to secure even a modest measure of parliamentary self-reform; and by Pitt's active opposition, in 1788–9, to the repeal of the Test Act. Across the Atlantic, Tom Paine's *Common Sense* (1775) had already taken an axe to most of the status-quo assumptions by asserting the right, in fact the duty, of the Americans to resist in terms of a defence of natural rights (for the taxed to be represented and free from forced billeting of British soldiers). The American lesson had, of course, not gone unheeded on this side of the Atlantic, especially by those who had always been critics of the war recently fought there. In the 1780s, proselytizing organizations like the Society for the Promotion of Constitutional Information and the Westminster Association, who numbered among their members not just preachers, professionals and artisans but also the radical fringe of the Whigs (the 3rd Duke of Richmond, the 3rd Duke of Grafton and the playwright –politician Richard Brinsley Sheridan, who met at Holland House, home of their silver-tongued leader, that child of a permissive Rousseau-ite nursery, Charles James Fox), began to flirt with a potentially democratic justification of government, one that began with the right of the people to choose or change their own rulers. That right, moreover, was said to be rooted not just in nature but in history. According to that view all governments had originated with the unforced, voluntary agreement of the people to assign their authority to representatives (be they kings or parliaments) for the express purpose of protecting their freedom and security. This agreement had always been understood as a mutual contract. The people would give their allegiance only so long as the government to which they had provisionally entrusted the protection of their rights respected them. Should those same authorities be judged guilty of violating rather than upholding those natural rights, the sovereign people were at perfect liberty to remove them.

This was heady stuff: part regurgitation of old 'Commonwealthmen' doctrines left over from the radicals of the 17th century; part American republicanism with a dash of Rousseau added for extra force. But it was the essence of what a succession of speakers—James Burgh, Priestley, Price, Horne Tooke, Major John Cartwright—had to say to the discontented of the 1780s. That such opinions were far from being restricted to a tiny minority of agitators out of touch with the

42

mainstream is borne out by the astounding sales of their often indigestibly severe opinions. Richard Price, for example, sold 60,000 copies (the kind of figure surpassed only by Tom Paine) of his daunting *Observations on the Nature of Civil Liberty* (1776). The fact that many of these opinions had been aired before, not least by John Milton, was far from being a sign of weakness (as some modern historians have assumed) but actually the secret of its appeal. For the late 18th century was becoming obsessed with the British past, especially the 'Gothick' Middle Ages—not just its political history, but its architecture, dress, furniture and armour, all of which saw compendious and beautifully illustrated histories published. So when Alfred the Great, the wise, the strong, the good, was trotted out yet again (by the anti-slavery campaigner Granville Sharp, for example) as the paragon of a popular monarch who worked in benevolent mutual collaboration with that mother of all parliaments, the Anglo-Saxon Witenagemot, history was taken not as some obscure and arcane irrelevance but as the model of what truly native British government was supposed to look like. The sealing of Magna Carta, another mythical moment when 'the people' had, through their barons and burgesses, exercised their right to call a despot to account, was also celebrated as an episode pregnant with significance for the present and future. It was just at this time, moreover, that the militant vegetarian–antiquarian–tramper Joseph Ritson's researches into Robin Hood were recasting that legendary character as a romantic popular hero (with wood engravings by Thomas Bewick).

Since the 16th century, the '88s' had always been critical years for Britain and for the fate of the monarchy; each generation adopted the epic of the last '88' as a touchstone for the next. The supporters of William III in 1688 claimed to be the heirs of Elizabeth's resistance to Catholic tyranny in 1588, the year of the Armada. In 1688, the Catholic James II had taken leave of his throne; in 1788 George III (whom some critics had accused of aiming at a 'Stuart' absolutism) had taken leave of his senses. By the time he was restored to them, in 1789, the fate of monarchy had been transformed by the stupefying events taking place in France. And those who were celebrating the centenary of the Glorious Revolution naturally embraced this latest revolution as the logical consummation of what had happened 100 years before. Providence, they thought, worked to a meaningful calendar.

On the face of it, the position of the two kings on opposite sides of the Channel in 1789 could not have been more different. While Louis XVI was being dictated to by the National Assembly and suspected (rightly) of planning a military coup to regain his absolute authority, George III was recovering his grip both on his sanity and on the nation. At the same time that Louis was obliged to leave Versailles for Paris to put the best face on his predicament and pretend, at least, to fold himself in the tricolour of the Revolution, George went on a tour of the West Country to recuperate. Everywhere he went he was regaled with booming choruses of 'God Save the King'; at Weymouth, indeed, he was surprised, while taking the waters, by a small but evidently loyal band concealed in the next bathing machine.

But none of these noisy demonstrations of loyalty deterred the true believers in a great British alteration from thinking that, if the walls of the Bastille could be stormed by the people of Paris, a day of reckoning with Old Corruption was not far off. In 1785 Joseph Priestley earned himself the nickname of 'Gunpowder Joe' by comparing the work of the radicals to 'laying gunpowder, grain by grain under the old building of error and superstition which a single spark may hereafter inflame so as to produce an instantaneous explosion'. When the Bastille fell, they hoped that its spark might carry right across the Channel. Glasses were hoisted at Swarley's Tavern; in the Bishop's Palace at Lichfield; in aristocratic Holland House. Charles James Fox celebrated it as 'much the greatest event that has ever happened in the history of the world and how much the best'. Although it was awkward to have the French, jeered at for generations by Whigs and Tories alike as the hopeless lackeys of despotism, complete what had begun in 1688 as a British revolution, it was after all the Americans who had already made the point that the 'true' spirit of Liberty, although born in Britain, had evidently migrated elsewhere. The fact that it had now returned across the Atlantic with the French General Lafayette, who had fought so ardently for the Americans, was only proof that the irresistible urge for popular self-government was the indivisible natural right of all mankind.

Yet the unfortunate Frenchness of the event did, for all their higher feelings, make the 'new Whigs' (the most radical of the party, committed to broadening the franchise, to secret ballots, to pay for MPs and the like) defensive. In 1789 they felt obliged to argue that cheering on the French revolution was not incompatible with true patriotism, but rather a sign of its good health. That was the message of Dr Richard Price's sermon on 'The Love of Our Country', preached, significantly, on 4 November 1789, almost to the day the 101st anniversary of William III's landing at Torbay, to the Society for Commemorating the Revolution at the Unitarian meeting house in Old Jewry, London. 'Country' properly considered, Price argued, was not just 'the soil or the spot of earth on which we happen to have been born; not the forests and fields, but that community of which we are members; or that body of companions and friends and kindred who are associated with us under the same constitution of government, protected by the same laws, and bound together by the same civil polity'. In other words, it is our politics and not our topography that gives us our true national allegiance. All the rest is just selfish bluster. And the politics of the great and glorious French Revolution, he said, were unmistakably connected with our own; were indeed the completion of what we had begun. Had not the meaning of 1688 been that the people had the right to resist tyrannical rule, get rid of the unlawful ruler and restore to themselves their undoubted right to self-government? And was that not precisely what the French were now doing? Their lesson was timely, for in Britain the representation of the people had become a bad joke; a 'shadow' freedom, the reality of which was corrupt oligarchy and a ministerial government that worked its will through paid yes-men in parliament.

If the fall of the Bastille and the transformation of the monarchy in France from an absolute to a popular monarchy was shocking, surely the shock was healthy; good for the constitution, like a cool dip at Weymouth or an excursion in the Lakeland drizzle. Price bridled at the craven 'servility' of the congratulations offered to George III on the recovery of his wits, 'more like a herd crawling at the feet of a master, than like enlightened and manly citizens rejoicing with a beloved sovereign, but at the same time conscious that he derives all his consequence from themselves'. They, in other words, were the true sovereign, and if he had been in the position of addressing the king, Price said, he would have spoken up thus:

> I rejoice, Sir, in your recovery. I thank God for his goodness to you. I honour you not only as my King, but as almost the only lawful King in the world, because the only one who owes his crown to the choice of his people. May you enjoy all possible happiness. May God shew you the folly of those effusions of adulation which you are now receiving, and guard you against their effects. May you be led to such a just sense of the nature of your situation, and endowed with such wisdom, as shall render your restoration to the government of these kingdoms a blessing to it, and engage you to consider yourself as more properly the *Servant* than the *Sovereign* of your people.

This was already daring enough. But at the end of his remarks Price abandoned all pretence of deference and unleashed a thunderclap of apocalyptic

47

revolutionary prophecy: 'Tremble all ye oppressors of the world! Take warning all ye supporters of slavish governments, and slavish hierarchies! . . . You cannot now hold the world in darkness. Struggle no longer against increasing light and liberality. Restore to mankind their rights, and consent to the correction of abuses, before they and you are destroyed together.'

It was the two central assumptions of Price's remarks—that the French Revolution was the continuation of the British (an assumption epitomized by one of the celebratory toasts, 'To the Parliament of Britain—may it become a National Assembly') and that the monarchy of Britain was, or ought to be, not an hereditary succession but accountable to the sovereign *people*—that provoked the Irish writer, orator and MP (for a pocket borough) Edmund Burke to write his devastating and vitriolic *Reflections on the Revolution in France* (1790). As much as anything else, it was Price's timing that so appalled Burke. He had greeted the French spring with cautious optimism, which by the autumn had turned to horrified disbelief. Everything that had happened after 14 July—the lynchings; the château burnings; the careless abandon with which the nobility liquidated their own privileges; and above all the expropriation of Church property to fund the national debt—struck him as a perverted act of national self-dismemberment. Most preposterous of all for Burke was the fiction that Louis XVI was an enthusiastic sponsor of all this demolition when he was, in fact, just the prisoner of the wrecking-gang. In November 1789—precisely when Price had seen fit to lecture George III on his duty to

48

consider himself the 'servant of the people'—the true state of Louis XVI's position had been exposed in the most brutal way. A march of Parisians to Versailles, led by the market women demanding bread, had degenerated into an attack on the palace as the marchers penetrated the private apartments of the royal family. Before it was over two Swiss guards were dead—although neither was, as Burke wrote, a sentry—and the king and queen, after making a nervous appearance on the Palace balcony at Lafayette's urging, were ignominiously taken back to Paris in a coach. Preceded by heads stuck on pikes, the royal couple did their best to put a brave face on their captivity and pretend to be 'united' with the people. 'This king . . . and this queen, and their infant children (who once would have been the pride and hope of a great and generous people)', wrote Burke, laying on the sensation with a trowel, 'were then forced to abandon the sanctuary of the most splendid palace in the world, which they left swimming in blood, polluted by massacre, and strewed with scattered limbs and mutilated carcasses.'

How was it possible that Dr Price—who was the butt of Burke's acid sarcasm—should celebrate such events as though from them flowed the milk of human benevolence? And how was it that he could have the audacity to claim kinship between the Glorious Revolution of 1688 and what for Burke were the utterly inglorious deeds of a century later? Only by utterly falsifying what that first, altogether British revolution had been about in the first place.

It was only in defiance of historical truth, he said, that Price could claim it had been licensed by

49

the people's right to choose their own form of government and hire or fire kings at their pleasure, or as they judged those monarchs protected the 'natural rights' of individual liberty. That had been the view of the men not of 1688 but of 1648—of Milton and the king-killing generation. William III had been invited to England, not as the people's choice, much less to make a fresh government from any sort of abstract principles, but to defend a form of law, Church and government that had always been there; the 'ancient constitution' violated by James II. It had thus been the most conservative of revolutions; hence its bloodlessness, hence its glory. And above all, Burke insisted, the 'ancient constitution' had the authority of countless generations—from Magna Carta, perhaps even Anglo-Saxon England—as its weight; pinning it to the earth of Britain rather than letting it be borne dangerously aloft by the hot-air balloon speculations of political philosophers like Rousseau. Governments could not simply be dreamed up from imagined first principles. Such 'geometric' or 'arithmetical' constructions were, by definition, lifeless. 'The very idea of the fabrication of a new government', Burke wrote, '. . . is enough to fill us with disgust and horror.' Governments, legitimate governments at any rate, drew their authority from the immemorial experience of their practical use. That, at any rate, was Britain's native way of doing things. 'This idea of a liberal descent inspires us with a sense of habitual native dignity.' So the 'spot of earth on which we happen to have been born' made light of by Price was, in fact, of the utmost importance in giving us a sense of our community. 'In England we have not yet been completely embowelled of our natural entrails; we still feel within us, and we cherish and cultivate, those inbred sentiments which are the faithful guardians, the active monitors of our duty.' Our territorial ancestry, complete with what Burke—heavily in love with heraldry—called 'armorial bearings', *was* our birthright, our political constitution. We damaged it at our peril.

As the prophets of international peace and understanding sang hymns to the coming universal communion of humanity, Burke thundered back, in effect: Nature! I'll tell you about *Nature.* You imagine it's all the same, daisychains and hands across the seas and songs of fraternity. But what *you're* talking about is the brotherhood of intellectuals who sip from the same little cups of chocolate, chatter away the same clichés and dream the same puerile dreams. But *nature*, my friends, is lived, not thought. Nature is familiarity, a feeling for place. Nature is a patriot.

The 'people' whom the demagogues so freely apostrophized had been revealed in France to be ignorant, credulous and bloodthirsty. Democracy was mobocracy. 'The occupation of a hairdresser or of a working tallow-chandler cannot', Burke insisted, 'be a matter of honor to any person. . . . Such descriptions of men ought not to suffer oppression from the state; but the state suffers oppression if such as they . . . are permitted to rule.' But they didn't know what they were doing. The unforgivable responsibility for giving them the illusion of their own importance and power lay with those who should have known better: class traitors, gentlemen or clergymen who toyed with democracy like a pastime and were rich enough to evade its

51

lethal consequences, who fantasized about exchanging their allotted role in the political order for mere 'citizenship'. In England it was the dukes and earls—Richmond, Grafton, Shelburne and, regrettably, his old friend Charles James Fox—who, by lending their voice to the destruction of their own nobility, were recklessly cutting the golden chain that tied one generation to the next, the past to the future. They imagined they could, like Lafayette, ride the tiger of the mobs to power and glory. But they would be the first to be devoured.

Burke's *Reflections* was, by the standards of the day, a commercial success as well as a polemical *tour de force*, selling 17,000 in the first three months (at a time when a generous print run for a novel would be about 1500 copies). It was seen by some of the radical Whigs as an act of apostasy from someone who had the reputation (not quite accurate) of having been a friend to the Americans. (Burke had, in fact, sought Anglo-American reconciliation, but once the conflict began was a British loyalist.) But what distressed Price (who died in 1791, his voice hopelessly drowned out by the thunder of Burke's rhetoric) was its parochialism: the insistence that the British political inheritance *was* unique; that at their birth Britons had received not 'natural rights' but a distinctly native inheritance, quite irreconcilable with universally applicable liberties. Nature, Burke seemed to be saying, could never be cosmopolitan.

In the humiliation of Marie Antoinette fleeing 'almost naked . . . to seek refuge at the feet of [the] king' Burke had seen and lamented the death of chivalry in France. Reverse chivalry—when a woman might spring to the defence of a violently abused man—would never have occurred to him. Such an occurrence he would certainly have characterized as 'unnatural'. But that is precisely what did happen. Barely a month after the appearance of Burke's *Reflections*, Mary Wollstonecraft, who had met Price when she opened a school in Newington Green, a stone's throw from his chapel, published her counter-attack, *A Vindication of the Rights of Men* (1790). She had obviously been stung to see Price the subject of Burke's withering scorn. He had been her first real mentor when she had returned to London from Yorkshire, a self-taught bluestocking nobody, and had encouraged and befriended her as he had many other women writers, such as the children's author (also a radical) Anna Letitia Barbauld.

Mary had needed all the help she could get, for she had led a gypsy life, constantly fretting about her siblings and never earning quite enough money from her reviews and essays. Her father, the son of a Spitalfields silk weaver, had tried a bit of this and a bit of that—farming in Essex, provincial swagger in Yorkshire—and had failed at each venture. Mary had perforce been mother hen to her sisters, even when one of them walked out on her husband for reasons unexplained but easily guessed. She had, of course, soaked herself in the tepid pool of Jean-Jacques Rousseau's sentimental education and had got all warm and sticky with dreams of emotional purity and immortal friendship. But one of Rousseau's truisms about nature—the nature of the sexes—struck her as monstrous. It was the philosopher's assumption, set out in his novel,

Emile, that girls had to be raised for one supreme purpose—to be a comfort and helpmate to their spouse and the mother (a nursing mother, naturally) to his children. Providence had ordained the sexes to be so unbridgeably different that any women who got it into their heads to be like, to act like, men were by definition biological and moral monsters, robbing their families of the quality that made an abode a home, *tendresse*.

Mary had seen her own mother's sad attempts to lavish such tenderness on her prodigal, drunken husband, and she thought it over-rated. Partly inspired by the example of the growing number of women who seemed to live from their pen, she wrote a little treatise on the education of daughters, arguing, in spite of *Emile*, that girls had the potential to be every bit as educated as boys. And she sent it to the man who seemed to be the hub of all the free spirits and radical writers in London, perhaps in England: Joseph Johnson.

Johnson, a short, neatly wigged, Liverpudlian bachelor, held court above his business at 72 St Paul's Churchyard, for centuries the favourite haunt of London's book publishers. To radical London he was the Johnson who really mattered—not just publisher of the *Analytical Review* (between 1788 and 1799) but patron and good uncle to his 'ragged regiment' of disciples. He was someone who could find a review to assign, a job to fill (for Mary he found a position as governess in Ireland, but with mixed results), a short-term loan or even (again, for Mary) a roof. She ate with him several times a week and was a regular at Johnson's famous Sunday dinners where the honest 'patriot' fare (a lot of boiled cod and peas) was spiced by interesting company: visionary artists like William Blake and Henry Fuseli; veteran stalwarts of the Society for the Promotion of Constitutional Information like the Reverend John Horne Tooke and Major John Cartwright; celebrity democrats like the black-eyed, red-faced Tom Paine; and, invariably, a group of articulate, unblushing, intelligent women like Barbauld and the actress Sarah Siddons. Accounts of Mary's appearances at Johnson's dinners describe an ungainly, strong-minded, immensely animated woman, her long curly hair powdered when it wasn't crowned with a beaver hat in the style of Benjamin Franklin or Rousseau. Self-consciously careless with her dress, she was a tremendous interrupter. The social philosopher William Godwin, who came to listen to Paine, found himself irritated by Mary talking incessantly over him.

The mix of stormy passion and tenacious argument, heart and head working like a right and left punch, which was already Mary Wollstonecraft's trademark, would have made her especially indignant at Burke's savage onslaught on the great and good Dr Price. But it was much more extraordinary that she should make the move from indignation to publication. Although her *Vindication of the Rights of Men* has been overshadowed by the more famous *Vindication of the Rights of Woman* (1792), published two years later, as well as by Paine's blockbuster *Rights of Man* (1791–2), Mary's intervention was not just the earliest counter-attack on Burke but one of the cleverest. Instead of doing what would have been expected (not least by Burke) of a woman and writing in a primly sanctimonious manner, Mary used Burke's own weapon of venomous irony to attack his credentials as the guardian of traditional institutions. If he were so deeply exercised about the sanctity of hereditary kingship, she wondered out loud, was it not rather peculiar that when King George had gone mad Mr Burke had been in such indecent haste to replace him (with the Prince Regent, Burke's patron's patron)? 'You were so eager to taste the sweets of power, that you could not wait till time had determined, whether a dreadful delirium would settle into a confirmed madness; but, prying into the secrets of Omnipotence, you thundered out that God had *hurled him from his throne . . .*' Was not that the very same dissolution of the bonds of loyalty that Burke had found so shocking in the French? The goal was to make Burke look not just wrong-headed but ridiculous, mocking his pet obsessions; his comical gallantry towards Marie Antoinette ('not an animal of the highest order'); his infatuation with the escutcheoned past; the myopia (more fun with Burke's famous eye-glasses, even though Mary used them herself) in not seeing that the 'perfect Liberty' was only perfect for those who had the property to enjoy it. More seriously, if the sanctity of the 'ancient constitution' were never to be tampered with, were we not then doomed to 'remain forever in frozen inactivity because a thaw that nourishes the soil spreads a temporary inundation?'

Mary was the sniper; Tom Paine the heavy artillery. In the early days of the French Revolution Paine had assumed that Burke, as an old 'friend of Liberty', would be sympathetic, and had actually sent him a cordial letter from Paris. The *Reflections* disabused him. Gripped by anger and urgency, in just three months Paine produced 40,000 words of Part I of *Rights of Man* (1791), his demolition job on the 'bleak house of despotism'. Much of it had been said before, by John Milton, Algernon Sidney and, indeed, by Paine himself: the rights of men, including their natural equality as well as individual liberty, are God-given at birth and, since they precede all forms of government, cannot be surrendered to those governments. On the contrary, governments were instituted to protect those rights, and are obeyed on the condition of such protection. But Paine added an extra note of sardonic ridicule at the mere idea of hereditary governments—aristocracies as well as monarchies. To entertain such a notion, much less defer to it, was no less absurd than believing in, say, inherited lines of mathematicians.

More important than what Paine said, however, was the way in which he said it. His own origins as a maker of stays and corsets in Norfolk, where he had grown up on a bare hill known as 'The Wilderness' facing the local gallows and had been taken to Quaker meeting houses, meant that Paine was not among those whom Burke wrote off as radical playboys with more money than morals or sense. Before his burst of fame in America, Paine had known what it had meant to be poor, itinerant, almost entirely self-educated. His real schooling had taken place amidst the bawling arguments of pipe-smoking tavern politicians. The rough-house clamour of American politics had added another string to his crude but powerful bow. And closeness to the language of the inns and the streets served him well in the combat with Burke since he understood, with an almost 20th-century shrewdness, that a battle of ideas was also necessarily a battle of language. Burke had deliberately chosen the most high-pitched vocabulary, alternating between Gothic histrionics when describing (at second hand) lurid scenes of mayhem in France and lordly grandiloquence when lecturing the 'swinish multitude' on their richly merited exclusion from public affairs. Paine called those set-piece performances 'very well calculated for theatrical representation, where facts are manufactured for the sake of show'. In calculated contrast, as if to make Burke's worst nightmare—the political education of ordinary people—come true, Paine chose to write with aggressive simplicity: 'As it is my design to make those that can scarcely read understand . . . I shall therefore avoid every literary ornament and put it in a language as plain as the alphabet.' Many polite readers who picked up *Rights of Man* were shocked less by the predictable twitting of the monarchy and the aristocratic establishment than by the coarseness of his language. As if anticipating the crinkling of noses and the fluttering of fans, Paine virtually belched his ideas in their faces.

The swinish multitude ate it up. Joseph Johnson had agreed to publish it in time for George Washington's birthday on 22 February (the general duly got a copy and thanked Paine). But on the appointed day Johnson, whose shop had already published attacks on Burke, including that of Mary Wollstonecraft, got an uncharacteristic attack of nerves. Paine was forced to shop around for another publisher, and when he found one hired a horse and cart to take the unbound sheets to the new premises. Johnson might well have regretted his panic, for *Rights of Man* sold out briskly and a second printing was needed three days after the first. By May there had been six editions and 50,000 sales of a book that, at three shillings, was not inexpensive. Even with foreign sales (for many copies undoubtedly went to Boston, Amsterdam, Paris and Dublin), this made Paine's work the most colossal best-seller of the 18th century, knocking Burke's readership into insignificance. Part II, with its even more radical 'welfare state' agenda (which divided the reformers), redistributing national income through progressive taxation to fund government obligations towards children, the aged, the infirm and the poor, did even better, selling, according to Paine, between 400,000 and 500,000 copies in the first 10 years. Even allowing for an element of exaggeration the figures make nonsense of the claims of some modern historians that radical opinions at this time were confined to a small and unrepresentative minority. At a meeting of the suddenly revived Society for the Promotion of Constitutional Information, a vote of thanks was passed to Paine in the sung form of a new version of the national anthem:

> God Save the Rights of Man
> Let Despots If they Can
> Them overthrow . . .

By the summer of 1791, with Louis XVI and Marie Antoinette caught at Varennes while trying to flee France, brought back in disgrace to Paris and held prisoner in their own Palace of the Tuileries, two sets of self-designated British patriots were at each other's throats. In May, in the House of Commons, the erstwhile friends and allies Edmund Burke and Charles James Fox had had a bitter and irreparable falling-out. Goaded by Pitt, Fox remained defiant that the new French constitution and the Declaration of the Rights of Man and Citizen were 'the most stupendous edifice of liberty' that the world had ever seen. And in private he accused Burke of being no more than Pitt's hired mouth, an accomplice to the dirty war of tarring him with the brush of being a republican. In the Commons on 6 May, a speech by Burke was a signal from Fox's ardent young band of radicals, whom Burke called 'the little dogs', to howl and hiss. Burke publicly aired his anger that 'a personal attack had been made upon him from a quarter he never could have expected, after a friendship and intimacy of more than 22 years'. Rehearsing other disputes that had divided them, but had neither compromised their closeness nor split the Whigs, Burke was about to say that this particular argument over the French Revolution was fatal to both. Fox interjected: 'There is no loss of friendship.' 'I regret to say there is,' responded Burke. 'I have done my duty though I have lost my friend.' Fox rose, became tearfully incoherent, but finally spoke unrepentantly of the disappearance of 'horrid despotism' in France. Burke responded again that he hoped no one would trade away the British constitution for a 'wild and visionary system'.

This courtly if emotional exchange disguised the polarization taking place, fast and furiously, in the provincial towns of England and even more ominously in Scotland. Certainly, London was also a storm-centre of both radical and loyalist politics. But the 'new Britain'—Manchester, Sheffield, Belfast, Birmingham and Glasgow, as well as older towns transformed by commerce and industry such as Derby, Nottingham and Bewick's Newcastle— was experiencing a real baptism of fire. It was in those places that meeting house 'rational religion', debating clubs, the printing and publishing trades and radical newspapers were all tied together. In Sheffield the bookshop owner John Gales, also the editor of the *Sheffield Register*, was the prime mover of the city's Constitutional Society, which rapidly acquired over 2000 members. The question of just how radical these organizations were to be often put a strain on their solidarity. Some wanted to follow the more 'Friends of the People', Fox-ite, constitutional line of pressing for parliamentary reform, perhaps even manhood suffrage as a 'birthright of freeborn Britons'; others quickly became intoxicated with millenarian visions of the coming just society as outlined in the gospel according to Tom Paine.

Amazingly, 14 July—the anniversary of the fall of the Bastille—replaced 4–5 November—the anniversary of both the Gunpowder Plot and the Glorious Revolution—as a critical day in British politics. On that same day in 1791 a huge crowd in Belfast—both Protestant and Catholic—cheered the dawn of liberty, especially for Ireland, while another crowd in Birmingham was trashing the precious library and laboratory of Joseph Priestley in the name of Church and King. The 'spark' had indeed caught for 'Gunpowder Joe', but it had lit a fire under the wrong people. By the spring of 1794 Priestley had emigrated to America, settling in

Northumberland, Pennsylvania, where he founded a cooperative community that at last corresponded, somewhat, to his social idealism.

Britain, on the other hand, seemed further off than ever from being converted into an Elysium of peace and freedom. Any 'Friend of the People' hoping to work some sort of miraculous constitutional change from within would have been sadly disenchanted when, on 6 May 1793, Charles Grey's measure of parliamentary reform (more equal representation and more frequent elections) was defeated by 282 votes to 41. That was about the size of the Fox-ite 'New Whig' remnant in parliament. So when, in May, a royal proclamation was issued outlawing seditious assemblies, the government expected and got Whig support; Fox voted against but the Duke of Portland, and of course Burke, were in favour. However, since the parliamentary road seemed, for the moment, to be a dead end, Paine's more revolutionary politics became more, not less, appealing. In January 1792, the shoemaker Thomas Hardy established the London Corresponding Society (the 'mother of mischief' according to Burke), with John Thelwall as its major theorist and spokesman; it was an overtly democratic Paine-ite organization pressing for manhood suffrage and annual parliaments. To the government, fretting about national as well as social disintegration, it suddenly seemed sinister that Hardy was a Scot—all the more so when, in December, Edinburgh was the chosen meeting place for a 'Convention' of Scottish 'Friends of the People'. Since the bloody change from a monarchy to a republic in France had produced a 'Convention' the very term (despite a quite different tradition of usage in Britain) seemed to presage a similar upheaval. The Edinburgh Convention numbered 160 delegates from 80 sister societies in no fewer than 35 towns. Government spies reported that there were Irishmen at the Edinburgh Convention—and for that matter Scots in Belfast and Dublin. When one of the conveners, the lawyer Thomas Muir, spoke of liberating 'enslaved England', the jump from Jacobite to Jacobin suddenly did not seem so fantastic. Part of the savagery of the government's counter-attack—arresting its leaders, trying them for sedition and sentencing them to 14 years' Australian transportation—was undoubtedly due to the fear that the Anglo-Scottish union was about to be subverted or that an attempt to replace parliament with a 'British Convention' might begin in some sort of northern democratic heartland stretching from Nottingham to Dundee.

Agents also noticed that the corresponding societies were packed with rowdy, violently verbose types: a new generation of uppity weavers, godly nailmakers, republican tailors and, most ominously for those who felt the hairs rise on the nape of their neck when they read of the revolutionary horrors in Paris, Sheffield cutlers. Raids occasionally produced the odd cache of pikes or axes, which only fed the hysteria. In the Commons Burke poured on the paranoia, comparing something that he called the Revolutional and the Unitarian Societies to insects that might grow into huge spiders building webs to catch and devour all who stood in their way. Less phantasmagorically, William Pitt warned that if the opinions of Tom Paine were allowed to spread unchecked among the common people 'we should have bloody revolution'.

With the connivance of the government, pre-emptive action was taken. The militia was called out in 10 counties, but they looked the other way when the target of the mob was the radicals. Presses were smashed; literature deemed 'seditious' taken and burned. Cartoonists like the genius James Gillray were hired to show, as graphically as possible, what would happen should a revolution happen in Britain. John Reeves, a sometime chief justice of Newfoundland now returned to Britain, was so disturbed by the brazenness of the clubs that in November 1792 he founded his own Association for Preserving Liberty and Property Against Levellers and Republicans 'to support the Laws, to suppress seditious Publications and to defend our Persons and Property'. As well as arming loyalists, the Association promoted the publication of tracts specifically to disabuse credulous working men of the views of Paine. Once war with the French had broken out in February 1793 a whole new seam of neurosis about the consequences of a French republican invasion could be richly mined. One of the tracts featured a patriotic master taking the time and effort to explain to his gullible apprentice just how wicked and dangerous Paine's opinions were. 'Right Master,' replies his journeyman, overcome with gratitude. 'I thank you for explaining all this and instead of going to the Liberty Club I will begin my work for I should not like to see the Frenchmen lie with my wife or take the bread out of my children's mouths.' The evangelical Hannah More, whose reputation had been built on improving literature for children, now took it on herself to supply timely patriotic definitions for all ages. Her *Village Politics* (1793) has 'Jack Anvil' explain to 'Tom Hod' that a democrat was 'one who likes to be governed by a thousand tyrants and yet can't bear a king'. The *Rights of Man* prescribed 'battle, murder and sudden death' and a 'new patriot' was 'someone who loves every country better than their own and France best of all'.

If, despite all the intimidation and danger, you were a committed 'Friend of the People' in the stormy years of 1792–3 what were your options? If you were prudent, and mistrustful of the excesses of Paine-ite revolutionary enthusiasm, you might make Thomas Bewick's choice and decide to button your lip, hunker down and hope that at some time, preferably in the not too distant future, British common sense, public decency and justice *would* prevail. In the meantime he would content himself with reading the local radical newspaper, *The Oeconomist* (distributed in London by, of course, Joseph Johnson); or relish the ferociously satirical attacks on Pitt in, say, his old friend Thomas Spence's *Pigs' Meat, or Lessons from the Swinish Multitude* (1793–5); get on with his birds and beasts, and smuggle, for those who wanted to look carefully between the illustrations, images of brutality, misery, daring and death. Or, from the relative safety of a Hepplewhite chair in your club, you might cheer on the dwindling band of 'New Whigs' in parliament—Fox, Sheridan, Charles Grey and Shelburne—who persisted in opposition to measures infringing the freedom of press or suspending habeas corpus and who refused to recant their benevolent views about the French Revolution. Or, if you were very brave, very angry or very drunk on revolutionary optimism you might take the plunge and join one of those artisans' clubs where you could drink rounds to the health of Paine, the imminent realization of a British republic and the death of despots. Given the ubiquitousness of government spies, you would be putting yourself in jeopardy, even for unguarded toasts. When John Thelwall, now the prime orator of the London Corresponding Society, swiped the froth off a head of beer and remarked (according to a spy), 'This is the way I would serve up kings,' the joke would come back to haunt him in the Old Bailey.

There was another option, of course: leaving Britain altogether. You could cross the Channel to inhale some of that heady air of liberty, equality and—especially—fraternity, and work for the day when you might return in the vanguard of the forces of freedom. The French seemed to be treating British radicals as brothers and sisters. Tom Paine had been made an honorary citizen. To go to the fountainhead of freedom and to drink deeply would be more than a gesture of political tourism. It was the promise of a new life.

Try as they might, however, not everyone could make the leap. At some point in the summer or autumn of 1792 John Thelwall took a little time off from lecturing on the cause of freedom and justice (to bigger and bigger crowds) to walk through Kent. In the guise of his literary *alter ego*, the Peripatetic Sylvanus Theophrastus, he arrives at the White Cliffs of Dover and looks out at the 'foaming billows' separating him from the land of liberty. The place for him is the essence of British sublimity, but there is so much to look at that he cannot decide whether the beach or the clifftop provides the more breathtaking view. He wants it all and scrambles up and down 'above a dozen times'. But then he gets too ambitious and tries to climb a near perpendicular rock 'with no better hold than a spray of elder, or a fragile tuft of thyme'. Three-quarters of the way there, the Peripatetic is well and truly stuck: no way up; no way down. Which describes allegorically, of course, Thelwall's political predicament. The Cicero of the corresponding societies, arch-republican demagogue to the authorities, he has no way up, no way down. So he perches 'though my heart beat an audible alarm . . . with all the calmness I was master of, beneath the hanging precipice, and contemplated the beautiful serenity of the spangled sea'. He turns 'a longing eye towards the distant cliffs of France; and could not but regret the impossibility of exchanging my present situation for the more honourable . . . danger of defending with the sword of justice, the gallant struggles of that brave people in the cause of their new-born Liberty'.

He can't do it. Ultimately he knows he is, in his way, a British patriot. His feet have to be on its ground. So somehow 'I contrived to let myself down, from precipice to precipice, till I arrived at last in safety on the beach, together with a fleck of chalk, and a sprig of thyme . . . Trophies purchased with more innocence . . . than all the sanguinary honours of the plunderers and destroyers of the world: the Alexanders and the Caesars, the Edwards and the Henrys, by whom the peace of mankind has been so repeatedly disturbed.' Poor Thelwall—who would end up trying to be a farmer in the Black Mountains of Wales at Llyswen before turning to elocution teaching in London—would always be on the verge of happiness.

CHAPTER 2

FORCES OF NATURE: THE ROAD HOME

In the spring of 1792, and of his life, William Wordsworth had none of John Thelwall's paralysing anxieties. Going to France was 'pleasant exercise of hope and joy!'

> For mighty were the auxiliars which then stood
> Upon our side, us who were strong in love!
> Bliss was it in that dawn to be alive,
> But to be young was very Heaven!

That, at any rate, was the way he remembered it 12 years later even when he was feeling a lot less charitable towards the French Revolution. The chronicle of his journey in and out of revolution forms part of *The Prelude*, the greatest autobiographical poem in English (or perhaps any other European language); the first section of which was written in 1798–9, exactly at the point when Wordsworth was undergoing a deep change of heart.

The momentous theme of *The Prelude* is the struggle to hang on—through memory—to the instinctive life of childhood, even while being pulled inexorably towards an adult sense of individual self-consciousness. Immersion in nature is the great ally in this war against the inevitable erosion of innocence by time and social experience. Nature is freedom; the business of the world a prison. The mature Wordsworth becomes a child of nature again through the act of intense recollection. What he describes is a Cumbrian childhood spent escaping from, fighting against, what we would now call 'socialization': against the rote-learning, fact-packed lessons at his school in Hawkshead. Instead, nature was his tutor and his playground:

> Oh, many a time have I, a five years' child,
> In a small mill-race severed from his stream,
> Made one long bathing of a summer's day;
> Basked in the sun, and plunged and basked
>   again
> Alternate, all a summer's day . . .
> or when rock and hill,
> The woods, and distant Skiddaw's lofty height,
> Were bronzed with deepest radiance, stood
>   alone
> Beneath the sky, as if I had been born
> On Indian plains, and from my mother's hut
> Had run abroad in wantonness, to sport
> A naked savage, in the thunder shower.

At St John's College, Cambridge, Wordsworth was in no hurry to oblige his father's expectation that he enter the Church or the law. Nor was he particularly enthralled with learning:

> Of College labours, of the Lecturer's room
> All studded round, as thick as chairs could
>   stand
> . . . Let others that know more speak as they
>   know.
> Such glory was but little sought by me.

Restive, anxious, dimly aware that something big
was waiting for him, in the summer of 1790 he
decided to go with a friend, Robert Jones, on a
walking tour of the Alps—in that generation very
much a statement of moral and political temper.
The two undergraduates landed in Calais—surely
not by accident—on 13 July, the eve of the first
anniversary of the fall of the Bastille, and
witnessed, first-hand, the ecstatic festival of flowers
and freedom. On their journey south and east
through France, they

> found benevolence and blessedness
> Spread like a fragrance everywhere, when
>   spring
> Hath left no corner of the land untouched.

At one point along their journey they found
themselves swallowed up in a throng of celebrating
villagers, 'vapoured in the unruliness of joy', who
gave them supper and got them to dance in a circle:

> All hearts were open, every tongue was loud
> With amity and glee; we bore a name
> Honoured in France, the name of Englishmen,
> And hospitably did they give us hail,
> As their forerunners in a glorious course.

Two years later, after his second journey to France,
the dewy innocence might have gone, but not the
political idealism. Still fending off family concern
about his profession, Wordsworth had gone to
London, where he met Joseph Johnson and the St
Paul's Churchyard circle during the height of the
Burke–Paine furore. He saw Burke himself in

the Commons:

> Stand like an oak whose stag-horn branches
>   start
> Out of its leafy brow, the more to awe
> The younger brethren of the grove …
> Declares the vital power of social ties
> Endeared by Custom; and with high disdain,
> Exploding upstart Theory, insists
> Upon the allegiance to which men are born.

But the retrospective eulogy of Burke as the personification of English nature—the gnarled and knotty oak defying the worst the revolutionary storm can hurl at him—is very much the recollection of the older Romantic conservative. Given the Paine-ite attacks on established authority that Wordsworth was still to write, it seems very unlikely that at this time he would have felt quite so warmly.

Much later, too, Wordsworth insisted that his second journey to France, in 1791–2, had been just a study-trip to learn the language. But this is where memory turns disingenuous. At that very moment, France was facing a desperate war launched by the Emperor of Austria (Marie Antoinette's brother) and the King of Prussia expressly to uphold the rights of monarchy and to liberate Louis XVI from the grip of those who had usurped it in the name of the people. It would have been rather like maintaining that a journey to Russia in 1920 was purely a matter of studying Pushkin. And Wordsworth did admit to a friend, albeit in rueful sorrow, that 'I went over to Paris at the time of the Revolution—in 92 or 93—and was pretty hot in it.'

Hot for revolution he certainly must have been, since all his contacts in France were fire-breathing expatriate militants like Robert Watt, Tom Wedgwood and the novelist and poet Helen Maria Williams, to whom, much smitten, Wordsworth had written a lyrically soppy poem on the spectacle of her in tears.

Which is not to say that he might not have had, from the beginning of his stay, some reservations. The beautiful account of his mixed feelings while roaming Paris:

> I stared and listened, with a stranger's ears,
> To Hawkers and Haranguers, hubbub wild!
> And hissing Factionists with ardent eyes,
> In knots, or pairs, or single . . .

has the undoubted ring of truth.

> Where silent zephyrs sported with the dust
> Of the Bastille, I sate in the open sun,
> And from the rubbish gathered up a stone,
> And pocketed the relic, in the guise
> Of an enthusiast; yet in honest truth,
> I looked for something that I could not find,
> Affecting more emotion than I felt.

Failing to find his friends in Orléans, as they had arranged, Wordsworth made his way down the Loire to Blois, now turned into a garrison town in the expectation that war, both foreign and civil, was not far away. But the war that broke out was in Wordsworth's own heart and mind. Although he 'became a patriot, and my heart was all/Given to the people' in Blois, his allegiances were torn by the fiercest emotions he had yet experienced, of both love and friendship. His love affair was the purest Rousseau melodrama, forbidden passion between tutor and pupil, but this time with the sex roles of *La Nouvelle Héloïse* reversed. His teacher was Annette Vallon, daughter of a fervently Catholic family who took the lonely young English poet under their wing, gave him all the affection he craved and tried to convert him to their hatred of the revolution. But the friendship that Wordsworth made with a young army officer from the Périgord, Michel Beaupuis, pulled him in precisely the opposite direction. Beaupuis struck Wordsworth as the model of selfless patriotism precisely because he had relinquished his aristocratic pedigree and rank to become a true citizen of the new France of equals, a soldier for liberty.

Beaupuis might also have struck Wordsworth as a kindred spirit because he too was moved, less by high-minded philosophical speculation than by the sight of physical distress. At home in the Lake District he had encountered woebegone old soldiers whose rags and tatters moved him inexpressibly, and, walking the streets of London Wordsworth had been moved by a blind beggar

who, with upright face,
Stood, propped against a wall, upon his chest
Wearing a written paper to explain
His story, whence he came, and who he was.

In Blois, too, right on cue, nature showed up to teach a lesson when Beaupuis and he chanced

One day to meet a hunger-bitten girl
Who crept along fitting her languid gait
Unto a heifer's motion, by a cord
Tied to her arm, and picking thus from the lane
Its sustenance, while the girl with pallid hands
Was busy knitting . . .

' 'Tis against that which we are fighting,' said
Beaupuis, and Wordsworth agreed

That a benignant spirit was abroad
Which might not be withstood, that poverty
Abject as this would in a little time
Be found no more . . .
That legalised exclusion, empty pomp
Abolished, sensual state and cruel power,
Whether by edict of the one or few,
And finally, as sum and crown of all,
Should see the people having a strong hand
In framing their own laws,whence better days
To all mankind.

The dream of a harmonious marriage between
liberty and equality turned out, of course, to be a
lot harder than shouting the slogan. As the war
sliced deeper into France, paranoia replaced
euphoria and a republic replaced the monarchy,
bloodily, on 10 August 1792, when Parisians
stormed the Tuileries, butchered the Swiss guards
and imprisoned the king. It was incumbent on
anyone harbouring reservations about the
Republic, or who had been born into privilege, to
demonstrate that they were purer than the pure.
Beaupuis predictably went off to die a citizen-
soldier's death, one of hundreds of thousands of

75

young men who were to sacrifice themselves for ideals that were being violated daily on the streets of Paris. Wordsworth mourned his fallen republican friend, but in the meantime he had put himself in danger by fathering a baby royalist. Born in December, the girl was given the name of Caroline and registered in Paris as the daughter of a Citoyen Williame Wordwort. He now had a painful decision to make. With war between Britain and the Republic very much on the cards (it was declared in February 1793) he could either stay and care for his mistress and infant daughter, especially now that they were more, not less, likely to need protection from the prying eyes of suspicious authorities; or, like some of the British expatriates, including Watt, who were already beginning to feel the chill, have second thoughts and worry about being cut off from their home, he could take the packet for Dover. Wordsworth chose the latter course, still procrastinating, telling himself he was going to London to raise money for both of his divided allegiances—the British revolutionary cause and his counter-revolutionary lover and their child. But it would be 10 years before he would see Annette and Caroline again.

As he departed, other staunch Friends of Liberty, many of them fellow-diners from 72 St Paul's Churchyard, were still arriving. The publication of the second, even more radical, part of *Rights of Man* in February 1792 had made Tom Paine public enemy number one in the charged atmosphere of bullish Britain. On 21 May he was summoned to answer a charge of seditious libel; but it seems likely that the government eventually became convinced that he would do less damage on the other side of the Channel than as a courtroom martyr, and gave him ample opportunities to escape. In the capital of what, since August, had become the French Republic, One and Indivisible, Paine was given a hero's welcome, made an honorary citizen, elected deputy for Calais to the National Convention and, although he spoke virtually no French, a key member of its constitutional committee. A fraternal 'British Club' (or, more grandly, 'The Association of the Friends of the Rights of Man Meeting in Paris') gathered at White's Hotel in the Passage des Petits-Pères, near the Palais-Royal, and its members, together with assorted American and Irish republicans, busied themselves drafting addresses to the Convention expressing the yearning of the People of Britain for their own liberation from the yoke of despotism and aristocracy. Among their number were the painter George Romney; the young businessman and essayist Thomas Christie; the Scottish poet and former soldier John Oswald, who drilled volunteers for the liberation of Britain; the democrat–aristocrat Lord Edward Fitzgerald, another former soldier, who was planning the same for Ireland; Helen Maria Williams and her lover, the wealthy businessman John Hurford Stone; and Tom Paine himself. Joining them, about a week after Wordsworth's departure, was Mary Wollstonecraft.

Much had changed for her since her guerrilla attack on the pretensions of Edmund Burke. The surprising fierceness of her criticism had inevitably given her the reputation of an 'amazon' among both friends and enemies. Horace Walpole had been less appreciative, calling her a 'hyena in petticoats'. Tom Paine and Joseph Johnson, however, saw that they had found a gifted and exceptionally tough polemicist; someone who was not going to run away from trouble, even in difficult and dangerous times. It may have been Paine, who was spending time in Paris even before his flight from the law, who suggested she write something on what women should ask of the dawning age of liberty and equality. Paine was close to the social and political philosopher the ex-Marquis de Condorcet, who was one of the very few writers in France to extend his progressive vision of social and political democracy to women.

Whatever or whoever spurred her to it, Mary leaped at the chance to air her own views on the subject. Six weeks of hell-for-leather writing produced *A Vindication of the Rights of Woman*. Perhaps she should have taken six months. But, chaotically organized, digressive and repetitive though the book is, none of those faults obscures or compromises its trenchant bravery, nor the fundamental correctness of its historical analysis of the relations between the sexes. Many of its insights—the conditioning of girls to correspond to male stereotypes of the doll-playing, dress-loving miniature coquette; the surrender of independence of mind and body for the slavery of idolization; the assumption that their anatomy disqualified them from serious thought—have since become commonplaces of the feminist critique of a male-ordered world. But when Mary Wollstonecraft set them out they were still profoundly shocking, even to those who thought themselves on the side of Progress and Liberty.

What may have been especially disconcerting

78

was her choice of arch-villains, namely the sainted Jean-Jacques Rousseau, whom Mary believed (not without reason) had done most damage by restating the traditional *canard* of the unbridgeable, biologically determined difference between the sexes as a modern point of view. It was Rousseau, whose 'ridiculous stories' were 'below contempt' and obviously based on no first-hand knowledge whatsoever, who had perpetuated the fable that all girls were good for was cooking, primping, idle prattle, and who had insisted that their entire education should be shaped around their destiny as wives and mothers. It was Rousseau who had argued that, the more like men they were persuaded to become, the less power they would have over them. 'This is the very point I aim at,' she wrote. 'I do not wish them to have power over men; but over themselves.' No wonder Rousseau had taken for his companion the 'fool' Thérèse, so 'conveniently humble'. Not being able to raise her to the status of a rational being, he had been determined to lower the rest of the sex to her level. Instead of dooming women to the imprisoning platitudes of their 'delicacy', Mary declared, they should be given identical educational opportunities; indeed, boys and girls should share the same schools right through their youth so that they could become easily familiar with each other's common humanity and reasoning faculties, and not be segregated either from each other or from their parental home. (Mary detested the idea of boarding schools.)

Rousseau had also been at fault for fetishizing the transports of romantic love, which encouraged marriages to be made (when they were not mere

79

property transactions) with expectations that were doomed to be disappointed since 'Love, considered as an animal appetite, cannot long feed on itself without expiring.' Hard on the heels of that inevitable disenchantment came betrayal, debauchery and bitterness. How much better to educate girls with enough strength of mind that they could become not just an adult doll but a true partner, a *friend*, and with that friendship withstand the inevitable decay of desire. Friendship was, after all, 'the most sublime of all affections, because it is founded on principle, and cemented by time . . . Were women more rationally educated, could they take a more comprehensive view of things, they would be contented to love but once in their lives, and after marriage calmly let passion subside into friendship – into that tender intimacy, which is the best refuge from care.'

But while Mary was writing these things she was also becoming seriously infatuated with one of Johnson's regulars: the middle-aged, eccentrically voluble Swiss artist Henry Fuseli. Weird and wonderful best describe Fuseli, whose work encompassed neo-classical histories; startling pre-Freudian 'Nightmares' of ash-pale virgins draped over yielding beds, upon whose loins squatted goblin-like succubi; Shakespearean phantasmagoria (Macbeth's witches and Bottom's new head); and, not least, a steady output of pornographic prints and drawings, featuring impractically phallic coiffures—for women. The model for many of these fantasies was Sophia Rawlins, whom Fuseli, hitherto a confirmed bachelor, had married in 1788. The peculiarity, not to mention the compulsiveness, of his erotic obsessions, often notoriously revelled in out loud, ought to have excluded Fuseli as a partner for Mary Wollstonecraft since *A Vindication* singles out sexual desire as the root of corruption in the relations between men and women; the source of romantic self-delusion; the destroyer of reason and friendship. But perhaps Mary saw Fuseli more as a detached analyst than as an accomplice of desire. At any rate, whether from desperation or from principle she flirted with him, offering herself as an intimate companion, a soulmate, rather than as a lover. Fuseli seems to have been disconcerted by her persistence, but in the summer of 1792 the odd foursome of Johnson (very definitely no womanizer), Mary, Fuseli and Sophia planned a six-week trip to France. By the time they got to Dover, Paris was in the grip of the fighting that ended the monarchy. The news was of bloody chaos. The party turned back and, dejected by this anti-climax, Mary became impulsive, knocking on Sophia's door to announce to the understandably astonished young wife that the three of them must establish a household together: 'As I am above deceit, it is right to say that this proposal arises from the sincere affection, which I have for your husband, for I find that I cannot live without the satisfaction of seeing and conversing with him daily.' She had no claims on him as a husband—those she would generously cede to Sophia—but mentally they had to be together. Sophia's horrified reaction was to slam the door after forbidding Mary ever to cross the threshold again.

Baffled, wounded and miserable, Mary Wollstonecraft decided to make the trip to France by herself. Although she made light of the risks, describing it as a romantic adventure ('I am still a Spinster on the wing. At Paris, indeed, I might take a husband for the time being, and get divorced when my truant heart longed again to nestle with its old friends'), she knew that even in ordinary times this would have been a brave, not to say foolhardy, journey. But these were extraordinary times. By early December 1792, when Mary finally crossed the Channel, the Revolution was entering its beleaguered and paranoid phase. It had escaped a Prussian occupation of Paris only by the skin of its teeth and the mobilization, thanks to the furious rhetoric of one of the Jacobin leaders, Georges Danton, of the entire Republic's human and material resources. In the knife-edge climate of elation and terror, today's heroes could be tomorrow's traitors; those who showed themselves most demonstrative in their loyalty to the Republic might find their professions of revolutionary ardour taken as a smokescreen for espionage. The position of the foreign communities in Paris was becoming especially precarious. Unless they showed themselves passionate enthusiasts for the war of national defence and liberation, more republican than the republicans, they were vulnerable to charges of being a 'fifth column'. It was this jumpy atmosphere that Wordsworth had decided to escape and in which Mary now found herself. The White's Hotel gang all helped to soften the shock. But Mary struggled with spoken French, discovering, like so many, that the thoughtful translations she had made in England had been no preparation for making one's way through the streets of Paris. She lodged with Aline Fillietaz, the newly married daughter of a schoolmistress acquaintance from London. The Fillietaz house was on the rue Melée in the Marais, which put it not only in the heart of one of the most militant revolutionary districts of the city, seething with clubs and pikes, but also directly along a main route from revolutionary prisons to one of the places of execution.

So, whether she wanted it or not, Mary had a ringside view of the drama of mass death and retribution. A few weeks after her arrival she saw Louis XVI being taken to his trial and, astonished at the dignity of his composure, confessed to Joseph Johnson that 'I can scarcely tell you why, but an association of ideas made the tears flow insensibly from my eyes.' But the letter shook with trepidation.

> Nay, do not smile, but pity me; for, once or twice, lifting my eyes from the paper, I have seen eyes glare through a glass-door opposite my chair, and bloody hands shook at me. Not the distant sound of a footstep can I hear . . . I wish I had even kept the cat with me!—I want to see something alive; death in so many frightful shapes has taken hold of my fancy.—I am going to bed—and for the first time in my life, I cannot put out the candle.

This was not the revolution, nor the life, Mary had expected. By the spring of 1793, Britain and France were at war with each other. French military reverses in the Netherlands and the defection of generals prompted the inevitable accusations of betrayals from within. The apparatus of summary 'revolutionary' justice was established. The fatal rhythm of denunciations, arrests and beheadings began. And it was precisely those republican politicians with whom the White's Hotel crowd had the closest relations—Condorcet and the moderate group known as the Girondins, many of whom had voted against condemning Louis XVI to death—who were now identified by the Jacobin revolutionary government as false patriots, enemies in fact to the *patrie*. By extension the British—whether they liked it or not, natives of an enemy country—were now, starting with Tom Paine, deeply suspect.

The most famous vote cast against the execution of the king was indeed Paine's, and many of those who wanted clemency actually invoked Paine as an example since, as he had said himself, his republican credentials were impeccable. Nonetheless Paine—who expressed the wish that the French Republic would abolish the death penalty altogether, perhaps the summit of his unrealistic optimism—argued eloquently that Louis 'considered as an individual' (rather than an institution) 'was beneath the notice' of the Republic; and that the Revolution owed compassion to its enemies as much as to its friends. To the Jacobins this was so outrageous an apostasy that their most militant spokesman, Jean-Paul Marat, shouted that the interpreter must be mistranslating Paine's words. When they were indeed confirmed, he declared that since Paine was 'a Quaker' and thus opposed to the death penalty on principle (his parentage was indeed Quaker), he ought not to be allowed to vote.

Paine voted anyway, but after the revolutionary government and the apparatus of the Terror was established in the summer of 1793, Paine found himself in the unusual position of being demonized as an enemy of the state in both monarchist Britain and republican France! The British Club had broken up shortly after the king's trial, but once its French patrons and friends had been purged from the National Convention, imprisoned, put on trial and executed, it seemed only a matter of time before the Britons would share their fate. One of Paine's fellow-lodgers, William Johnson, became so unhinged at the prospect that he attempted to commit suicide on the staircase of their hotel, stabbing himself in the chest and rolling operatically down the steps. After the British navy took Toulon in late August, occupying the naval base and town, any kind of association with Britain was a deadly liability. Paine was arrested, along with Helen Maria Williams and some other members of the club, and incarcerated in the Luxembourg, once a royal palace. He missed his date with the guillotine only by a fantastic stroke of luck. Cell doors were marked to indicate the intended victims of the next day's executions. His were by accident left open. In haste the mark was made on the inside and, when the doors were later slammed shut, became invisible. Or so Paine's version of the story goes.

Just as bad for Mary, the *bête noire* of *A Vindication*—Jean-Jacques himself—was everywhere. The image of the patron saint of the Republic of Virtue appeared on placards, on drinking glasses and on patriotic pamphlets. The women's clubs that had agitated for their inclusion in the franchise and for legal rights were shut down by the Jacobins and their leaders arrested or beaten up on the streets if they opened their mouths. The duties of women to the Fatherland were exactly as Rousseau had prescribed: indoctrination in the arts of 'tenderness'; a solace for citizen–soldiers, breast-feeders for the *enfants de la patrie.*

Mary had no choice but to play by the rules of the enemy; to find some sort of refuge from fear and insecurity. It materialized in the good-looking shape of the American revolutionary soldier and author, Gilbert Imlay. Imlay was now in the business of selling revolutionary happiness, or more specifically the real estate on which happiness could be planted in farming settlements and small towns. His *Topographical Description of the Western Territory of North America* (1792) was, like Imlay himself, an attractive thing of many parts: travelogue, land survey and commercial promotional literature. He certainly understood the power of romance and something drew him towards the alternately exuberant and insecure Mary Wollstonecraft. A love affair began, which quickly turned serious. As 'Mrs Imlay', Mary's status as an American citizeness protected her from the hostility and suspicion directed at the British, subjects of a king with whom the Republic was at war. By June she was settled in a cottage at Neuilly on the western outskirts of the city, tending a garden and cooing over the *soupers à deux* she was sharing with Imlay. The author of *A Vindication*, who had made such a powerful case against the delusory and destructive nature of romantic passion, was now in the rhapsodic throes of it. Sensing, already in August, Imlay's reservations about being smothered in so much emotional intensity, she wrote to him with the note of imploring desperation that she had despised in sentimental novels: 'Yes I will be good, that I may deserve to be happy; and whilst you love me, I cannot again fall into the miserable state, which rendered life a burden almost too heavy to be borne.' Mary Wollstonecraft had become a dependant.

By January 1794 she was pregnant, and became anxious and weepy whenever Imlay disappeared on business trips. The more clinging she became, the more regularly he disappeared, leaving her overwhelmed by despondency at the ebbing of 'tenderness'. Only the prospect of the baby pulled her out of this morbid brooding. Determined to go through a modern pregnancy, she made sure she had regular exercise and when her girl, named Fanny, was born in May, Mary horrified the midwife by getting up from her bed the next day, refusing the purification ritual of covering herself in ashes, and resuming, almost immediately, her routine of country walks. Needless to say, she nursed Fanny herself—even though, as she wrote frankly to Ruth Barlow, her 'inundations of milk' were sometimes inconvenient. But Imlay was away a lot, and when he wasn't he fell sick. And the little life added to hers had given Mary a fresh aversion to the tide of death running through France. 'My blood runs cold and I sicken at the thought of a Revolution which costs so much blood and bitter tears.'

With the fall of Robespierre and his execution in reaction to the Jacobin Terror, there was a little more breathing room. Tom Paine and the rest emerged from prison, permanently changed by their ordeal. Now that travel around the country was easier, Imlay took advantage of it to see to his shipping business in Normandy. Swooping up and down between love-sick euphoria and suicidal gloom, Mary followed him to Le Havre with the baby only to find him crossing the Channel repeatedly. Trying to calm her, Imlay wrote from London that she should perhaps come home. Despite writing that 'England is a country which has not merely lost all charms for me, but for which I feel a repugnance' she made the crossing, only to have her worst fears confirmed. Imlay would not turn himself into a husband and father, not least because he had a new love interest. Mary took an overdose of laudanum. Although shocked by the attempted suicide, Imlay was not shocked enough to want to resume their old life. Instead, he came up with the perverse plan of distracting her by sending her off to Norway on business to track down a missing shipment of silver.

Of all the roles she chose to assume in her wandering life, Mary Wollstonecraft, commercial investigator, was the oddest. But off she went with little Fanny and a maid as her only companions, making her way through Sweden and Norway, trying, and not surprisingly failing, to track down her feckless partner's cargo of bullion. In an inn built of logs, painted red and yellow and overlooking the dark sea, Mary, who had been so brutally manhandled by politics and passion, did at last find something akin to a state of grace in nature. She swam, sat on the rocks in the windy northern sunlight and jotted in a journal. In the 'Letters' she planned to publish as a meditation on the times, she wrote that the Norwegian fishermen were indeed the children of nature she had been searching for: instinctively, artlessly free, without the need of ranting philosophy to instruct them in their liberation.

The restoration of her sanity, however, was only temporary. Returning to London, she discovered that Imlay's reluctance to set up house did not extend to establishing a ménage with an actress, his new mistress. One night in October 1795 she went out in a torrential rainstorm, meaning to drown herself. Battersea Bridge, chosen for the jump, proved somehow disconcertingly public, so she paid a boatman to row her up-river to Putney. She walked up and down for half an hour to make sure her dress was saturated enough to sink her, then paid her halfpenny toll to get on the bridge, climbed on to the railing and jumped. 'Let my wrongs sleep with me!' she had written in the suicide note addressed to Imlay. 'When you receive this, my burning head will be cold . . . I shall plunge into the Thames where there is the least chance of my being snatched from the death I seek.'

But she hadn't reckoned with the ubiquitousness of modern philanthropy. The Royal Humane Society had been set up, subsidized by public money, specifically to reward boatmen who pulled would-be suicides from the river. The Thames was full of rowers just waiting for a jumper. Mary was duly rescued and taken to the Duke's Head tavern in Fulham to recover. Mortified and wretched, she lost no time proposing to Imlay that they live together in a *ménage à trois*, so that at least their daughter would know her father. For a moment Imlay wondered, and brought Mary to see their house before (in all likelihood) the actress put her foot down.

Mary Wollstonecraft was 37 and seemed to have lost everything except her child: her faith in the liberating humanity of revolution; in a marriage based on friendship rather than passion; in the possibility of a truly independent woman's life. As for the benevolence of nature, it must have seemed a cruel joke. A letter to Fuseli asking for her letters back became a cry of pain: 'I am alone. The injustice, without alluding to hopes blasted in the bud, which I have endured, wounding my bosom, have set my thoughts adrift into an ocean of painful conjectures. I ask impatiently what—and where is truth? I have been treated brutally; but I daily labour to remember that I still have the duty of a mother to fulfil.'

Her friends, especially the long-suffering Johnson, who published Mary's *Letters Written During a Short Residence in Sweden, Norway and Denmark* (1794–5), did what they could to help. But then they had other things on their minds than the personal fate of Mary Wollstonecraft. The same week that she jumped into the Thames saw a huge demonstration of at least 100,000 people against Pitt, the war with the French and 'famine'. Britain seemed closer than it had ever been to revolution.

Through the spring of 1794 the British government had been bringing prosecutions against those whom it deemed to be the writers, publishers and purveyors of seditious literature. Its object was to employ the usefully vague medieval charge of 'compassing the death of the king' to make into an act of outright treason publications and discussions on the concept of a republic or even on manhood suffrage (for how would *that* be accomplished, one prosecutor argued, without the overthrow of the lawful constitution?). Testimony given by a government witness (later discredited as a drunk and a perjuror) that Thomas Walker, the Manchester radical, had been heard to say 'Damn the King' was the kind of thing taken seriously as evidence. In almost all the cases the accused were defended by Thomas Erskine, one of the genuine champions of British freedom, whose name deserves to be better known. Erskine put his fortune and reputation on the line to insist on the principle that utterance or publication alone (without any evidence of a conspiracy to commit 'tumult' much less regicide) could not be incriminating, and especially not retroactively after the government established ever broader categories of sedition and treason. In May 1794 Thomas Hardy, John Thelwall, John Horne Tooke and 11 other members of the London Corresponding Society were arrested. The right of habeas corpus (no imprisonment without trial) was suspended the same month, and by late in the year 2000 people were being held without due process. A mass meeting at Chalk Farm just north of London declared that Britain had 'lost its liberties'.

Thelwall, Hardy, Horne Tooke and the rest—perhaps in keeping with the medievalism of the charges—were incarcerated in the Tower of London. Traumatized by Hardy's imprisonment, fearful that he would pay with his life for the 'treason', his wife miscarried and died. Thelwall was kept in solitary confinement for five months before being taken to the 'dead hole' of Newgate, which, deprived of almost all light and air, was even worse. On 25 October the prisoners were formally arraigned for 'conspiring to overthrow the government and perpetrate the king's death'. Three days later the first trial, that of Thomas Hardy, opened. Jostling crowds surrounded the Old Bailey. They weren't there to cheer on the prosecution. For nine hours the Attorney-General, Sir John Scott, laboured to stitch together shreds of circumstantial evidence into a treasonable conspiracy to depose and kill the king. 'Nine hours!' shouted the fat ex-Lord Chancellor Thurlow when he heard. 'Then there is no treason, by God!' And the government's case did indeed rest almost entirely on analogies with France in respect, for example, of what had been meant by a 'Convention'.

At the end of the week's proceedings Erskine responded for the defence with a mere seven-hour speech. Echoing a pamphlet published by William Godwin, he insisted that whatever had been said (by Hardy, for example—and he had said a lot) had to be proved to be an actual plot to kill the king in person, not just complaints about parliament or even the monarchy as an institution, since that had still been protected as free political debate. By such unconscionably elastic definitions of treason Hardy was being tried for his life on account of activities that were undoubtedly peaceful and lawful. 'I hope,' said Erskine, brilliantly throwing back at the prosecutors the imputation of disloyalty, 'never to hear it repeated in any court of justice that peacefully to convene the people on the subject of their own privileges, can lead to the destruction of the king; they are the king's worst enemies who use such language.' At the end of his heroic oration he croaked to the jury: 'I am sinking under fatigue and weakness,' and then indeed sank. Appreciative of great theatre, the jury applauded. Hardy was acquitted and spoke to the roaring crowds outside: 'My fellow countrymen, I return you my thanks.' The crowd untethered the horses from the carriages of the accused and pulled them down the Strand, past the Palace of Westminster and along Pall Mall. When the subsequent trial of Horne Tooke opened on 17 November and that of Thelwall on 1 December, the verdicts seemed hardly in doubt before they got under way, although Horne Tooke played it safe and pleaded—disloyally but not incorrectly—that he had been a moderate compared to other indicted firebrands. Thelwall had prepared not so much a defence as a manifesto of British Rights of Nature and was about to give it his oratorical all until Erskine buttoned his lip. Miffed at the loss of an opportunity to address posterity he published it in 1796.

The bitter winter of 1794–5 only made Pitt's government more feverishly defensive. The war was going badly. French armies occupied first the Austrian Netherlands; then the Rhineland and finally the Dutch Republic, where an old ally, the Stadholder William V, was deposed in favour of a new revolutionary Batavian Republic. Harvests were disastrous, sending the price of wheat rocketing by 75 per cent. At the same time an export slump caused lay-offs in the textile industry. In London, the population responded with violent action. The steam-powered Great Albion Flour Mill was attacked by rioters. In the summer mass meetings were held at St George's Field. On 28

October 1795 another—said by the London Corresponding Society to be 200,000 strong, although others put it at between 40,000 and 100,000—assembled in a field by the Copenhagen House tavern in Islington to hear the 22-year-old Irishman John Binns attack the war and denounce the Pitt government. The chant was 'Peace! Bread! No Pitt! Down with George.'

On the following day the coach taking George III to open parliament was mobbed in the Mall by an angry crowd, some of them holding bread loaves wrapped in black crepe and shouting, 'No war, no famine!' In Parliament Street the coach was pelted with mud and stones, smashing its windows. At some point on the journey a projectile made a small hole that the king thought had been caused by a bullet. When he reached the House of Lords he is said to have stammered, 'My Lords, I . . . I . . . I have been shot at.' His route back to St James's Palace was no friendlier, with more missiles and broken windows. The state coach was abandoned and torn to pieces when spotted in Pall Mall; one of the royal grooms fell under its wheels, breaking his thighs and dying of the injuries. When the king tried to reach Buckingham House in a private coach, he was recognized (no one else, after all, looked like George III). The coach ground to a halt in the mêlée, and it was said that someone opened a door and attempted to drag the king from it. Only the appearance of the Horse Guards riding to the rescue saved the situation from becoming even uglier. The threat to lay hands on the king was taken especially seriously, since the previous year there had been a 'pop-gun plot' (probably a fiction invented by spies) to fire a poisoned dart at him from a custom-designed air-gun. Stories were also rife of other plots for a revolutionary coup, to take place simultaneously in London, Dublin and Edinburgh, in which the magistracy and judges would be locked up, aristocrats put under house arrest and parliament liquidated.

The mobbing of the royal coach was, of course, a godsend to Pitt's government, so much so that suspicious radicals speculated Pitt and the Home Secretary, the Duke of Portland, might have orchestrated it themselves (although their coaches were roughly treated as well). Riding the tidal wave of loyal addresses of indignation and loyalist passion, in December Pitt introduced two bills for the protection and policing of the realm. The first made meetings of more than 50 people illegal. If an assembly refused to disperse when ordered, those present could be charged with a capital crime. The second enlarged the scope of sedition still more broadly to encompass any advocacy of changes to the government, other than by acts of parliament. In other words: no pamphlets, no petitions, no meetings, no reform. Wordsworth, who on returning to England had published in 1793, in the form of a letter to the Bishop of Llandaff, a ferociously Paine-ite assault on the hereditary principle, would now have to keep his peace. Up in Newcastle Thomas Bewick—no Paine-ite revolutionary democrat—gritted his teeth. Later he remembered this as a scoundrelly time when 'Knaves and their abettors appeared to predominate in the land; and they carried their subserviency to such a length that I think, if Mr Pitt had proposed to make a law to transport all men who had pug noses, and to hang all men above 60 years of age, these persons . . . would have advocated it as a brilliant thought and a wise measure.'

Not surprisingly, the combination of propaganda, gang intimidation, genuinely patriotic volunteer militias, censorship, political spying and summary arrests succeeded in stopping the momentum of democratic agitation. Critics and reformers like William Godwin who had come to the aid of the accused in the treason trials now withdrew from direct political action, and tried to reflect on social utopias away from the furore. In any case, Godwin had come to mistrust any proposals that made the state the agency of betterment. His *Enquiry Concerning Political Justice* (1793) was the perfect tract for the disillusioned, since it argued that the only obligation for reasoning individuals was the realization of their own freedom and happiness. Any institutions that got in the way needed removing; so no religion, no system of government, no criminal law (it was, Godwin believed, hypocritical for societies to punish crimes it had generated itself), no systematic education, no accumulation of property beyond what was required to satisfy individual needs, and especially no marriage, an institution that held couples hostage to their transient passions.

That last sentiment was perhaps the only opinion that he held in common with Mary Wollstonecraft. He remembered her, not particularly warmly, as the person who wouldn't shut up when he had wanted to listen to Tom Paine at one of the Johnson dinners. But when Godwin read the Scandinavian letters he declared that 'If ever there was a book calculated to make a man in love with its author, this appears to me to be the book.' Love and Mr Godwin, short, earnest, pedantic, almost inhumanly cerebral, had not kept close company. Yet women—actresses, writers whom he called 'the Fairs', some of them hot with romance—set their cap at him. But it was Mary who melted his chilly soul. And he in turn made her a more reflective, quieter person. After all the miseries she had inflicted on herself through the years of torment with Imlay, Godwin's mixture of coolness and clumsiness seemed positively winning. She relaxed in the growing certainty of his feeling, and the woman who had gone on record as mistrustful of sex now took shameless pleasure in initiating Godwin, reassuring his anxieties: 'If the felicity of last night has had the same effect on your health as on my countenance, you have no cause to lament your failure of *resolution*: for I have seldom seen so much live fire running about my features as this morning when recollections—very dear, called forth the blush of pleasure, as I adjusted my hair.'

Mary became pregnant. In March 1797 William Godwin, the sworn enemy of marriage and churches, got married to 'Mrs Imlay' (her first union being considered merely a republican civic convenience and thus not binding) at St Pancras Church. Mary was satisfied that she had not 'clogged my soul by promising obedience', and the two of them let it be known that they would not continuously cohabit, but continue to respect each other's independence and see others of the opposite sex, sharing lodgings some of the time but keeping their own respective places. It was bravely said. But as Mary's belly grew, Godwin found himself unaccountably enjoying the small pleasures of domesticity and companionship. Theirs was growing into exactly the kind of intimate conjugal friendship that Mary—without ever having experienced anything like it—had prescribed as the formula for enduring married happiness.

Which is what made the end so unbearably sad. When the time came for her labour, on 30 August, she called a local midwife. But after the baby, another girl (the future author of *Frankenstein*), was born, the placenta failed to descend down the birth canal, threatening sepsis. A physician, hurriedly summoned from Westminster Hospital did what he could, but the placenta ruptured in fragments as Mary lay haemorrhaging in agony.

Eventually the bleeding stopped. Mary was strong enough to tell Godwin that she would never have survived had she not been determined to continue sharing her life with him. The next day she felt much better and was happy to have her old, best mentor, Joseph Johnson, visit. The following day she seemed better still and Godwin thought it was safe enough for him to take a walk. When he got back he found her convulsed with shivering fits and obviously running a high fever. She never got better. A week later, on 10 September 1797, Mary Wollstonecraft died of septicaemia.

She was 38. Godwin, the supreme rationalist, was distraught. He wrote to a friend, 'My wife is now dead . . . I firmly believe that there does not exist her equal in the world. I know from experience we were formed to make each other happy. I have not the least expectation that I can now ever know happiness again.' It was the best

98

and most unlikely epitaph: that she had been the bearer of happiness to the man who had declared war on marriage. Through Mary, the thinker had learned to feel. Through Godwin, the creature of feeling had recovered her power of thought. Wollstonecraft is properly remembered as the founder of modern feminism; for making a statement, still powerful in its clarity, that the whole nature of women was not to be confused with their biology. But nature, biology, had killed her.

On 17 October 1797, the Austrian Empire gritted its teeth and made its peace at the Italian town of Campo Formio with a 28-year-old Corsican called Bonaparte, whom no one (in Vienna at any rate) had heard of a few years before. Napoleon did so without waiting for permission from his civilian masters in the Directory. But since much of Italy, including some of the greatest cities and richest territories, now passed either into French control or under its influence, the Directors were hardly likely to repudiate their military prodigy. The ending of the war with Austria now allowed France to redeploy a large number of troops to a different theatre and its one remaining enemy. Within a month more than 100,000 of them were camped between Rouen—William the Conqueror's old capital—and the Channel coast. The point of the massive troop concentration was not lost on Pitt's government. Suddenly the world seemed a more dangerous place.

Since the war with the French Republic had begun in 1793 it had been an axiom in Westminster that, sooner or later, the revolutionary origins of that state would prove its military ruin; that an army built from rabble would, after an initial burst of self-deluded energy, collapse in on itself. The Terror's habit of guillotining its own generals, should they be careless enough to lose the odd battle, only confirmed this diagnosis. But with Bonaparte's Italian campaign, so shocking in its speed and completeness, and with the French tightening their grip on a whole swathe of continental territory from the Netherlands down through the Rhineland, threatening even the Swiss cantons, it seemed that this bandit state had done the unthinkable and actually created a formidable fighting machine. Its troops did not run away. It seemed to manufacture more and more guns; and it obviously knew how to transform conquest into workable military assets, taking money, horses, wagons and conscripts as it rolled along. James Gillray might be starting to draw caricatures literally belittling this Bonaparte as a scrawny scarecrow wearing plumed hats a size too big. But William Pitt and his intelligent, inexhaustible secretary of war, the Scot Henry Dundas, knew he was no joke. Tom Paine, for one, believed he would be the long-awaited Liberator of Britain; urging him to prepare a fleet of 1000 gunboats, he did his best to persuade the future Emperor that in the event of an invasion there would be a huge uprising, for 'the mass of the people are friends to liberty'. Initially, at any rate, Bonaparte was impressed enough with Paine to appoint him leader of a provisional English Revolutionary Government to travel with the invasion fleet when the order was given to sail. But the order never came, Bonaparte turning his attention instead to Egypt.

The prospect of Paine's return was not, however, high on the list of the British government's concerns. Even before the magnitude of Bonaparte's victories in Italy had sunk in, something happened in the spring of 1797 that did indeed seem to turn the world upside down: mutiny in the Royal Navy. The base at Spithead in the Solent, off Portsmouth, had been the first to go; then the Nore in the Thames Estuary. At one point the mutineers managed to blockade the Thames itself. Their demands were pay and the cashiering of some officers, not any kind of radical agenda. But the commonplace was that a third of the navy's 114,000 manpower was Irish, and since Ireland had apparently become a breeding ground for revolutionaries and known agents of the French, the mutinies suddenly took on the aspect of a conspiracy. In fact, the 'Irish third' was a myth. Irish sailors—often the victims of impressment—numbered no more than 15,000. But even this was enough to scare the Lords of the Admiralty, who had had a frighteningly narrow escape the previous December. A fleet of 43 French ships and 15,000 troops, commanded by the general thought to be the most dangerous of all, Louis-Lazare Hoche, and the Irish republican Theobald Wolfe Tone, had been prevented by foul weather from making a landing at Bantry Bay on the southwest tip of County Cork.

Ireland was, as always, the swinging back door to Britain. Had Hoche managed to land his troops, they would have had an immediate numerical superiority over the defending British garrison of at least six to one. For a country known to be so vulnerable it was, as Wolfe Tone had correctly

101

pointed out to the Directors in Paris, complacently defended. There were perhaps only about 13,000 regular British troops stationed there, who in wartime might be reinforced by another 60,000 militia. And even these estimates of the defence were based on the loyal turn-out of the Volunteer movement during the American war; since then, especially in the last few years, the political situation in Ireland had drastically changed.

If it had changed for the worse, moreover, it was largely the fault of Pitt's own mishandling of the situation; his refusal to act on his own intelligent instincts. Since the creation of an Irish parliament in 1782, an articulate, energetic political class—both Catholic and Protestant—had been able to air its grievances against the narrow ascendancy of the Protestant oligarchy who ruled from Dublin Castle. The American lesson of the risks of imposing taxation without representation seemed even more pertinent in Belfast than in Boston. A meaningful degree of political devolution and electoral reform—not least the enfranchisement of the Catholic majority—was urged. But for all the flamboyant rhetoric of the lawyer Henry Grattan, the leader of this movement, there was no thought of a revolutionary break-away. A freer Ireland was supposed to be a more, not a less, loyal Ireland—and the hope was that George III would in fact be less, not more, of an absentee. When the French Revolution broke out, Pitt's first thought was that the natural conservatism of Irish Catholics could be used to tie the Irish reform movement closer to Britain and make sure they did not enter some sort of unholy alliance with the non-conformist Dissenter radicals, especially in Belfast. The Dissenters' sympathy for the Revolution was only too clear, not least from their jubilant celebration of the anniversary of the fall of the Bastille. But the precondition of a rapprochement between the Catholics and the British government was, obviously, their emancipation, or at the very least the relief of their legal and civic disabilities, limiting their rights to vote and hold political office.

It was in the mid-1790s, then, that a scenario to be repeated time and again over the next two centuries miserably played itself out. The prospect of a British government selling out the Protestant ascendancy threatened a backlash to the point of a complete breakdown of the Dublin Castle system of government. And the leaders of the ascendancy were able to use the generalized social panic spread by the Revolution—and apparently confirmed in the violent acts of armed militias, such as the Catholic 'Defenders' and the Protestant Peep o' Day Boys, in Irish country towns and villages—to persuade Pitt that this was no time to be toying with liberalism. In 1795 a new Whig viceroy of Ireland, Earl Fitzwilliam, came to the point rather more abruptly than Pitt cared for, peremptorily dismissing a number of high officers of the Castle and making known his plans for a sweeping emancipation of the Catholics that would give them equal rights with Protestants. He was recalled after only seven weeks in office.

The removal of Fitzwilliam—however clumsy his tactics—was a true turning point in the swift downhill ride of Irish politics towards sectarian misery, terror and war. For it finally disabused the 'United Irishmen'—an organization formed in 1791

103

with many Protestant as well as Catholic members—of any remaining optimism that fundamental justice and reform would be gained from continued collaboration with the British government. Increasingly, as wartime conditions began to pinch, the question of precisely what quarrel Ireland had with *France* became voiced. Young Irish republicans like Lord Edward Fitzgerald (the cousin of Charles James Fox) and Arthur O'Connor had been in Paris invoking a connection between the two causes that went back to 1689, attempting to persuade the French government to extend its 'liberation' strategy of revolutionary assistance to their own country. But the conversion of Wolfe Tone, the Protestant secretary of the Catholic Committee, from a mainstream constitutional reformer into a full-fledged republican nationalist, prepared to wear the uniform of a French general, was symptomatic of the line Irish politicians were now prepared to cross to realize their dream of national self-government. Once, not so long ago, Tone had hoped to work *with* the British government to move towards autonomy. But after that government broke up the United Irishmen (forcing its members into Britain itself, to make contact with Scots and English revolutionary radicals), and following Fitzwilliam's removal, Tone's public utterances defined the enemy oppressor and conqueror as 'England'.

A deteriorating military situation in Europe and a consciousness of their limited resources in Ireland meant that Dublin Castle could not afford to dispense with the help of Protestant militia—like the Orange Order, founded in 1795—to counter

Defenderism, and thus instantly aggravated the situation. By the beginning of 1798, then, the tragic spectacle of modern Irish history was already on view: rival, armed sectarian irregulars committing mutual atrocities against the backdrop of an embattled Britain fighting to close its own back door against invasion.

While the French army was encamped on the Normandy coast, Irish agents had been sent to England and Scotland to sound out the possibility of a domestic uprising in the event of an invasion. They returned deeply pessimistic, but much more optimistic about a rebellion in Ireland itself. For months, the familiar game of 'after you' was played out, reminiscent of the disastrous strategy used by the Scottish Jacobites during the first half of the century: the French waited for signs of insurrection, while the United Irishmen waited for news of a French expedition. Finally, in the spring of 1798, the Irish acted first, attacking Dublin Castle and bringing out much of the southeast in revolt. However, Ulster in the north, the key to success, remained ominously quiet. The customary atrocities were committed by both sides and at Vinegar Hill on 21 June the Irish were brutally routed by British troops, giving the new viceroy, the now aged but still vigorous Cornwallis, his last, bloodiest success in a career devoted to cleaning up the messes made by the British Empire.

French help did come, but it was too late and landed at Killala on the shore of County Mayo in the west, as far away as it was possible to be from the decisive southeastern theatre of conflict in Leinster and Munster. But the western province of Connacht *was* poor, angry and overwhelmingly

Catholic. It had strong Defender support in the villages and country towns and an impromptu army, led by schoolteachers, farmers and priests, and armed with pitchforks and pikes. Connacht rallied to the French. Before the British and the yeomanry could regroup the insurgents had some success, at Castlebar; but before long their supplies of men and munitions dwindled and capitulation was inevitable. To cap the disaster, a small fleet with Tone on board, which had barely made it past the British blockade at Brest, was caught off the coast of Donegal. Tried and found guilty of treason, Tone committed suicide in prison before he could be hanged.

A bald summary of the military ebb and flow of the events of what became known as 'the year of the French' does not, however, properly record the magnitude of the misery of 1798. At least 30,000 Irish were slaughtered; an economically and politically dynamic world turned into a charnel house of invasion, repression and sectarian massacres—although, once the immediate military threat had passed, the government sensibly commuted many of the sentences passed on rebels. More decisively, hopes of Irish freedom were replaced by the fact, in 1801, of Irish absorption into Britain: the completion of the last cross on the Union Jack. The parliament at Dublin (retrospectively considered the root of the problem) was abolished and Irish members would now sit at Westminster. But this move was anything but a quid pro quo. The number of Irish boroughs, and so the number of representatives in parliament, was steeply reduced and the Irish debt (unlike the Scottish equivalent a century earlier) remained separate—and a serious taxable burden on the people of Ireland. Henry Grattan, who had lived through all this, was only telling the truth when he declared that the union was 'not an identification of people, as it excludes the Catholic from the parliament and the state . . . it is . . . not an identification of the two nations; it is merely a merger of the parliament of the one nation in that of the other; one nation, namely England, retains her full proportion; Ireland strikes off two thirds . . . by that act of absorption the feeling of one nation is not identified but alienated.'

But 1798 was not just 'the year of the French'; it was the year of the British too. For when the French landed in Ireland, some of those who had believed most fiercely in the imminent brotherhood of man decided, philosophically, to come home. A large number of the 'Friends of Peace' had argued that 'Pitt's war' was a thinly disguised instrument of oppression, giving pretexts for attacking free speech and closing down the avenues of protest while making the monied richer and the labouring people poorer. (Joseph Johnson probably still felt that way when he and J. S. Jordan, Paine's publisher, were indicted for publishing attacks on the loyalist Bishop of Llandaff.) Many, however, were coming to have almost as dim a view of Bonaparte and the France of the Directory, which seemed, to those who had been there and those who had heard, just as much a tyranny imposed by the propertied classes. Perhaps, too, with a powerful 'Army of England' arrayed across the Channel, they were beginning to concede the power of Burke's axiom in the *Reflections* that there was something unnatural about cosmopolitanism; that the impartial distribution of affection only testified to the shallowness of those sentiments. Nature, he had said, was particular, local. 'To be attached to the subdivision, to love the little platoon we belong to in society, is the first principle, the germ, as it were, of public affections. It is the first link in the series by which we proceed toward a love to our country and to mankind.' In other words, there was no humanitarianism except through patriotism.

At any rate, this was certainly the emotion budding in the warm breast and mighty brain of the 26-year-old Samuel Taylor Coleridge. In the spring of 1798 a quarto edition of three of his long(ish) poems announced, simultaneously, his disillusionment with France and his concern about the fate of Britain. The fact that the publisher of the poems was Joseph Johnson is itself eloquent about the shifting direction of the apostles of nature. Like so many of his generation Coleridge had fervently believed—at Cambridge University and afterwards—that the cause of the French Revolution, the cause of Jean-Jacques Rousseau, opened a new age in which mankind would live according to the rules of nature. The first of the poems, 'Fears in Solitude', written during the height of the invasion panic—before Napoleon took his expedition off to Egypt instead, to attack Britain's Indian empire from the rear—is an extraordinary work of conflicted anguish and ecstasy. Coleridge grieves for the normalization of the continuing war:

We send our mandates for the certain death
Of thousands and ten thousands! Boys and
  girls,
And women, that would groan to see a child
Pull off an insect's leg, all read of war,
The best amusement for our morning meal!

But he has also come to accept that, given the nature of the enemy, there may be no alternative and his verses swell into a patriotic threnody:

O native Britain! O my Mother Isle!
How shouldst thou prove aught else but dear
  and holy
To me, who from thy lakes and mountain-hills,
Thy clouds, thy quiet dales, thy rocks and seas,
Have drunk in all my intellectual life,
All sweet sensations, all ennobling thoughts . . .
. . . O divine
And beauteous island! thou hast been my sole
And most magnificent temple . . .

The embrace of homeland is followed by the repudiation of the hypocrite aggressor. The second stanza of 'France: An Ode' recalls in sorrow the euphoria of 1789:

When France in wrath her giant-limbs
  upreared,
And with that oath which smote air, earth, and
  sea,
Stamped her strong foot and said she would be
  free,
Bear witness for me, how I hoped and feared!

At school at Christ's Hospital the 16-year-old Coleridge had indeed written an ode celebrating the fall of the Bastille, and it was to be 10 years before any sort of recantation crept in. At Jesus College, Cambridge, he had continued to be a notorious trouble-maker, one of the rowdiest supporters of the Unitarian Reverend William Frend when the university brought proceedings to remove him from his fellowship for his attacks on the Church and his 'seditious' opinions. Although his prodigal ways had driven Coleridge to enlist briefly (and under an assumed name) as a trooper in the 15th Dragoons, his political and social idealism (as much as a cripplingly embarrassing case of saddle sores) got him out of uniform again, certified by the discharging officer as 'insane'. (Coleridge was always a superb actor.) En route to the mandatory summer walking tour for democrats, where he followed the Pennant tour of the Brito-Celtic sublime, at Oxford Coleridge met the equally ardent young student, Richard Southey. Together the two idealists planned to establish in America a social utopia, a 'Pantisocracy', in which (to the delight, perhaps, of Mary Wollstonecraft if she could but have known it) men would do the house cleaning. The nearest Coleridge got to the banks of the Susquehanna river, though, was Bristol, where for 10 months in 1795–6, during which he met William Wordsworth, he gave public lectures and edited his paper, *The Watchman*. Throughout this period Coleridge remained a coruscating critic of Pitt and his government, referring to the prime minister as 'the fiend' and to his speeches as 'Mystery concealing Meanness as clouds envelop a dunghill'. He attended a dinner in honour of Charles James Fox, went to see the trials of Horne Tooke and Thelwall, and became a friend of the latter, the 'Peripatetic', even while scowling at his atheism. Above all, the ex-trooper's lectures and articles were full of hatred for the war itself, as a misery inflicted by the rich and powerful on the poor and helpless who paid for it with their taxes and their blood.

In 1798 Coleridge's tune changed dramatically. *The Watchman* had, predictably, folded, leading its editor to comment that 'I have snapped my squeaking baby-trumpet of sedition and have hung up its fragments in the chamber of Penitences.' The extinguishing by the French of the independent Confederation of Swiss Cantons had made it unmistakably clear that the threat was not from a liberator but from a common-or-garden military aggressor. Switzerland, moreover, was not just another anachronism to be knocked over. To the Romantics who, like Wordsworth in 1790, had hiked all the way there (after celebrating Bastille Day in France) it was the temple of liberty and the place, *par excellence*, where the fortress of nature had preserved a people in simplicity, innocence and freedom. Rousseau himself had been born in the shadow of Mont Blanc; William Tell had been reinvented (along with Robin Hood in Britain) as one of the classic heroes of defiance against tyranny; the oath sworn on the Rütli meadow, binding the cantons against their Austrian overlords, had been immortalized by Henry Fuseli. To violate its sanctity, as the French had done, was to unmask themselves as squalid oppressors, all the more detestable for mantling themselves still in the tricolour and pontificating hypocritically about the Rights of Man. Appalled at the betrayal, Coleridge let fly his curse:

> O France, that mockest Heaven, adulterous, blind,
> And patriot only in pernicious toils!
> Are these thy boasts, Champion of human kind?
> . . . To insult the shrine of Liberty with spoils
> From freemen torn; to tempt and to betray?

Disillusionment with France did not make Coleridge a reactionary. His dilemma now was how to sustain his 'social affection' for the downtrodden beyond the posturing and polemics, the sound and the fury, that had turned ordinary people into cannon fodder. The answer came to him in the third of the three poems in the Johnson-published quarto, 'Frost at Midnight', where he looks at his infant son and imagines him far and free from city din:

> But thou, my babe! shalt wander like a breeze
> By lakes and sandy shores, beneath the crags
> Of ancient mountain, and beneath the clouds.

Nature would be both consolation and instruction, but its head tutor now would be not Rousseau but God. Looked at with the honesty and seriousness it deserved, nature did have the power to transform each and every life—but not in the sense of drafting a political agenda. Constitutions and revolutions now seemed absurdly beside the point compared with the illumination to be had from the embrace of the natural and the simple. A vote would never make one happy. A snowdrop in February, the arc of a lark's flight, the babble of a crawling babe just might.

Needless to say, these insights did not come to Coleridge in the bustling commercial port of Bristol. He had taken a cottage at Nether Stowey in north Somerset where, on a previous trip, he had met someone whom he thought of as the epitome of the honest, natural man, the tanner and enthusiastic democrat Thomas Poole. Poole had found Coleridge the house, but, more important, it put him within walking distance (given that Coleridge thought nothing of walking 40 miles) of Wordsworth, who was living with his sister Dorothy at Racedown in Dorset. In the years since his return from France, Wordsworth, encouraged by his sister, had also moved away from the shallow apostrophizing of 'mankind' and towards an active sympathy with the plight of particular individuals, often the outcasts of society: crippled veterans, itinerant beggars, ragged waifs and orphans, destitute labourers. In 1795 Dorothy described the 'peasants' of the southwest as 'miserably poor; their cottages are shapeless structures (I may almost say) of wood and clay; indeed they are not at all beyond what might be expected in savage life'. During the second half of 1797 and the spring of 1798, after Wordsworth had moved closer to Coleridge, taking a rather grander house at Alfoxden, the two planned something unprecedented. They proposed to compile a collaborative anthology of their work, which would use the plain speech of the labourers and cottagers of the West Country people, and be utterly free of the ornamental fantasies of the pastoral tradition. The 'Lyrical Ballads' would not be pretty. They would look at the broken bodies and ruined hovels with a clear eye and an open heart. Often they would sound impolite, and their meter might tread as heavily as a hob-nailed boot on a parlour floor. But to be true to the sovereign force of nature meant, above all, not treating it as a bookish idea, much less a political slogan; it meant living with it as a physical reality. *That* would be their revolution.

Some of their greatest and certainly their most intensely compassionate work resulted from this collaboration. Following the plodding round of 'The Old Cumberland Beggar' from house to house, Wordsworth adopted precisely that body of men whom the powerful had judged most expendable of all.

> But deem not this man useless—Statesman! ye
> Who are so restless in your wisdom, ye
> Who have a broom still ready in your hands
> To rid the world of nuisances . . .

Why? Because the beggar, through his visits, knitted together in a common act of sympathy a mere aggregate of men and women and fashioned them into a true community, a village. And he also brings together the past with the present:

> While from door to door,
> This old man creeps, the villagers in him
> Behold a record which together binds
> Past deeds and offices of charity
> Else unremembered . . .
> . . . Among the farms and solitary huts,
> Hamlets and thinly-scattered villages,

114

Where'er the aged Beggar takes his rounds,
The mild necessity of use compels
To acts of love . . .

Although he may not have owned up to it yet, Wordsworth's growing preference for individual acts of charity over collective acts of policy; his budding Christian sense of the importance of individual, face-to-face encounters, often deep in the country; and his dawning realization of the unforced strength of tradition, all put him much closer to Burke than Paine. But to some of the locals, who were bemused by the poets hobnobbing with their inferiors (especially since Coleridge decided to express his social sympathy by wearing the clothes of the Somerset country people), these eccentricities started to seem dangerously peculiar. It was rumoured that the gentlemen spoke French. Perhaps some sort of plot was being hatched in the Quantocks in the year of national peril? The appearance of John Thelwall, who—naturally— had *walked* the 150 miles from London, only confirmed their suspicions. After his acquittal for treason, undeterred by the spies who stuck to him like leeches, Thelwall had become the star lecturer on the provincial radical circuit, in 1796 alone giving 22 lectures in places as far apart as Derby and Norwich. When it became obvious that Thelwall was the reason that the Quantocks poets were attracting talk he decided to move on, taking the spies with him. He believed that, despite fierce arguments with Wordsworth and Coleridge over atheism, he and they were essentially of a like mind; it was a view, alas, not reciprocated.

Among the pilgrims who came to Nether

Stowey and Alfoxden, none was more awe-struck than the 19-year-old William Hazlitt. To Wordsworth and Coleridge, Hazlitt—painfully shy and slightly peculiar—was a puppyish oddity, an amusement. Nothing in his manner suggested that this gauche, pop-eyed aspiring painter and son of an Irish Unitarian minister in Shropshire would become the greatest essayist in the English language. Hazlitt, who in January 1798 had walked 10 miles in the frozen mire to Shrewsbury to hear Coleridge deliver one of his stupendous Unitarian sermons, was by his own overwrought account 'dumb, inarticulate, helpless, like a worm by the wayside, crushed, bleeding, lifeless'. From the minute Coleridge opened his mouth, his voice rising 'like a steam of rich distilled perfumes', Hazlitt was a goner; the big man with the long, dark, flopping hair and full lips put him in mind of St John crying in the wilderness, 'whose food was locusts and wild honey'.

Later that week the great man actually came to visit Hazlitt's father on Church business. William, as usual, sat staring at the floor, tongue-tied except when blurting out speeches on some topic on which he happened to feel passionately and supposed (not wrongly) that Coleridge felt the same—Burke, Mary Wollstonecraft, William Godwin. On the table was a haunch of Welsh mutton and a dish of turnips. Flooded with happiness at talking to, and being talked at by, Coleridge, Hazlitt savoured each mouthful as if he had never tasted food before. Then, in a daze of veneration, after being invited to Nether Stowey in the spring, he followed the poet six miles down the road (passing the Romantic qualification of having good walking legs).

In Somerset, Hazlitt was taken to Wordsworth's manor house and met Dorothy; slept in a blue-hung bed there opposite portraits of George I and George II, and saw William return from Bristol and 'make havoc' with half a Cheshire cheese. He got to take morning walks with the poets and listened to them recite drafts of their verses with, he said (tantalizingly), 'a decided chaunt'; Coleridge was always more theatrical, Wordsworth more quietly lyrical. On one of those walks, just before Coleridge left for Germany to study philosophy and go wandering in the Harz mountains, they took another long saunter along the path above the seashore, then 'loitered on the "ribbed sea-sands"' and examined odd species of seaweed; it was there, finally, that Hazlitt thought he understood what they meant by living naturally. A fisherman told them there had been a drowning the day before and that he and his mates had tried to save the boy at the risk of their own lives. 'He said,' wrote Hazlitt later, 'he did not know how it was that they ventured, but, "Sir, we have a nature towards one another." '

'One another!' *This* was 'social affection' in action, and what Hazlitt thought he saw in the poets' shared households in Somerset was an unforced community based on mutual sympathy: unaffected family life; easy conversation with the people of the villages; the rediscovery of unspoiled humanity far from the fads and frenzies of metropolitan fashion.

When, in 1802, Hazlitt wanted to see the poets again he had to go north, for both of them had resettled in the Lake District: Wordsworth was

117

living with his sister and brother John in a little cottage at Grasmere, and Coleridge in the much grander Greta Hall nearby. But something had cooled along with the climate of their countryside. Nature now seemed, not to connect them with the daily world beyond their immediate company, but rather to detach them from it. The words 'solitude' and 'solitary' started recurring, especially in Wordsworth's poems; and when he introduced figures, hewn almost from the rocky landscape, they were seen as desolate apparitions silhouetted against the bare hills. To Hazlitt, the only serious connection of 'the gang' seemed to be with each other. Grasmere had become a little commune of family and friends, reading to each other, taking possession of the countryside by carving their names into rocks and trees; sharing meals. If they still thought of themselves as poet–philosophers, what they preached, Hazlitt found, was not any sort of public reformation (much less revolution) but rather the recasting of individual lives by re-establishing the simplicity and intensity of the connection to nature experienced in childhood. Coleridge's idea of a great change was to turn the Lake District yellow by surreptitiously sowing laburnum seeds in the woods.

This intense self-absorption irked Hazlitt, now 25 and a struggling artist who kept himself alive by hack journalism. He knew perfectly well that, for all the ostentatious simplicity of their lives in the Lakes, the poets could not have afforded it without the help of gentleman patrons like Sir George Beaumont. So when Coleridge ruled out Hazlitt as a travelling companion for his friend Tom Wedgwood (the ex-British Club member from

Paris), describing him as intellectually brilliant but personally '99 in 100 singularly repulsive—: brow-hanging, shoe-contemplative, strange . . . he is jealous, gloomy, and of an irritable Pride—addicted to women', and when Wedgwood maliciously repeated this to the horrified and hurt Hazlitt, the disenchantment was total. He was the essayist, after all, who would write the definitive piece on 'The Pleasures of Hating', and in the years ahead he seldom missed an opportunity to sink his sharp little teeth into Coleridge's ailing, opium-addled reputation. It was personal but it was also political. Hazlitt never forgave Wordsworth or Coleridge their apostasy; the indecent eagerness with which they echoed Edmund Burke when he made Nature not a revolutionary, but a patriot.

In 1802 the signing of the Peace of Amiens briefly opened the sea lanes to safe passage in and out of France. Tom Paine, who had never really recovered from the typhus he had contracted in jail, but who was suffering even more from a clinical aversion to Napoleon ('the very butcher of Liberty and the greatest monster that Nature ever spewed') had finally given up on France as the haven of freedom and social justice. He sailed from Le Havre to the United States where, after predictably quarrelling with George Washington and John Adams, the country's first two presidents, he moved to the 300-acre farm in New Rochelle, New York, presented to him by the grateful state in 1784. He lived there almost until the end of his days, amidst a few hogs and cows. Pilgrims who came to visit him (and there were many) were disconcerted by his return to a state of nature, so relentlessly frugal that he dried out his used tea leaves after a pot to recycle them for further use. Poverty finally forced him to sell the farm, and he died in New York City in 1809, near penniless.

Not everyone shared his horror of the state of despotism that France had become. William Hazlitt, for example, had become enthralled by the Napoleonic epic and would, in fact, never free himself of it, later writing a biography that is perhaps the dullest of all his works. In 1802 he somehow scraped up enough money to go to Paris, where he stood in the Louvre, agog at the masterpieces, while conveniently overlooking the fact that the First Consul had accumulated the contents of the museum by plundering the churches and galleries of Europe. In the Salon Carré he saw Charles James Fox—touring Europe during the brief period of peace—now grown fat and grey but still Hazlitt's indomitable hero for refusing to truckle to Pitt's wartime security state.

And much as he despised Bonapartist France, Wordsworth too made the summer packet boat crossing along with his sister Dorothy. He had no intention of recapturing his youthful passions, but rather proposed to put a seal on them. He had decided to marry and, before he could do so with an easy conscience, needed to set eyes once more on Annette and his daughter, Caroline; perhaps assure himself that they would not stand in his way. For her part Annette had practical reasons for seeing her old lover. She needed to be certain that, once he was married, he would continue to pay the modest maintenance he had been sending for Caroline's upbringing. And since, in Napoleon's misogynist state, mothers of illegitimate children had no rights over their offspring, she also needed to feel certain that Wordsworth would not try to take their child from her. The reassurances were duly given. The poet, who found he could not give much else, bestowed on mother and child a volume of his verses. They went their separate ways.

Both Coleridge and Wordsworth were now fast turning into all-out propagandists for John Bull. When the truce with France broke down in May 1803, and an invasion seemed even more likely than in 1798, Coleridge wrote in back-to-the-wall proto-Churchillian mode, revelling in insularity, in the concept of Britain as the last refuge against European tyranny: 'Englishmen must think of themselves and act for themselves . . . let France bribe or puzzle all Europe into a confederation against us. I will not fear for my country . . . the words of Isaiah will be truly prophetic. "They trod the winepress alone and of the nations there was none with them." '

In these Boneyphobic years it was Coleridge, not Hazlitt, who was in tune with the vast majority of Britons. The threat was not, after all, imaginary. In 1803–4 there were at least 100,000 French and allied troops camped at Boulogne, and 2300 vessels (most of them, admittedly, small) waiting for the order to sail. When Napoleon put the Bayeux Tapestry on display for the first time the point was not lost, neither on the massed ranks of the army of England nor on the defenders 20 miles across the narrow straits. By the end of 1804, Britain was also at war with Spain.

William Pitt, however, had not survived 10 years of brutal, global war only to go down with an arrow in his eye. Recognizing the scale of what he was up against on his return to office in May 1804, he and the new First Lord of the Admiralty, Henry Dundas, mobilized national resources on a scale and with a thoroughness not seen even in his father's heyday as a war leader 50 years before. More impressively, they did it for the most part without coercion, unlike the Prussians or the Russians. (Although more than once impressment officers, tipped off that he was lecturing, had tried to seize the irrepressible Thelwall, who took to carrying a loaded pistol and on one occasion pressed it to the temples of the assailant who tried to take him.) While the loyalism of the early years of the war had been exhibited mostly by the gentry and patriot middle classes, who delivered men-at-arms to the government reserve, the extraordinary numbers who volunteered to fight against the Napoleonic threat of invasion did so in a much more spontaneous manner. It is a phenomenon that recent histories call, without anachronism, 'national defence patriotism'. Sometimes the authorities' worst problem was avoiding the chaos of being inundated with manpower, virtually all of it untrained and much of it undisciplined. A Defence of the Realm Act ordered lists to be compiled of every able-bodied male between 17 and 55, so that a home guard could be formed and called on in the event of an invasion. In 1804, at the height of the scare, more than 400,000 came forward—around half of those asked. Many of the keenest came not, as the government had predicted, from the countryside but from the southern ports (most immediately in the front line) and the industrial towns of the Midlands and the north which, just a decade earlier, had been written off as hotbeds of disloyalty and sedition. By late

1804, the country had been transformed into 'Fortress Britannia'. Out of a population of 15 million, 3¾ million men were of an age to bear arms. And over 800,000—one in five—were in fact part of the national defence; 386,000 as volunteers, of whom 266,000 were in the army and 120,000 in the navy.

The Scottish contribution to this massive mobilization was huge. Highland contingents—to the satisfaction of Dundas, a Lowlander Scot, who, since he had a holiday house on Loch Earn, rather fancied himself an honorary Highlander—were conspicuous. It was, after all, an alternative to emigration, and during this war the Black Watch, the Gordon Highlanders and the Cameron Highlanders all achieved mythic status. Much was made of the fact that the first blessed martyrs of the land war—Sir Ralph Abercromby, killed in Egypt in 1801, and Sir John Moore, killed in Spain in 1809—were Scots. Although Scottish soldiers had served in America and India, it was in *this* war, above all, that Scotland's sense of itself was enhanced, rather than diminished, by being British.

The king, of course, was the symbolic focus of all this genuine patriotic feeling. When George III reviewed 27,000 volunteers in Hyde Park in October 1803 a crowd of a half a million watched the spectacular parade. Bad memories of the mobbed coach in October 1795 must have seemed a very long way away. He was able, now, to enjoy public appearances again and between 1797 and 1800 even attended 55 theatre performances to drink in the applause of the audience. It was in these years and for this king that 'God Save the King' (rather than 'God Save the Rights of Man')

123

became, definitively, the national anthem. Burke's loyalism, defined by him as a popular sentiment, appeared, at this moment anyway, to have been vindicated; the territorial imperative of defending hearth and home established as the most natural instinct of all.

It was exactly at this moment that the mythology of Merrie England, of the sceptred isle, was born, complete with especially passionate revivals of the appropriate Shakespeare histories. *Anything* historical found an enthusiastic following, a market, as now, perhaps for the first time, the past became a pastime, but a serious pastime—a way to discover Britishness. The romance of Britain had begun as radical geography and had come of age as patriotic history. Books for children sprouted illustrations and scenes that told little Johnny and Jane Bulls their island story. King John at Runnymede, Queen Elizabeth at Tilbury, Bonnie Prince Charlie at Glenfinnan, all sprang off the page. They reappeared in Madame Tussaud's new waxwork museum, and in popular paintings by illustrator–artists like Thomas Stothard. Meeting the craving to make contact with the ancestors, books on historical costume, furniture, sports, weapons and armour all appeared. And after the great authority on medieval arms and armour, Samuel Rush Meyrick, was invited by George IV to reorganize the collection at Windsor Castle so that phantom knights could be stood beneath the big histories painted by Benjamin West, an entire generation of country gentlemen went to their barns and attics to clean the rust off ancient swords and helms and reassembled them in their newly Gothicized 'Great Hall'.

124

As well as the chronicle of their own war, history had become patriotic entertainment. And the biggest boon to the business was its most fantastic showman, Horatio Nelson. He may have been not much over 5 feet tall, with only one arm, blind in one eye, prematurely grey hair and no teeth, but in every way that counted Nelson was larger than life. As a naval commander he was a genius, and no one was more convinced of that than Nelson himself. He came along at precisely the moment when the Romantic cult of genius was itself being born. Conventionally, the pantheon of God-kissed talent was reserved for the great artists—Shakespeare, Milton, Michelangelo. But Nelson's astounding career and his own equally prodigious talent for self-promotion made it possible for a military man to be treated this way too. From the start, the impresarios of patriotic entertainment made him their star. The victory at the battle of the Nile in 1798 had, after all, everything calculated to pull in the crowds— Mameluke warriors, camels, crocodiles and the French going down *en masse* to Davy Jones's locker. Henry Aston Barker set box-office records with his 360-degree panoramic 'Battle of the Nile'. But for William Turner, ex-coachmaker and painter, even huge pictures in the round didn't do justice to the epic. Off Fleet Street Turner built a water theatre called 'the Naumachia, after the Roman flooded arenas. Queues formed round the block to get into Turner's 1½-hour Nelson spectacular, complete with ear-splitting cannon and smoke machines. (The other Turner would inspect what was left of the *Victory*, along with his fellow artist Philippe de Loutherbourg, whose unerring

125

instinct for public taste had taken him from Derbyshire wonders to naval battle pieces, so that he could achieve in 1808 his astonishing *coup de théâtre, The Battle of Trafalgar, as Seen from the Mizen Starboard Shrouds of the* Victory.)

But it was hard to upstage the little man himself. Everything about him, even (or especially) his passion for Emma Hamilton, was a gift to the cult of celebrity. Although Pitt and the king and the stuffed shirts at the Admiralty cringed at his refusal to disguise his relationship with the much-painted woman who was, after all, the wife of the British ambassador to Naples, Nelson's reputation for naughtiness did nothing to harm his popularity; quite possibly the reverse. He was already the glamorous, charismatic outsider, and all his well-known vices of vanity, recklessness and arrogance were sold, not least by him, as part and parcel of the heroic bravura. Nelson played on his cult like a harp. He dressed to kill and be killed, jangling with decorations, whether on parade or the poopdeck, so it was no surprise when all that glittering hardware did, in fact, make him the perfect target for the French mizenmast sharpshooters, one of whom hit his target at the battle of Trafalgar on 21 October 1805. Nelson had known that the battle would be decisive for the preservation, not just of British maritime dominance, but the very independence of the island. Had Napoleon been able to unite the French and Spanish fleets in a single armada, he might well have been able to launch an invasion. The Grande Armée was still camped on the Channel coast. So his heroic death guaranteed life to Great Britain.

Like James Wolfe a generation before, Nelson

virtually designed his own apotheosis—his translation to the immortals. The huge ceremony in January 1806 completely overshadowed William Pitt's funeral the following month and, for that matter, was on a scale that outdid royal ceremony. Like Winston Churchill's funeral a century and a half later, everything was finely designed to tap into deep patriotic emotion. The body, preserved in alcohol, was unloaded from the shattered hulk of the *Victory* at Greenwich, then borne to a lying-in-state, where the hero's coffin could be viewed by ordinary sailors and the people whose love he had cultivated and genuinely cared for. Black barges carried the bier downstream, like Arthur to Avalon, to a four-hour service at St Paul's Cathedral, where royals were allowed by their own anachronistic protocol to attend only in their capacity as private individuals. But unlike Churchill, this was where Nelson stayed in the black marble sarcophagus originally meant for Cardinal Wolsey, buried right beneath the centre of the dome.

Politically, as his enthusiastically vindictive role in propping up the autocratic Bourbons of Naples made clear (a commitment backed up by torture of political prisoners and a carnival of hangings, all under Nelson's direction), the vice-admiral was a dyed-in-the-wool reactionary. But he still belonged to the streets and the taverns, to the ordinary seamen and dockers, and had got their blood up and pulse racing in a way none of the epauletted grand dukes could ever manage.

It was a time hungry for heroes, for as much as Britain loved him, the king was old and increasingly mad. The Prince of Wales was a fat, often drunken lecher; his brothers, like the Duke of York—who had been the sole official representative at Nelson's funeral—just as dissolute. No one was surprised, only appalled, when it was revealed that, to please his mistress, the courtesan Mary Ann Clarke, the duke had been awarding military promotions to anyone on her 'A' list. Scandals like this put a face on that ancient radical bugbear 'Old Corruption' and gave an opportunity, even in the midst of war, for the critics to find their voice again. In 1807, the same London crowds who had turned out in hundreds of thousands to pay their last respects to Nelson now cheered the patrician Sir Francis Burdett, as well as an even more unlikely hero, the naval commander Thomas Cochrane—ex-privateer, notorious eloper, jailed (and then escaped) for stock-exchange fraud. This pair were the new radical candidates for the two Westminster seats, one of which had, until his death in 1806, been held by Charles James Fox.

Dissent—political and religious—had not, in fact, gone away. It was just busy with moral causes untainted by the accusation of flirting with the enemy. In 1807 a huge petitioning campaign, driven by a Nonconformist army, mobilized not in barracks but in chapels and meeting houses, had succeeded in making the slave trade illegal in the British Empire, though not in freeing slaves in British colonies. A year later Burdett and Cochrane swept away the official Whig candidates on a programme of impeccably patriotic revivalism. Give us back the True Britain, they said, the Free Britain, the Britain that had been stolen by the dukes and the dandies. Give us our birthright: annual parliaments, a secret ballot, manhood suffrage! Figures from the recent past, like Major Cartwright, resurfaced from a silence imposed by intimidation, their voices louder than ever. With them on their banners were figures from the not-so-recent past—Robin Hood and the Civil War parliamentarian John Hampden, rediscovered as the heroes of an alternative history; the people's history.

When this new army of Christian soldiers and Magna Carta warriors marched to win what they insisted were the 'natural rights' of blacks and Britons, they seemed unstoppable. By contrast, the performance of the armies commanded by the dukes kept on stopping. The nursery rhyme about the 'Grand Old Duke of York' refers to one of his many wartime fiascos, the latest occurring on the Dutch island of Walcheren in 1809 when an enormous expedition of 40,000 troops, supposedly laying down a beachhead on Napoleonic Europe, was cut down by fever and had to be ignominiously evacuated. In its first few years the campaign against the French in Portugal and Spain, known as the Peninsular War, seemed, equally, to specialize in gallant defeats and pyrrhic victories. Frederick Ponsonby wrote to his mother, Lady Bessborough, after the British won the battle of Talavera with droll disenchantment: 'We had the pleasing amusement of charging five solid squares with a ditch in front. After losing 180 [troopers] and 222 horses we found it was not so agreeable and that Frenchmen don't always run away when they see British cavalry, so off we set and my horse never went so fast in his life.' One of Wordsworth's most stinging poems was written in despair at the 'Convention of Cintra', when it seemed that Britain had abandoned the Spanish resistance. None of this bad news, of course, prevented the Prince of Wales from throwing a party at his grand London residence, Carlton House, featuring a 200-foot-long table into which had been carved an artificial canal for wine, its banks lined with silver and gold, and the wine driven by miniature pumping machines; a small-scale industrial revolution engineered to amuse the Quality. Only Arthur Wellesley, the Duke of Wellington, would draw huge and enthusiastic crowds, bonfires and marching bands whenever he scored a victory.

But in 1810, there was no inkling of a Waterloo around the corner, except in India and the Caribbean. Napoleon, in fact, seemed largely unbeatable. The Spanish guerrillas deserved admiration, but the French controlled all the great cities of the peninsula from Madrid to Seville. One by one his adversaries had made their peace. The Habsburg Emperor of Austria, Francis I, had even married his daughter to the man once reviled as the Corsican ogre. King Frederick William of Prussia and Tsar Alexander of Russia had both made treaties. Unchallenged on most of the continent, but thwarted in his invasion plans and frustrated by the Royal Navy from making any serious inroads on the empire, Napoleon attacked Britain in a campaign designed to cripple the island economy. Sealing off continental Europe against its exports he created the embryo of a common market on the other side of the Channel. It very nearly worked. European industry, protected by the blockade and driven by the technical innovations of French technology (in chemistry and engineering for example), surged. In Britain, with export demand on the floor, a deep slump set in. Handloom weavers, who had been heavily in demand as factory-spun cotton yarn surged in output, were now the first victims of the sharp downturn of trade. Unemployment and food prices soared at the same time.

In 1811 and 1812, well-organized gangs calling themselves the soldiers of 'General Ludd's Army' after their originator, a worker named Ned Ludd, smashed hand-powered machines in the Midlands and factory machines in Lancashire. The Luddites, who signed themselves 'Enoch', did their work with sledge-hammers. Letters were sent to employers, especially those notorious for cutting wages, that General Ludd's soldiers were coming their way. Legislation was enacted making machine-breaking a capital crime, but it persisted almost as long as the economic crisis.

In 1812 a ruined businessman, driven to distraction, shot and killed the prime minister, Spencer Perceval, at point-blank range in the ante-chamber of the House of Commons. To the horror of the governing classes, the assassin was noisily toasted in the inns of London, Birmingham and Manchester. So when, at last, in 1813 news arrived of Wellington's spectacular victories in Spain and of the destruction of Napoleon's Grande Armée in the Russian snows, no one with any sense took much comfort from the happy, drunken, patriotic uproar. Some 12,000 regular troops—more than Wellington had to use against the French—were stationed at home to deal with the marches, riots and machine-wrecking that had become a regular feature of British life. After Wellington's decisive defeat of Napoleon at Waterloo in 1815, when a quarter of a million demobilized soldiers were thrown on to an already depressed labour market, the situation became even more serious. The one ray of light amidst the gathering economic gloom ought to have been lower food prices, now that the blockade and the artificially high demand of the war had gone. But in response to complaints from landowners that their incomes would collapse, a Corn Law had been passed, letting in foreign grain only when home prices hit a designated ceiling. The effect, as intended, was to keep British farmers' profits artificially high. So bread remained punishingly dear at a time when the Quality looked as though it were embarking on an orgy of house-building, each construction more extravagant than the last. Brighton Pavilion, the Prince Regent's Indo-Sino-Moorish funhouse, was being rebuilt, sporting iron columns and a gaslit ballroom, at the same time as 45,000 paupers, many of them bearing scars from the battlefields of India, America and Europe, were hammering on the doors of Spitalfields poorhouse.

For some of the angriest, most articulate radicals, these shocking contrasts were an insupportable obscenity. Thomas Bewick's old sparring partner, Thomas Spence, had taken to making much, symbolically, of his slight stature, casting himself as Jack and calling his latest publication *The Giant Killer*. Shortly before his death in 1814, he did some revolutionary sums, calculating that since the estimated rental value of the houses and estates of England and Wales was £40 million and stock another £19 million, and since the population of the country was 10½ million, each taxpayer was shelling out about £6 annually to support 'the drones in luxury and pomp'.

Even Spence's fury, however, pales beside the wrath of William Hazlitt. He had finally given up his dreams to be a painter and was scraping along as a writer, in almost any genre, for any newspaper that would pay him. He served an apprenticeship in the new job of parliamentary reporter, but also reviewed theatre performances, art exhibitions, even boxing matches, and in so doing transformed each of the journalistic media he tried. But his vocation in these bitter years was to attack the class he felt had turned Britain into a sink of corruption and unnatural social cruelty. What especially made his blood boil was to be told that the misfortunes of the poor were only to be expected in the shift from a wartime to a peacetime economy; just a structural dislocation—nothing, really, to get agitated about. Hazlitt, responding in a series of vitriolic essays in the *Examiner*, begged to differ: 'Have not the government and the rich had their way in everything? Have they not gratified their ambition, their pride, their obstinacy, their ruinous extravagance? Have they not squandered the resources of the country as they pleased?' And what had his old heroes—Wordsworth and Coleridge—to say about any of this? Nothing. They had become, to Hazlitt's horror and disgust, Tories.

In 1816 he defined for his readers, in an unforgettably savage portrait of a country in pain, the character of a 'Modern Tory'. He was, wrote Hazlitt (*inter alia*):

> a blind idolater of old times and long established customs . . . A Tory never objects

to increasing the power of the Crown, or abridging the liberties of the people, or even calls in question the justice or wisdom of any of the measures of government. A Tory considers sinecure places and pensions as sacred and inviolable, to reduce, or abolish which, would be unjust and dangerous . . . accuses those who differ with him on political subjects of being Jacobins, Revolutionists, and enemies to their country. A Tory highly values a long pedigree and ancient families, and despises low-born persons (the newly created nobility excepted), adores coronets, stars, garters, ribbons, crosses and titles of all sorts. A Tory . . . deems martial law the best remedy for discontent . . . considers corporal punishment as necessary, mild, and salutary, notwithstanding soldiers and sailors frequently commit suicide to escape from it . . . sees no hardship in a person's being confined for thirty years in the Fleet Prison, on an allowance of sixpence a day, for contempt of the Court of Chancery . . . A Tory . . . is averse to instructing the poor, lest they should be enabled to think and reason . . . and reads no poetry but birthday odes and verses in celebration of the battle of Waterloo. A Tory . . . lavishes immense sums on triumphal columns . . . while the brave men who achieved the victories are pining in want. A Tory asserts that the present sufferings of the country . . . are merely temporary and trifling, though the gaols are filled with insolvent debtors, and criminals driven to theft by urgent want, the Gazette filled with bankruptcies, agriculture declining, commerce and manufactories nearly at a stand, while thousands are emigrating to foreign countries, whole parishes deserted, the burthen of the poor rates intolerable, and yet insufficient to maintain the increasing number of the poor, and hundreds of once respectable house-holders reduced to the sad necessity of soliciting admission into the receptacles for paupers and vagabonds ...

Much of what he said was inaccurate and unjust, since the Whigs were hardly less, indeed perhaps more, narrowly aristocratic, and there were certainly many Tories—Coleridge and Wordsworth, for example—who were deeply moved by the plight of the poor, but their solution was to rekindle a sense of social and moral responsibility in the governing classes, not to challenge their legitimacy. In 1808 Wordsworth organized an appeal for the children of two smallholders who had died in a terrible blizzard, and took in one of the daughters himself at his home at Dove Cottage. But it was exactly this personal, traditional charity that Hazlitt judged so patronizing and sentimental. When Coleridge proposed to deliver what he called (reverting to the old Unitarian days, when Hazlitt had sat wonder-struck by his eloquence) a 'Lay Sermon' on the ills of the time, even before he had seen it he exploded at its presumptuousness. Reading it would not have abated his anger. Hazlitt took exception to men who had once advertised themselves as the mouthpieces of the common people now consenting to the gagging of those who wished to combine in their own defence; or who were prosecuted for expressing discontent, like his own friend Leigh Hunt, who was jailed for describing the Prince Regent as 'this "Adonis in loveliness" . . . a corpulent man of 50! . . . a violator of his word, a libertine . . .'

Wordsworth, whom Hazlitt still revered as a great poet, was perhaps the most culpable of all, for he had accepted a post from his local magnate, the Earl of Lonsdale. While Hazlitt was scribbling furiously away in John Milton's old lodgings at 19 York Street, Westminster, a holy place of the British republican tradition, Wordsworth was living in his new home at Rydal Mount supported by the earl and by his sinecure as Distributor of Stamps for Westmorland. It was even known that the old country tramper, the friend of beggars and poor veterans, had got himself up in knee breeches and silk stockings to go and dine in London with his noble superior, the Commissioner of Stamps. Hazlitt's reaction was acid: 'Cannot Mr Wordsworth contrive to trump up a sonnet or an ode to that pretty little pastoral patriotic knick-knack, the thumbscrew . . . On my conscience he ought to write something on that subject or he ought never to write another line but his stamp receipts. Let him stick to his excise and promotion. The world has had enough of his simplicity in poetry and politics.'

Undeterred, in 1818 Wordsworth campaigned in the *Kendal Chronicle* for the earl's sons when the radical Henry Brougham had the unmitigated gall to contest one of the two county seats of Westmorland, both of which had been safely in the family's gift for generations. Lonsdale and his family, the Lowthers, were everything that Hazlitt hated. They owned hundreds of thousands of acres of north-country land, an estate so big that it was said the earl could walk across the Pennines from the Cumbrian to the Northumbrian coast without ever leaving it. They owned coal mines, and in the middle of the worst slump in living memory the earl was building a vast Gothic Revival castle, Lowther Park, with fantastic turrets and timbered halls—his very own dream palace of Merrie England, Walter Scott-style.

Hazlitt was not alone in his contempt for this synthetic version of tradition, which pretended to embody the old paternalistic virtues while acting out its fantasies through cupidity and brutality. Thomas Bewick was now an elderly gentleman, the successful author and illustrator of *History of British Birds* (1804) and *A General History of Quadrupeds* (1790). Although still full of creative energy, his eyes had been so badly damaged by the fine work of his wood engravings that he needed help from his son and pupils to execute, in 1818, his long-cherished project of an illustrated *Aesop's Fables* (1813). He continued to insist he was no Frenchified revolutionary. Unlike Hazlitt (who had gone on a grief-stricken four-day bender at the news of the battle of Waterloo) he was no admirer of Napoleon. But Bewick was astonishingly forthright about 'the immense destruction of human beings, and the waste of treasure, which followed and supported this superlatively wicked war'. And now it was over, he thought Britain had become a plunder-land for an unholy marriage of old titles and new money: 'The shipping interest wallowed in riches; the gentry whirled about in aristocratic pomposity.' For Bewick, theirs was a system of power sustained, above all, by lies about the true nature of the countryside with which they

137

affected to be intimate, but from which they were actually cut off behind the elegant gates of their Palladian or Gothick mansions. Bewick was displeased, for example, to be told that his engravings of cattle and sheep commissioned for landowners should resemble, not what he had drawn from sight, but paintings of them (done by other artists, who were happy to flatter for a fee) shown to him in advance: ' . . . my journey, as far as concerned these fat cattle makers, ended in nothing. I objected to put lumps of fat here and there where I could not see it . . . Many of the animals were, during this rage for fat cattle, fed up to as great a weight and bulk as it was possible for feeding to make them; but this was not enough; they were to be figured monstrously fat before the owners of them could be pleased.'

The very opposite of this deceit was pictured in Bewick's own *Quadrupeds*: the bulls of Chillingham, a herd of wild cattle preserved in woodlands owned by the Earl of Tankerville but prized and cherished by Bewick's close friend, the engraver and agriculturalist John Bailey, who lived at Chillingham. The cattle, with their dazzling white coats and black muzzles, were said to be the survivors of an ancient, undomesticated breed that had wandered the woods of Britain before the Romans had arrived. For Bewick and Bailey, these creatures were the *real* John Bulls of Britain: untameable, unpolluted by cross-breeding, unsuitable for fancy farm shows. In order to make his drawings without them either disappearing back into the woods or, more alarmingly, charging him, Bewick had to wait patiently in cover by night and then approach at dawn, crawling on his hands and knees, in an attitude that, his own account makes clear, was as much one of respect, wonder and happiness as of prudence. The result, an image of massive power, is the great, perhaps the greatest, icon of British natural history, and one loaded with moral, national and historical sentiment as well as purely zoological fascination.

Rural authenticity in an age of lies mattered deeply to such as Bewick. And he responded, like tens of thousands of others, to someone who seemed to exude it: the two-legged, bellowing bull called William Cobbett. Cobbett was pure country, although his appeal went straight to town. Born in 1762, he had grown up working on his father's farm at Farnham in Surrey, moving to London at the age of 19, where he worked as an attorney's clerk. But his real apprenticeship and his education had been served, along with countless other ploughboys, in the king's army in New Brunswick. He had then spent some years in Philadelphia teaching and writing before returning to England in 1800 with a reputation already made for pithy, popular journalism, couched in the language of country people. Astoundingly, he met with Pitt and William Windham, his spymaster, who were interested in subsidizing a pro-government daily paper that Cobbett called *The Porcupine*, which would shoot its quills at the Friends of Peace and anyone suspected of disloyalty. For three years at least Cobbett dutifully banged the patriotic drum, urging the government to give the people inspirational popular histories with role models like Drake and Marlborough, and promoting (to the horror of evangelicals) as martial training violent sports like 'single stick', in which men with one arm tied behind their backs whacked each other with cudgels until 'one inch of blood issues from the skull of an opponent'.

Around 1803–4, when the country was going through its patriotic paroxysm, Cobbett went through an almost Pauline moment of conversion. His Damascus road was a village called Horton Heath. It was one of the few still to have an unenclosed common, and he noted that the villagers used the green to accommodate, cooperatively, 100 beehives, 60 pigs, 15 cows and 800 poultry. Notwithstanding Arthur Young's truisms that such commons were an uneconomic waste, Cobbett believed that, on the contrary, they served the *village* economy very well indeed. Then he began to make some calculations in earnest. A report published in 1803 admitted that there were around 1 million paupers in England and Wales; the vast majority, of course, in the countryside. One in seven in Wiltshire was a pauper, receiving Poor-Law relief; one in four in Sussex. Cobbett relayed this horrifying news to his readers in his new, furious voice: 'Yes in England! English men, women and children. More than a million of them; one eighth part of our whole population!' Oliver Goldsmith, written off as a hopeless sentimentalist, had been right!

What was more, Cobbett felt deeply that, while the platitude was to crow about how rich Britain was, the condition of the common people of rural Britain must have been getting progressively worse over the past half-century. Misery, on this scale he thought, was *modern*! He blamed the *nouveaux riches*; the capitalists; the money men who had bewitched the traditional squires and landlords

140

from their old roast beef and plum pudding paternalism and let their labourers fend for themselves on the market. They were the 'bullfrogs' who gobbled down at a gulp the small tenants. 'Since the pianofortes and the parlour bells and the carpets came into the farmhouse, the lot of the labourers has been growing worse and worse.'

Cobbett's *Weekly Political Register*, in which these evils were enumerated, was an extraordinary, almost revolutionary, broadsheet. It used not just aggressively earthy language but the kind of village-pump and alehouse talk calculated to be read out loud. And its main feature, as Hazlitt justly observed, was William Cobbett: 'I asked how he got on. He said very badly. I asked him what was the cause of it. He said hard times. "What times," said he, "was there ever a finer summer, a finer harvest . . . ? Ah," said he, "they make it bad for poor people for all that."' Throughout his long journalistic career, Cobbett also remained an active farmer and benevolent landlord, housing bachelor labourers in one of his own houses, paying his adult male farm workers on average 15 shillings a week or what he claimed was 20 times the going market rate—and still making a profit.

Living as close to the people as he did, Cobbett took violent exception to the kind of language used to characterize ordinary people—'the peasantry' or Burke's 'swinish multitude'. Cobbett felt that such an epithet actually maligned hogs, with whom he warmly identified ('when I make my hog's lodging place for winter I look well at it and consider whether, in a pinch I could . . . make shift to lodge in it myself'). The problem with the conditions endured by labourers he saw at Cricklade in Gloucestershire was that their dwellings fell *below* pigsty standards 'and their food not nearly equal to that of pigs'.

Since parliament seemed deaf to this misery, Cobbett signed on for the usual radical platform: the purge of 'Old Corruption'; the sweeping away of placemen and sinecures and rotten boroughs; but also and always, social justice for the poor. His aim, as he saw it, was not to accelerate social disintegration but its opposite: the rebuilding of the ties of social sympathy that he thought had once— not so very long ago—connected farmers with smallholders and labourers. It was his genius to bring the distress of the country and town together. He knew, of course, that they could and would understand each other, if for no other reason than that the industrial towns of Lancashire, Yorkshire and the Midlands were crammed with first-generation migrants from Arthur Young's capital-intensive, labour-extensive, commercialized countryside. Both were now suffering. Weavers and knitters had no work; hedgers, farm-hands, ditch-diggers and shepherds were now hired for shorter periods and in the winter sometimes not at all.

Not surprisingly, Cobbett's landscape does not look anything like Wordsworth's idyll of God-sheltered Lakeland. It is, instead, usually filthy, diseased, on the edge of starvation, at its worst reminiscent of shocked evangelical reports of destitution and poverty in India, with squatters and beggars huddled by the road. And he saw that in what were sometimes assumed (wrongly) to be the poorer regions—the north and northwest—the labourers were actually better off. In the great engine of agrarian prosperity, on the other hand—the grain belt of the Home Counties and East Anglia, where land had been most heavily exploited to maximize profit—the condition of the labourers was worst; he predicted, accurately, that it would be there, if anywhere, that a new peasants' revolt would catch fire.

The red-faced, loud-mouthed, piggy Cobbett rode and rode through the counties, poking into barnyards and poorhouses, picking on the bailiffs and absentee landlords who had the most infamous records, and reporting everything in his newspaper. Despite its editor being harassed by the government, who were understandably livid at his betrayal, as they saw it, and despite his doing time in Newgate for an article (not actually published) attacking flogging in the army, Cobbett's *Weekly Political Register* sold, at its height in 1817, 60,000 copies a week, overwhelmingly more than any other publication. He was certainly no saint. A vicious anti-semite, he also hated blacks and, until he saw that abolitionism was popular in his working-class constituency, insisted that the 'greasy Negro' in the Caribbean had a far better time of it than the British working class. But there is no doubt that no one since Tom Paine had quite got to the ordinary people of Britain in the way that Cobbett did and turned them into political animals.

There is also no doubt, however, that the new crusade for the restoration of 'natural rights' and old liberties was sent on its way by another surge of religious enthusiasm amongst the middle-class and working people of the country. Some of it was fuelled by disgust at well-publicized scandals in the heart of the ruling order.

When the notorious 'Impure' Harriette Wilson published her instantly best-selling memoirs in 1825, it emerged that her long list of aristocratic clients included the Duke of Wellington (who shared her with the Duke of Argyll) and the Marquis of Worcester. His amusement was to dress her up in a replica of his uniform as an officer of the 10th Hussars and accompany her out riding in that get-up (the only way, she claimed, to get him out of bed). Along with the predictable strain of moral outrage at the shamelessness of the new Sodom, there was also a distinct tinge of millenarian urgency. A great change *was* coming, and the regiments of the righteous would be its advance guard. The Unitarian meeting house and the evangelical chapel and schoolroom were often the places where petitions were drafted and marches and assemblies organized. Their demands included both political and moral reform: an end to the monopoly of the Church of England and to slavery, as well as to the worm-eaten parliament. On the fringe of this mass enthusiasm, and hoping to tap its anger, were men who were genuine revolutionaries, like Bewick's old print-shop sparring partner the millenarian communist Thomas Spence. Slightly less extreme were journalists like Thomas Jonathan Wooler, the editor of *The Black Dwarf*, always in and out of prison for inciting the overthrow of the government. Spies were once again sent to infiltrate the most dangerous cells but this time as *agents provocateurs*, engineering conspiracies that would allow the authorities to make arrests and break the organization.

In November 1817, two deaths occurred which

144

seemed to symbolize the polarization of the country. The only genuinely popular member of the royal family other than the king, Princess Charlotte Augusta, the beautiful and apparently liberal-minded daughter of the Prince Regent, died and the country fell into a paroxysm of grief, uncannily anticipating the mourning for a 20th-century princess to whom the same qualities would be attributed. Augusta was said to be the princess who *understood* the lives of ordinary people; who, given the age and decrepitude of her father and uncles, might well be in the line of succession and who, at any rate, might have produced an entire dynasty of compassionate, intelligent monarchs. At almost the same time, three radicals who in the spring of 1817 had been duped by one of the most energetic of the government secret agents, William Oliver, to lead a 'rising' of a few hundred stocking knitters and weavers at Pentridge in Nottinghamshire were convicted of sedition and sentenced to be hanged and—in the modern 19th century—quartered, though in the end they were just hanged until dead.

The rising had from the beginning been a trap set by the home secretary, Lord Sidmouth, to smoke out artisan revolutionaries before they could do damage. Wordsworth and Coleridge bought the government's line, and defended the politicians for stamping on the spirit of insurrection before it grew into a godless Jacobinical hydra. But along with the horrified Hazlitt, a younger generation of their admirers—including the poets John Keats and Percy Bysshe Shelley—recoiled and wrote angry verses denouncing the apostasy.

With the knowledge that the government was

waiting for a pretext to use its muscle, the organizers of reform meetings took great care not to oblige them. So when, in the summer of 1819 while Cobbett was away in America, a mass meeting was called at St Peter's Fields on the outskirts of Manchester, the organizers—the Manchester Patriotic Union Society—took every precaution to ensure that the assembly would be peaceful. No opportunity would be given to the forces of 'order' to represent the meeting as a bestial, Jacobin mob bent on pillaging property and tearing down Christian civilization. 'It was deemed expedient,' wrote the weaver Samuel Bamford in his account of what quickly became known as the Massacre of Peterloo, 'that this meeting should be as morally effective as possible, and that it should exhibit a spectacle such as had never before been witnessed in England.'

The crowd of some 50,000–60,000, gathered from all over the northern counties, duly appeared on 16 August in an orderly procession beneath banners for 'Universal Suffrage', some of them singing Primitive Methodist anthems, more like a revival meeting than a revolution. But the local magistrates were not interested in awarding marks for good behaviour. They were out to break the meeting. Among the speakers were the white top-hatted 'Orator' Henry Hunt and Samuel Bamford. Orders were given to the Manchester and Salford Yeomanry—merchants, manufacturers, publicans and shopkeepers—to arrest Hunt, which was done in short order: they roughed him up and pulled his trademark white hat over his head. But in cutting a way through the crowd, the yeomanry trampled a small girl who happened to be in the way of their

146

mounts and killed her. At that point they found themselves surrounded by furious demonstrators, hemming in the horses and showering them with abuse. The yeomanry began to panic; regular cavalry—hussars—were sent in to try and extricate them. They did so with sabres unsheathed, slicing a path through the tight-packed people. A desperate rush to escape the troops ensued. Eleven people were killed; 421 seriously wounded, 162 with sabre cuts. At least 100 of the hurt were women and small children.

Bamford described the mêlée with poetic economy:

> The cavalry were in confusion: they evidently could not, with all the weight of man and horse, penetrate that compact mass of human beings; and their sabres were plied to hew away through naked held-up hands, and defenceless heads; and then chopped limbs, and wound-gaping skulls were seen; and groans and cries were mingled with the din of that horrid confusion. 'Ah! ah! for shame! for shame!' was shouted. Then, 'Break! break! they are killing them in front, and they cannot get away . . . For a moment the crowd held back as in a pause; then was a rush, heavy and resistless as a head-long sea; and a sound like low thunder, with screams, prayers, and imprecations, from the crowd-moiled . . . and sabre-doomed, who could not escape.

Lord Sidmouth congratulated the Manchester magistrates on their firmness. William Wordsworth appears to have felt much the same way. Others were nauseated by what had taken place, comparing it with the worst atrocities inflicted by European absolute despots on their populations. There was something evil about Peterloo, which for many mocked the pretension of the government to be upholding British traditions against innovation. Peterloo was not, the critics believed, a British event. Shelley was in Italy but that didn't prevent him from writing a savage anti-government poem, 'The Mask of Anarchy' ('I met Murder on the way/He had a mask like Castlereagh'), which marked his divorce from the older generation of poets.

In the shocked aftermath of Peterloo the radicals themselves divided into those like 'Orator' Hunt, cheered on the streets of London by 300,000 people as he was taken to his appeal hearing, who felt it was important to persist with lawful, constitutional change, and other less patient types who had been driven over the edge. Arthur Thistlewood, for example, a down-at-heel gentleman radical who had planned the Cato Street conspiracy (to assassinate the cabinet and attack the Tower of London, the Bank of England and parliament), was the perfect subject for a show trial followed by execution and government repression. By the end of 1820 most of the leaders of the democratic movement—Sir Francis Burdett, 'Orator' Hunt and Thomas Wooler—were in prison. Since 1819, when the Six Acts were passed, magistrates had the right to search houses for seditious literature or arms and to ban meetings of more than 50 persons, and a new stamp duty of sixpence put most popular publications safely beyond the reach of literate working men and women.

This was the moment when William Cobbett reappeared from America, bearing (until he dumped them in Liverpool) the bones of Tom Paine. Cobbett had obviously inherited Paine's mantle as the People's Friend. As a crowd-puller and the man who could articulate anger the people's way, he was desperately needed. But something odd had happened to William Cobbett. Instead of mobilizing against the repressive Six Acts, he decided to mobilize his loyal following against tea. Roasted wheat or American maize, he told them over and over, is much better for you. Instead of attacking the infamy of Peterloo, he attacked the infamy of potatoes. Instead of honouring the memory of Paine, he went on at numbing length about his new currency policies and the 'Jew dogs' who had turned London into the 'Jew Wen'. A pity, he thought, that England couldn't return to the sensible policy of Edward I and make them wear badges.

With the tribunes of the people out of harm's way or, like Cobbett, self-destructed, and with a measurable improvement in the economy, the government could congratulate itself that a British revolution had indeed been nipped in the bud. But theirs was an unmerited and unwise complacency. The shoots of anger had been clipped, but the roots of anger ran deep. Bewick, for one, had not been pacified. The last straw for him was the cynicism with which Wellington and Castlereagh, the foreign secretary, had allowed Britain to be hitched to the heavy wagon of pan-European policing, orchestrated by the Austrian foreign minister, Klemens von Metternich, at the Congress of Vienna in 1815. To do the bidding of foreign despots while remaining obstinately deaf to the cries of Britons was, for Bewick, a dangerous as well as a morally reprehensible policy. Waxing prophetic, he warned that the oligarchs and aristocrats and bishops had

> sinned themselves out of all shame. This phalanx have kept their ground, and will do so, till, it is to be feared, violence from an enraged people breaks them up or perhaps, till the growing opinions against such a crooked order of conducting the affairs of this great nation becomes quite apparent to an immense majority, whose frowns may have the power of bringing the agents of government to pause upon the brink of the precipice on which they stand, and to provide in time, the wise and honest measures, to avert the coming storm.

Bewick was writing in the 1820s, a few years before his death in 1828, and the sustained note of moral urgency he strikes was typical of the decade, notwithstanding its deceptively quiet politics. They were the years when, from the west of Ireland to Bewick's Newcastle, town halls, chapels, assembly rooms and taverns were filled to overflowing with earnest crowds, often addressed by evangelical preachers. The targets now were not so obviously political as religious and social. In Ireland they included the delivery of the promise, made by Fitzwilliam 20 years earlier, to remove the ban on Catholics taking public office and standing for parliament, the great aim of the Catholic Associations led by the charismatic Kerry lawyer and landlord Daniel O'Connell. It was a movement with which Dissenting, Nonconformist religion in England and Scotland now made common cause, since they sensed that their adversaries were indeed the same. In the industrial towns a new, largely middle-class campaign for parliamentary reform, launched in Birmingham by the banker Thomas Atwood, tapped into the atmosphere of moral crusade. In 1824, a cause that might have been dear to Bewick's heart was consummated when the Society for the Protection of Cruelty to Animals (Royal, when Queen Victoria became its patron) was established. By parliamentary statute, it became an offence to inflict gross cruelty on cattle being driven to Smithfield. But the same act also outlawed the traditional pastimes of bull-baiting and November bull-running—one of the staples of popular village life, especially in the Midlands. When a bull-run was held at Stamford in Lincolnshire, despite the new law, it took a company of dragoons and police to enforce the suppression.

The army of righteousness was very much on the march, and their most successful crusade was the abolition of slavery. Originally a Quaker speciality, the abolitionist cause had swollen into a great evangelical campaign that crossed party and confessional lines. Although it had to contend with some crude working-class racism it had strong popular support in Yorkshire and Lancashire, and it was at Oldham in 1832 that Cobbett finally announced his own conversion to the cause. The abolitionist George Thompson, who risked his life lecturing against slavery in the United States, claimed to have spoken to 700,000 in Liverpool alone.

All these campaigns were revolutionary in ways that neither Tom Paine nor Mary Wollstonecraft could have imagined. They gave rise to the first professionally organized popular pressure groups. To defeat the Protestant landlords' chosen incumbents in Ireland, O'Connell used paid agents, carefully compiled voters' lists, and organized travel for those who needed it to get to the polls. The abolitionists were prepared, if necessary, to organize a systematic boycott throughout the country of West Indian sugar, which, given the enormous numbers involved in the campaign and the existence, since the Napoleonic wars, of commercially farmed sugar beet, might well have inflicted huge economic damage on West Indian slave owners. And they all brought the old instrument of the petition into the age of mass mobilization. Hundreds of thousands of signatures would be gathered, sewn into one immensely elongated sheet designed specifically for the spectacular effect, and delivered to the floor of the House of Commons by a supporting MP. If the organizers had done their job properly, the petitions would be so weighty that they would need four or even eight members to carry them into the chamber. In the first three years of the 1830s, 4000 such petitions were brought to parliament. The best research now suggests that fully one in five adult males had signed their name on an abolitionist petition in 1787, 1814 or 1833. Even more astonishingly, the petition of the women of Britain bore 187,000 names and needed four members to lug it on to the floor of the House in a scene that would have made Mary Wollstonecraft happy had she been alive to witness it.

In the hands of the new social church, politics became a theatre of virtue; one in which the assumption of authority by old, tight-hosed lechers at court and parliament seemed increasingly grotesque. The traditional symbols of power—coats of arms and battlemented manors—now gave way to the travelling exhibition, organized by men such as the great abolitionists, the MP William Wilberforce and the writer Thomas Clarkson, who displayed whips and chains, models of slave ships and the commodities used in the trade of humans. Instead of an image of the king, Clarkson's famous print of the sardine-can slave ship with hundreds of bodies crammed between decks, or Blake's horrifying prints of the sadistic treatment meted out to rebel slaves were seen everywhere in Britain, in public places and private houses alike.

By the end of the decade party divisions seemed less important than moral boundaries separating the righteous from the heedless. Abolitionism finally brought together in the same big tent William Hazlitt and William Wordsworth; the privileged inside the system and the vocal outside it. And the campaigns were capable of bringing about changes of heart in men who had sworn they would never tamper with the best of all constitutions. As prime minister, the Duke of Wellington felt that he had no choice but to assent to Catholic emancipation as the price of buying off O'Connell's formidable Catholic Association. And the Whigs, who for many years were no keener than the Tories on parliamentary reform, were now faced with the possibility of their own redundancy should they not find some way to harness the steam-driven energy of moral radicalism to their own old coach and four.

The summer of 1830 unexpectedly gave them their chance but it also confronted them with an end to procrastination. The countryside—the same countryside that plodded gently along in Constable's landscapes; the country that was still celebrated as the solid heartland of Old England, the imperturbable realm of squire and parson—went up in smoke, exactly (suspiciously, some thought) as Cobbett had predicted. He made no secret, in fact, of his sympathy: 'Never, let what will happen, will these people lie down and starve quietly.' The winter had been very bad. As usual, the consequences were high prices, labourers unemployed or put on short hire, and starvation wages. But this time the 'army' of 'Captain Swing' made itself felt, burning hayricks and smashing threshing machines. Swing cut a huge swathe through southern England, as far west as Dorset and as far east as East Anglia and Lincolnshire. Pitched battles between yeomanry and rebels broke out in Hampshire, Cobbett's home county, Kent and east Sussex, close to where he had addressed a crowd of 500 at Battle—a coincidence that put him on trial in 1831, with the predictable acquittal. Nearly 2000 Swing prisoners were put on trial and 19 were executed, but more than 200 other death sentences were commuted to Australian transportation.

The great argument for pre-emptive reform came from France, where another revolution in July 1830 had removed the Bourbon king Charles X and replaced him with Louis-Philippe, the son of the Duke of Orléans who had sat in the first

Revolution's Convention as 'Philippe Egalité'. The power of historical memory was sobering and unhesitatingly used by Whig historians and orators like the young Thomas Babington Macaulay. Only timely reform, they argued, would prevent a *modern* revolution from happening in Britain. But the Tory prime minister, the Duke of Wellington, who had accepted Catholic emancipation, put up the barricades. 'The state of representation', he said, 'was the best available' and he 'would never introduce and always resist parliamentary reform'. As it became known that King William IV felt much the same way, the monarch's popularity evaporated.

But the consensus that repression without reform would calm the country was collapsing within the political elite. It was now an argument about the wisest means of collective self-preservation. By November 1830 Wellington was gone, and the first Whig administration since before the Revolution of 1789 took office on condition that a measure of parliamentary reform would be introduced. The new prime minister, Charles Grey, Charles James Fox's protégé, had first attempted a Reform Bill almost 40 years before. This, at last, would be the endlessly delayed vindication of that '40 years' war'. Since this Whig government was at least as aristocratic as the Tories (Grey himself was an earl), few were prepared for the thunderbolt that struck when the details of reform were unveiled in the Commons in March 1831. Macaulay described with pardonable over-excitement the state of shock on the Tory front bench: '. . . the jaw of Peel fell, and the face of Twiss was as the face of a damned soul and

Herries looked like Judas'. They could be forgiven their consternation. Some 140 boroughs with fewer than 4000 residents were to lose either one or two members (60 being wiped out altogether), who were to be redistributed to the new towns of industrial Britain and to London.

Between the time that this first bill went down to defeat in the Lords and its reintroduction, the more apocalyptic warnings of the Whigs seemed about to be fulfilled. Riots broke out in Derbyshire, Nottingham and Bristol, where the Bishop's Palace was burned to the ground. In the coal and iron country of south Wales (where there had already been a serious strike in 1816), hunger fused with political anger when a crowd at Merthyr Tydfil attacked a courtroom, liberated pro-reform prisoners and took over the town. A detachment of cavalry from Swansea was ambushed and hundreds of troops had to be sent from Monmouth before some sort of order was restored.

Against this background of gathering chaos and violence, a new election was called. The campaign was, for once, taken to almost every town in the country, big and small, with very clear principles dividing the contending parties. The result was a Whig majority big enough to demand from a mortified William IV the instant creation of 50 new peers, enough to carry the measure through the Upper House, where it had been twice rejected. The Reform Bill became law in June 1832. Most historians have insisted on its deep social conservatism: the preservation, not the destruction, of the aristocratic flavour and dominance of land. And that was, in fact, the intention of the Whigs. 'No-one,' as Macaulay wrote, 'wished to turn the

156

Lords out of their House except here and there a crazy radical whom the boys on the street point at as he walks along.' On the contrary, by betting on anti-revolutionary instincts of the £10 household suffrage (granting the vote only to men holding property worth £10), the Whig grandees like Lord John Russell, Earl Grey and Viscount Durham believed that it was *more* likely to preserve the stabilizing power of the aristocracy from the threat of all-out 'American' democracy. Their aim was to split a potentially much more dangerous alliance between middle-class moralizing activists and truly radical, universal-suffrage democrats.

The strategy worked. The reform made half a million Britons new voters and created a new House of Commons, one that had room for Daniel O'Connell, 'Orator' Henry Hunt, Thomas Atwood and William Cobbett—the last, somewhat improbably, the member for industrial Oldham. This was a parliament in which a vague air of common-sensical liberalism had indeed stopped revolution in its tracks (although there would still be countryside riots, the worst in Kent in 1838). And yet the changes did matter. When Cobbett threw one of his 'Chopstick Festivals' for 7000 labourers to celebrate the Reform Act, supplying 70lb of ham and wagonloads of mutton, beef and veal, he knew he was seeing the bloodless death of 'Old Corruption'; the sweeping away of 'potwallopers', placemen and pocket boroughs.

Conversely, there was a reason why King William IV was so beside himself with rage that he could not bring himself to sign the act, leaving it to royal commissioners. In 1829, with the passing of the Catholic Emancipation Act, the monopoly of the Church of England had gone. Now the independence of the House of Lords had been irreversibly compromised by the threatened instant creation of a politically pliant majority. And with the recognition of the campaigning success of Thomas Atwood's Birmingham Political Union, so soon after O'Connell in Ireland, the way was open (although it would not be immediately taken) for the machinery of modern party politics, using all the techniques of mobilization pioneered by the abolitionists and the emancipators—hustings, mass petitions, newspaper campaigns—to contest power in Britain.

A year later, in 1833, the reformed but still undemocratic Commons made Britain the first nation to outlaw slavery in all its colonies, at a time, notwithstanding recent historical writing, when the demand for slave-products was increasing and not diminishing. It had been destroyed, overwhelmingly, by the force of moral argument; by the final victory of the view that argued for a common human nature. Which is not to say that when the Houses of Parliament burned down in 1834 the fire could be taken as some sort of providential announcement of a new age of moral miracles. The victories had still been only partial. Catholics now had access to office but in Ireland had lost the 40-shilling freehold vote. It was replaced, as in the counties of mainland Britain, by the suffrage bar—of the £10 annual household rental—which effectively excluded the vast majority of those who had lined up behind Paine, Cobbett and Hunt. True manhood suffrage would have to wait until 1918. Even in the Caribbean, slave-holding plantation owners had to be

158

compensated for their losses; and initially a system of transitional 'apprenticeship' created a twilight world between servitude and genuine freedom.

Nothing had quite worked out as any of the forces of nature had imagined. The British had not walked their way to democracy and social justice. The ramblers and peripatetics had, in fact, been overtaken by a high-speed, steam-driven, economic revolution which they were powerless to arrest, much less reverse. And yet, industrial Britain—the most extraordinary transformation in the history of Europe—had happened, so far without bloody revolution. An age which had begun with fast roads had been replaced by another with unimaginably faster railway trains. Some of them, to Wordsworth's dismay, were violating the sanctuary of the Lakes; belching smoke, making a demonic noise and bringing working people virtually to his doorstep. There were walkers all right, hordes of them, carrying with them Thomas West's and his own guide, in a hurry to mark off the obligatory stops on the route. He had himself become a tourist site.

This wasn't what he wanted at all. Like Rousseau, Wordsworth believed that the British countryside ought to be the antidote to, not the accomplice of, modernity. But the opposites had somehow come together, got *inside* each other; country people wanting town things; town people yearning for a piece of the countryside. And they got it. The most industrial society in the world was also the most attached to its village memories. Within every early Victorian town were green spaces and places: miniaturized corners of the country, created as a palliative or memento of what had been lost. The railway companies gave their workers allotments beside the tracks where they could grow vegetables and flowers or keep a pig and some chickens, an echo of the strips and common land they had lost in the enclosures. It was not Cobbett's imagined Merrie England of village greens, small ale and roast beef, but people were still better off for having the allotment than they would have been without. For the first time, too, thanks to pioneers of green spaces like John Claudius Loudon, a 'park' meant not the private estate of an aristocrat but a public place where there were no barriers of class or property; designed, as in the park at Birkenhead, opened to the public in 1847, with rambles and cricket pitches, ponds and meadows; the kind of place where ordinary Britons could come and give their children something of nature's pleasures. Such places were not, I suppose, sublime. But neither were they at all ridiculous.

CHAPTER 3

THE QUEEN
AND THE HIVE

Somewhere—beyond the 24-ton lump of coal; the 80-blade Sportsman's Knife; the mechanical oyster opener billed as 'The Ostracide'; beyond the Gutta Percha Company's steamship furniture (convertible into a buoyant liferaft in case of mishap); beyond the tea party of stuffed stoats—were the glass beehives, designed by John Milton 'Inventor of London'. The little queen, in her pink watered-silk gown and tiara, stopped in front of the exhibit and peered in at the teeming occupants. What struck her most was their virtuous indifference to public inspection. There was honey to be made and they got on with making it. 'Her Majesty and Prince Albert frequently bestowed their notice on the wonderful operations of the gifted little insects whose undeviating attention to their own concerns in the midst of all the various distractions of sound and sight that surrounded them afforded an admirable lesson.' It was a lesson that did not need labouring. There would be times when Victoria would feel the indecency of visibility. Ten years on, robbed of the long, protecting shadow of her husband, she would pull the curtains; douse the gaslight; bury herself in blackness.

But not on this sparkling May Day 1851; 'the *greatest* day in our history, the most beautiful and imposing', she wrote to her uncle, King Leopold of the Belgians. On this day, inside the Crystal Palace,

161

Victoria was perfectly content to be the queen of the humming hive. She could return the stares of 30,000 season-ticket holders and feel nothing but a welling of sacred exhilaration. A misty drizzle had been falling as the queen and Albert rode up Rotten Row (a corruption of *Route du roi*—the Royal Way). But as if deferring to the majesty of the occasion (as Victoria noted), it had given way to the pearly sunshine of a Hyde Park spring. Passing through the Coalbrookdale iron gates and walking into the Palace, heralded by a blaze of trumpets, the space a mass of palm fronds and heaped flowers, Victoria was momentarily blinded by the radiance as 300,000 panes of glass, each exactly 49 inches by 10, flooded the space with intense light. It was, *assuredly*, the light of the Lord, who had, like her, recognized the goodness of her husband's great work. Now, as he stood by her side, together with Vicky (the Princess Royal), in her Nottinghamshire lace and white satin with wild roses in her hair, and little Bertie, dashing in his Highland kilt, they were all washed by the effulgence. With the perfume of the eau-de-Cologne falling from the 20-foot crystal fountain, and her ears full of the euphony of a 600-voice choir and of the five organs strategically placed to exploit the building's shuddery resonance, Victoria felt borne aloft into a state of sublime transcendence. She was not alone. The usually hard-bitten reporter of the *Daily News* waxed spiritual when he heard a sound akin to 'the noise of many waters heard in some apocalyptic vision, making the hearts of the hearers vibrate like the glass of the edifice that inclosed them'.

The prophetic visions swimming in the head of

the Prince Consort—harmony; peace; unity within and between nations (sentiments exhaustively enumerated in a long speech, while his starstruck queen gazed adoringly on)—did not, on this particular May Day, seem unrealistically sanctimonious. The Great Exhibition *was* in its way a sort of miracle. Although the Crystal Palace was the largest enclosed space on earth (more than one third of a mile long), it had been built from scratch in Hyde Park in just over six months (the principal construction taking just 17 weeks). Once Fox and Henderson, the glass and iron manufacturers, had received the basic design it took them a week to prepare full estimates, and the architect had taken just eight days from his original conception to draft a full set of working drawings.

Despite initial apathy, even resistance, in parliament and carping in the press, Prince Albert's enthusiasm finally inspired philanthropy, which was quick on its toes when it came and as sure of its mission as the designers and builders. Funding for the exhibition had been launched by some £70,000 of private subscriptions, after which guaranteed money had flowed in. But then the entire occasion confounded conventional expectations. The welcoming grace of the prefabricated and infinitely extendable building made nonsense of the romantic cant about the infernal grimness of industrial society. The rigidity of iron had been bent into lacy, feminine curves. Painted in the hues of medieval heraldry—yellow, red and blue—the interior, which had a Gothic Revival 'medieval court' as well as an array of piston-driven heavy machinery, seemed to announce the happy marriage of past and future. Although

163

manufactures were supposed to be the death of artisanal craft, the Palace showcased both engineering and the best that artisans could produce. Every one of those panes had in fact been hand-blown. Together the iron and the glass wove a filigree web that, instead of blocking out open space, seemed to contain it as if in a delicate membrane. (There was in fact some not unjustified anxiety about whether the Crystal Palace would be leak-proof and wind-resistant.)

The fiercest critics of the machine age also routinely cast it as the enemy of nature. The true Merrie England, they said, was the village green, the cosy cottage and the benevolent squire. But when the members of the royal commission that had been set up to organize the exhibition, with Prince Albert at its head, picked May Day as opening day they knew what they were doing.

Their chosen architect, who had not submitted designs for the original competition, was the young, but well-connected landscape designer Joseph Paxton whose own career—as both greenhouse designer and board member of the Midland Railway—exemplified the easy fit between horticulture and industrialism. (He had doodled the first sketch of the building in a bored moment at a railway board meeting.) So when the proposed siting in Hyde Park was attacked, especially by Colonel Charles Sibthorp, MP for Lincoln and a truculent enemy of all things modern, as a 'tubercle' on the lungs of London, Paxton rose to the challenge. He raised and bent the framing ribs of the 'transept' to form a semicircular roof enclosing the two ancient 90-foot elms whose impending destruction Sibthorp had made the test case of the 'humbug' exhibition's expensive vandalism. Instead of being casualties of the show, the elms were now its green presiding guardians, offering extra shade (along with the fabric awnings) to anyone sweating in the glassy humidity, and a promise that the industrial future need not sound the death knell for the British landscape.

If nature and industry, the bees and the glass hive, could be reconciled, so could other perennial antagonists: science and religion; aristocracy and enterprise; technology and the Christian tradition. The membership of the royal commission over which Prince Albert presided had been thoughtfully composed so as to include all possible cultural constituencies other than protectionists. There were entrepreneurial aristocrats like Francis Egerton, the Earl of Ellesmere, and the Duke of Buccleuch and Queensberry; free-trade politicians like William Gladstone and Richard Cobden; a Gothic Revival architect, Charles Barry, who had designed the new Palace of Westminster; and a self-made developer, Sir William Cubitt. There was room both for the founding force of the National Gallery, Charles Lock Eastlake, and for the President of the Geological Society, Sir Charles Lyell, whose own work had thrown serious doubt on the literal truth of the Book of Genesis. The driving spirit of the show, who had persuaded Albert to lend his patronage, was the extraordinary Henry Cole, who had been the editor of the *Journal of Design and Manufactures* between 1849 and 1852, and had produced the first commercial Christmas cards and the first sets of children's building blocks. Cole may have started with the idea that the exhibition would be a showcase for the best of British design (he himself had created a famous all-white Minton tea service); but by the time it was finished, he and Prince Albert shared a more messianic vision. The Great Exhibition would not be just a grand national and international bazaar; it would be a template for the peaceful future. Carried away by his personal mission, and encouraged by Cobden, Albert had already thought—out loud during an extraordinary speech at a banquet in York for the Lord Mayor of London on 25 October 1850—that the post-exhibition world would be an indivisible human community of growers, makers, and, not least, happy shoppers. In such a world, war between states would become an anachronistic absurdity, replaced by the peaceful competition of commerce. Shows like the Great Exhibition would be the alternative to the military parades of martinet autocracies.

Machinery, which had been depicted by the fearful and the ignorant as a Moloch, delivering humanity into its maw and spitting them out again as labour units of the profit calculus, without regard for the communities, the families and the individual lives it had devoured, would now be seen as socially and morally benevolent. At this precise moment, when the word 'Victorian' entered the English language, another word, 'industry', did a semantic somersault, conveying henceforth not the expenditure, but the saving of physical labour. Together the two spelled a third of the age's favourite doctrine: progress. The big machines themselves, brightly burnished and hissing odourless steam, mesmerized the crowds, who stood for hours watching them from behind crimson ropes. Broad-gauge locomotives like the Great Western's green giant *The Lord of the Isles,* capable of generating 1000 horse-power, were ogled as friendly Titans, not least because the railways had been crucial in accomplishing the professed objective of the exhibition: to bring Britons, divided by both class and geography, together. Of the 6 million-plus visitors who came to see the Exhibition during the six months it was open, from May to October, at least three-quarters of a million came by railway train. Transport on this scale had hitherto been achieved only at times of military mobilization, by armies on the march and civilians fleeing from their advance. But the greatest mass movement of population to this point in all of British history was entirely peaceful; the triumph, not of state power, but of curiosity and commerce. Excursions, including lodging, were organized by Thomas Cook, and visitors from relatively humble backgrounds, the 'respectable working class', could take advantage of a special cut-price admission. Hundreds of thousands did.

There had been other industrial exhibitions. Embarrassingly, it had been Napoleonic France that had invented the genre. But this was the first time that an entire nation was redefined by a trade show. Let tinpot tyrants parade their hussars and their field cannon. The workshop of the world would boast Nasmyth's steam hammer. 'These, England's triumphs are', wrote Thackeray in his May Day ode to the Exhibition in 1850, 'the trophies of a bloodless war.'

So the Great Exhibition was meant to dispel virtually all the social and political nightmares of mid-19th-century Britain, replacing isolation by commercial connection. But would the *classes* of Britain itself be quite so harmoniously reconciled? The poetic pieties were doubtless all very nice, thought the octogenarian Duke of Wellington, still the commander of the London garrison, but they were no substitute for guns and cavalry to keep the dangerous rabble at bay. Wellington believed that 15,000 troops at a minimum were needed, along with an overpowering display of police, to safeguard the metropolis. He was still haunted by the narrow escape of spring and summer 1848, when London had been the scene of mass Chartist demonstrations for political equality, threatening to spread the revolutionary contagion that had overthrown governments from Paris to Rome and Vienna. But three years later there were no bloody barricades; only the patient queue for the turnstiles.

The prospect of masses of the great unwashed freely mingling with the quality in what was already, at 2 million, the most populous city the world had ever seen worried guardians of order like Wellington. Never mind the piety of spreading peace among nations, the active encouragement of foreigners to visit London for the Exhibition seemed criminally irresponsible. Bearded revolutionaries (their full whiskers thought to be an unmistakable sign of political deviance) would be stalking the streets of Kensington in the guise of innocent tourists. Surveillance and containment would stretch to breaking point. Prince Albert was only half joking when he wrote that

> The opponents of the Exhibition work with might and main to throw all the old women into

a panic and to drive myself crazy. The strangers, they give out, are certain to commence a thorough revolution here, murder Victoria and myself, and to proclaim the Red Republic in England; the plague is certain to ensue from the confluence of such vast multitudes and to swallow up those for whom the increased price of everything has not already swept away. For all this I am held responsible.

But both Albert and Paxton stood their ground. Because of the attempts that had been made on her life (four in the 1840s) it was assumed that the queen would be given a private tour of the exhibition by the prince on opening day before the public was let in. But as far as Albert was concerned, if the exhibition was to be a demonstration of the unique virtues of the constitutional monarchy it was essential that the queen be seen in the midst of her loyal subjects. Against the objection that ill-intentioned parties might insinuate themselves among the ranks of the respectable, the bolder Albertian view prevailed. Dignitaries dominated the proceedings on 1 May, which included a blessing pronounced by the Archbishop of Canterbury that gave the terms 'nave' and 'transept' used for the building an odour of authentic sanctity. But Victoria made a point of walking round the displays—including Mr Milton's glass beehive—and she would come back with the family 13 times before it closed.

Paxton's views about the populism of the event were even more audacious. His proposal to make admission free after the end of May was greeted with incredulous horror. But his insistence (shared by Cole and Prince Albert) that the Great Exhibition was the best possible display of the British 'third way', neither republican nor autocratic, extended to arguing that bringing working people into the Palace would soften, not sharpen, their sense of separateness from the ruling classes. It would show them the cushily upholstered future waiting for the thrifty and industrious—the worker bees of the Workshop of the World. Soothed by the spectacle, they would be transformed from agitators into consumers. The result was that a compromise was struck. After 26 May, admission would be set at one shilling from Tuesdays to Thursdays, with even cheaper season tickets for women. On the first 'shilling day' 37,000 people came to the Palace. Subsequently the number averaged between 45,000 and 65,000 a day. No revolutionary hordes materialized. In fact, over the six months of the exhibition's life not a single act of vandalism was reported. By October 1851, between 90,000 and 100,000 were coming every day. As *The Times* rightly reported, 'the People have now become the Exhibition'.

The first great British show of the 19th century was defined, above all, as a family outing—starting with the royal family. There is no doubt that, had the Great Exhibition not been her husband's pet project, it would have been considerably less likely to have aroused so much of Victoria's enthusiasm. But she believed it to have been emphatically his creation (poor Henry Cole would never emerge from the long shadow of that myth) and 1 May 1851 was, for Victoria, primarily the product of Albert's persevering benevolence. She responded, too, to the prince's strong conviction that the exhibition should be a vision of domestic Britain, strengthened, rather than stressed, by its industrial transformation. The overstuffed displays of home fabrics and furniture, dinner plates and nursery toys, pianos and cast-iron garden seats all seemed to translate the picture of Britain's economic power into a middle-class idyll. The royal family's personal memento of the occasion was not the ceremonial views so much as the artist Franz Xaver Winterhalter's family group called *The First of May* (1851), depicting the scene when the old Duke of Wellington, on his own 82nd birthday, came to bring a present to his godson, the one-year-old Prince Arthur, on his. In the background of this modern Adoration of the Magus holy sunbeams bathe the Crystal Palace.

It went without saying that this sunlit bourgeois future would also warm the chillier prospects of the British working class. Or so Prince Albert hoped. Encouraged by Thomas Bazley, the Manchester businessman who prided himself on the benevolent treatment of his workers—and who seems to have invented Friday paydays—the Prince Consort set himself to think how the exhibition could give some momentum to redesigning the domestic lives of working people for better health and comfort. As President of the Society for Improving the Dwellings of the Working Classes, he commissioned Henry Roberts to build a gabled, two-storey, four-unit model apartment house for working families. Built from hollow bricks to reduce the price, these dwellings incorporated tall windows for maximum light and a central staircase for better ventilation, and could be extended through modular replication, either horizontally or vertically. The show houses were erected in Hyde Park beside the exhibition and, after it was over, dismantled and rebuilt on Kennington Common (significantly the site of the Chartist demonstrations) where they still stand, albeit in woebegone condition.

Decades later, in the 1880s, emerging, just a peek, from her widow's shrouds, Victoria too would also interest herself in the housing of the poor. Shocked by published reports on the slums of London, and doubtless moved by a conviction that it was what Albert the Good would have wanted, she wrote to Gladstone's government urging them to turn their attention to the problem, and her benevolent nagging resulted in a royal commission. The issue was important to the queen because she subscribed to the contemporary liberal commonplace that if industrial Britain had proved uniquely stable in a world of war and revolution, it was due not just to the political, but also to the social, constitution with which the country was blessed. That constitution rested on the moral bedrock of family life of which the queen was the chief exemplar, as wife, then bereft widow and, always, mother. She was, in fact, the first British sovereign–mother; although often, in her 64-year reign, the paradox gave her no joy—she fretted that her duty to be a good woman 'amiable and domestic' was at odds with both her character and her duty to reign, especially in an empire where so much emphasis was placed on the ideal of Christian manliness.

But then Victoria believed that this dilemma was, to some extent or other, also the lot of her sex. She felt that all over Britain there must have been countless good daughters, wives and mothers, torn between their obligation to be the 'angel at the hearth' (in the poet Coventry Patmore's famously sentimental poem 'The Angel in the House', 1854) and the unforgiving necessities of daily life: children to be nursed; work to be done; tables to be laid; prayers to be said. And the mother–queen flattered herself, even when she was immured at Windsor or Osborne or wrapped up in the bracing world of Highland 'Balmorality', that she understood the condition of Britain's women; the burden of their duty and the weight of their fortitude.

But did she?

In the autumn of 1832 the 13-year-old Princess Victoria, *en route* to Wales, had her first glimpse of industrial Britain. The visits to a cotton mill at Belper and a school at Bangor, where she laid the foundation stone, were carefully orchestrated to disarm the hostility of the 'labouring classes' and symbolize the union between the future sovereign and the ordinary people. Who could hate a rosebud? But somewhere near Birmingham, Victoria's coach rolled through coal country and she saw something deeply un-English: black grass. She wrote in her journal:

The men, women, children, country and houses are all black. But I can not by any description give an idea of its strange and extraordinary appearance. The country is very desolate every where; there are coals about and the grass is quite blasted and black. I just now see an extraordinary building flaming with fire. The country continues black, engines, flaming coals,

173

in abundance every where, smoking and burning coal heaps, intermingled with wretched huts and little ragged children.

The naivety of this wide-eyed picture of a British inferno is hardly surprising. The whole purpose of Victoria's upbringing to this point had been isolation. After her father, the Duke of Kent, the fourth son of George III, had died on 23 January 1820, eight months after her birth on 24 May 1819, she was brought up almost entirely in the company of women: a small, stuffy world dominated by her mother the duchess (in whose room she slept) and her governess Baroness Lehzen, and riddled with petty court and family intrigues. At Kensington Palace, Victoria was to be fenced off from squalor and wickedness, otherwise known as King George IV and his successor King William IV, her uncles. In an age in which Evangelical fervour had taken hold, not just of the middle classes but of a significant part of the aristocracy too, the purity and piety of the heiress presumptive were touted as a desperately needed correction for a monarchy badly compromised by scandal. The queen–saviour was intended to have been George IV's daughter, Princess Charlotte Augusta, whose virtue and liberal intelligence were supposed to give the raddled monarchy a fresh start. But, to genuine and unforced national grief, she had died in childbirth. Her widower (who was also Victoria's mother's brother and thus her uncle twice over), Leopold of Saxe-Coburg-Gotha, later king of the Belgians, obviously saw the little princess as Charlotte's natural successor; he passed on advice books, and began to tutor her as he would have done his wife.

'Our times are hard for royalty,' he wrote to her when she was just 13, 'never was there a period when the existence of real qualities in persons of high station has been more imperiously called for.'

It was the truth. When George III had died in 1820, his passing had been marked by genuine sorrow for an endearingly simple man. Although in later years he was blind and behaved as if mad, he was always thought to have understood the hardships of the humble as well as, if not better than, the pomp of the mighty. But when George IV was lowered into the vault at St George's Chapel, Windsor, in 1830 (by undertakers who were drunk), while his successor, his brother King William, made a scene of himself by chatting noisily throughout the funeral service, it was a demise conspicuous for its lack of regret, much less grief. Massively bloated and terminally debauched, George IV and his excesses had seemed to moral critics like Hazlitt and Cobbett especially offensive at a time when so many, in both the countryside and industrial towns, were in dire want. When, at the time of his coronation, he had had the doors of Westminster Abbey locked against his wife, the estranged Queen Caroline, and then had her tried for adulterous treason, violent rioters had shouted support for her cause.

William IV's contribution to the monarchy's public standing was not much more auspicious. In contrast to his elder brother, the famous bluff simplicity of the sailor king—he had served for decades in the Royal Navy—went down well. But the new king squandered much of that popularity by his entrenched and publicly declared opposition to parliamentary reform. It did not, moreover, go unnoticed that, while he had no surviving legitimate

175

children, he had no fewer than 15 illegitimate ones—a record for the British monarchy. Perhaps it was because she was scandalized by the king's insistence on keeping company with his current mistress, the actress Mrs Jordan, that the Duchess of Kent went out of her way to forbid Victoria his company (although the girl seems to have been personally quite fond of her uncle). The duchess was certainly concerned to keep the priceless political capital of Victoria's moral, as well as physical, virginity intact. But she also bitterly resented what she thought the king's niggardly refusal to grant her what she thought her proper share of the civil list.

Necessity, however, can be the mother of politics. And, much as the duchess hated it, a virtue was made of the frugality imposed by financial stringency, so severe at one point that mother, daughter and governess had to move out of Kensington Palace to more ordinary, even suburban, residences at Ramsgate and Sidmouth. Compared with the distasteful luxury of the court, the Kent household could be made to seem a model of austere self-denial. Victoria's childhood suppers, she recalled, were very simple (up to a point)—bread and milk from a little silver basin. Wherever she was, Victoria was subjected to the full Evangelical regime of constant prayers and self-inspection for the blemish of the day. She inherited the forbidding guidance manual written for Princess Charlotte by the arch-evangelical Hannah More, *Hints Towards Forming the Character of a Young Princess* (1805). And she kept (or was made to keep) a Behaviour Book, in which all these failings, as well as a strict accounting of how she had spent her time, were mercilessly recorded. One much-underlined, self-chastising entry, that for 21 August 1832, reads, 'Very very very TERRIBLY naughty!'

It may have been that the duchess and Baroness Lehzen schooled the girl in Christian correctness and domestic propriety only too well. For as she grew, and became more solemnly conscious of the destiny awaiting her, Victoria also became deeply unsettled by what seemed to be her mother's craven dependence on the Irish adventurer Sir John Conroy, ostensibly her household secretary but, even to a young girl, quite evidently something more. Although she still slept in the duchess's bedchamber, she was beginning to keep her own company and commune with the past. 'I am very fond of making tables of the Kings and Queens,' she wrote to Leopold, '. . . and I have lately finished one of the English Sovereigns and their Consorts as, of course, the history of my own country, is one of my first duties.' Anne Boleyn was 'extremely beautiful, but inconsiderate'; Elizabeth I 'a great Queen but a *bad* woman'.

And as her trim figure filled out, so Victoria became awkwardly aware that she was the most desirable catch in Europe. Like any mother trawling for a suitable match, the duchess threw banquets and balls to show her off, the invitation list prominently featuring eligible bachelor princes—Dutch, Portuguese and German. As a Saxe-Coburg-Gotha himself, Leopold of the Belgians was keen to promote the cause of the princes of his own family, Ernest and Albert; but a first encounter with the latter at Victoria's 17th birthday ball was not promising. Although undeniably good looking in a grave, erect kind of

177

way, Albert seemed silent and prim, and turned so ashen white during the dancing that he needed to leave in haste lest, it was thought, he should faint. Victoria was also growing more curious about the public world beyond the court and society; she read the newspapers, and became initiated into the rituals of royal philanthropy that would become one of the mainstays of the modern monarchy. In 1836 she visited an asylum for 'vagrant girls' and, closer to home, all but adopted a distressed gypsy family, the 'Coopers', whom she had discovered camping near the gates of her childhood home, Claremont House, but whose family virtue in adversity she pronounced so exemplary as to make it clear that these gypsies, at any rate, were good English Christians. 'Their conjugal, filial and paternal affection is *very great* as also their kindness and attention to their sick, old and infirm.'

As she moved out a little into the wider world, Victoria became more reluctant to do her mother's bidding so meekly. She was becoming painfully aware that the duchess and the adhesive Conroy were shamelessly exploiting her prospects in order to feather their own nests. Should she become queen while still a minor, they could establish a kind of regency. But when William IV died, on the night of 20 June 1837, Victoria had already turned 18. The duchess was put on notice what this would mean when one of the first acts of the new queen was to move her bed out of her mother's room and insist on dining alone. She was, henceforth, to be very much her own mistress.

William IV's extended decline into fatal sickness (punctuated by startling revivals of good cheer when he would summon ministers to dine, stipulating that they each consume two bottles of wine) had given Victoria ample time to contemplate her impending translation. She faced her situation with striking self-possession. To Leopold she wrote, with a winning combination of modesty and courage, 'I look forward to the event, which, it seems, is likely to occur soon, with calmness and quietness; I am not alarmed at it, and yet, I do not suppose myself equal to all; I trust, however, that with *good will*, honesty and courage, I shall not, at all *events fail*.' The astonishing tone of clear purpose continued on the famous night itself, when she was woken (first by her mother) to find the Lord Chamberlain and the Archbishop of Canterbury sinking to their creaking knees: 'Since it has pleased Providence to place me in this station, I shall do my utmost to fulfil my duty toward my country; I am very young and perhaps in many, though not in all things inexperienced, but I am sure that very few have more real good will and desire to do what is fit and right than I have.'

Breakfast was taken with the prime minister, William Lamb, Baron Melbourne, in whom Victoria was lucky enough to find a supremely skilled and almost tearfully dedicated guardian; the next in succession, after her uncle Leopold, in her line of surrogate fathers. From their first meeting the relationship was one of mutual devotion, which bordered, almost, on compulsive love. The age difference was not a barrier; it was, in fact, the permitting condition of the reciprocal adoration. Lord Melbourne was a Whig grandee who had lived the kind of life from which Victoria might have been expected to recoil. But as far as she was concerned he had been more sinned against than sinning, and this was not entirely untrue. When his wife Caroline had been jilted by her lover, Lord Byron, Melbourne's instinct was to care for her as best he could. When he was named in a divorce suit by Lady Caroline Norton's husband, he accepted the role even though it seems more likely the relationship had been platonic. A year before he met Victoria his only son, Augustus, had died. So he came to the queen with an allure of battered gallantry, more than ready for his avuncular role.

Romanticized in the newspapers as 'England's Rose', Victoria needed a tutor who could help develop a public persona, gently build her confidence and launch her on the vast and terrifying stage of British history. Rose she may have looked, with that pink complexion, those round cheeks and blue eyes; but Melbourne understood very quickly that she also came with her fair complement of thorns. In the 4-foot-11 doll, he already saw the formidable woman—impetuous and headstrong. So he never made the mistake of talking down to Victoria, or of treating her as a child in need of basic schooling. Instead, he spoke to her as someone sophisticated enough to appreciate his shrewd political information and his droll, elliptical humour; even his waggish take on English history. (Henry VIII? 'Those women bothered him so.') Victoria's journal entries describing their meetings are full of complicit laughter.

Those meetings were a constant feature of the young queen's life. Reporting on politics—the state of the economy and international affairs; playing chess with Victoria; accompanying her riding; dining with her (seated always on her left); poring together over the royal collection of prints and drawings—Melbourne spent on average four or five hours with her each day. She watched the faded peacock preen himself and strut, in a tottery sort of way, for her benefit; lean over at dinner to impart a sly titbit of intelligence; or just tuck in ('He has eaten three chops and a grouse—for breakfast!'). And she carefully noted down his pearls of wisdom even when they scarcely amounted to dazzling insight ('People who talk much of railways and bridges are generally Liberals'). Their intimacy was not without costs— the occasional jeering shout of 'Lady Melbourne' came the queen's way at Ascot. But such costs were more than compensated for by the benefits. Victoria now had a pseudo-father who was not always disappearing back to Belgium and, with Melbourne's encouragement, she decisively liberated herself from the tentacles of the unfortunate duchess and Conroy. Two months after her accession, in September 1837, the queen inspected her guardsmen and lancers in Windsor Great Park and carried the event off with extraordinary dash and confidence. Her account is strikingly reminiscent of that 'great' queen but 'bad woman' Elizabeth I. 'I cantered up to the Lines with all the gentlemen and rode along them. Leopold [the horse, not the king] behaved most beautifully, so quietly, the Bands really playing in his face. I then cantered back to my first position and there remained while the Troops marched by in slow and quick time. . . . The whole went off beautifully and I felt for the first time like a man, as if I could fight myself at the head of troops.'

She needed to be sure-footed: the economy had

taken a sharp turn for the worse, and radical movements, such as Chartism, were beginning to attract a serious following, so not everyone was in thrall to the spell of the Rose of England. But at least Victoria was not an active liability, and among the propertied classes won relieved respect from unforced acts of kindness and a disarming frankness that was half ingenuous, half knowing. She was also becoming quickly convinced of the soundness of her own judgement. When she knighted the Jewish Moses Montefiore in 1837 over a fit of raised eyebrows at court, she wrote that he was 'an excellent man . . . I was very glad to do what I think quite right, as it should be.'

As for spectacle, Victoria sensed—again, perhaps, guided by Melbourne—how important it was to the survival of the monarchy. George IV had been determined to stage a coronation of stupendous lavishness, complete with pseudo-medieval banquets in Westminster Hall (and in Scotland at Holyroodhouse) at which the King's Challenger would enter in chain mail ostensibly to do combat with anyone who presumed to question the succession. But the more elaborately got up he was—and George IV was an apparition in ostrich plumes—the more grotesque he appeared. It seemed right that, when the chain-mailed Challenger cantered over to kiss his sovereign's hand, he fell off his horse. William IV had no time or taste for such flummery. But Victoria's accession was a heaven-sent opportunity for the impresarios of monarchy, with a canny sense of publicity, to present a tableau—almost a modern masque—of the rebirth of Britannia's innocence and virtue. Images of sweet nature abounded. Victoria's train was carried by eight ladies dressed in white satin with wreaths of silver ears of corn in front, and wreaths of pink roses (by now the talisman of the new reign) behind. And despite having to bear the considerable weight of robes and regalia, Victoria carried off the occasion with satisfying aplomb. When the 87-year-old Baron John Rolle tripped as he attempted to mount the steps before the throne to do homage, the queen's instinct was to rise and go down to help him, an act of consideration that was widely noticed. When it came to Melbourne's turn, she noticed tears welling in his eyes. Her even more spectacular wedding ceremony a few years later would further capture the popular imagination.

Her strong-minded piety, although an undoubted asset, could sometimes threaten to become a headache for the worldly wise prime minister. She disliked Baron John Lyndhurst, she told him, because he was a bad man. 'Do you dislike all bad men?' he asked roguishly. 'For that comprises a large number.' And although she indulged, even enjoyed, Melbourne's raffish past she was quick to make censorious judgements. Toleration for human frailty was the one quality he failed to impart. So when the shape of her mother's unmarried lady-in-waiting Lady Flora Hastings started to become suspiciously round, Victoria assumed it was a pregnancy and demanded that she be punished (another echo of the Virgin Queen) for her immorality by being removed from court. A medical inspection to which the unfortunate young woman was subjected judged that her condition was a liver tumour, not a pregnancy. Initially the queen refused to believe she was actually ill, provoking some criticism at court for her lack of sympathy; but once she was persuaded by Melbourne of the truth she steeled herself—also at his firm suggestion—to go and see the dying woman. Victoria held her hand, and on departure cried, 'Poor Lady Flora.'

When Melbourne's administration fell, to be replaced by a Tory government under Sir Robert Peel, Victoria took the change as a personal affront. She tearfully stormed over the removal of her friend and mentor, expressed her disgust at the uncouth chilly manners of Peel (a mere manufacturer, after all), and adamantly refused to abide by the convention that her ladies of the bedchamber change with the altered government. Although Melbourne did his tactful best to explain that the queen really had no choice, Victoria refused to understand that this was a constitutional, not a personal, matter. The precondition of the monarchy's survival was its distance from political partisanship. She herself might see her ladies as her own attendants, but the fact was that they had been Whig appointees and retaining them meant—as far as the incoming government was concerned—tolerating a fifth column in the Palace. Eventually Victoria conceded, but only with a fuming sense of indignity.

By the time Melbourne was departing in 1839, plans were advanced to find Victoria someone else to lean on: a consort. It had been King Leopold, in cahoots with her old governess Lehzen and Baron Christian von Stockmar of Saxe-Coburg, who, in the summer of 1839, had suggested she might like to think again about her cousin Albert. She initially took strong exception to being cajoled, even by the two men she trusted most—Melbourne and Leopold ('the whole subject was an odious one and one I hated to decide about'); but eventually she relented. When Albert arrived in England, in October, Victoria was immediately startled by the 'beauty' of his person, especially on the dance floor where a few years before he had cut such a pallid figure. She was overcome by the 'exquisite neck'; 'such a pretty mouth with delicate moustaches and a beautiful figure, broad shoulders and fine waist; my heart is quite going—it is quite a pleasure to look at Albert when he galops and valses.' When allied to his moral seriousness, his evident intelligence and unimpeachable virtue, the 'angelic' good looks prompted her to make up her mind— fast. To the amused delight of the cartoonists, it was obvious that it had been the queen who had proposed. 'At about half past twelve I sent for Albert; he came to the Closet where I was alone and after a few minutes I said to him that I thought he must be aware of why I wished him to come here and that it would make me too happy if he would consent to what I wished (to marry me); we embraced each other over and over again.'

Expeditious was the word. Victoria supplied the ring, asked Albert for a lock of his hair, wallowed in the long kissing sessions, and decreed that two or three days was quite enough for the honeymoon. 'You forget, my dearest love that I am the sovereign and that business will stop and wait for nothing.' A more serious shock was the discovery that the queen would lay down the law as to who would be his personal secretary. While she would fight like a tigress (especially with Peel) to resist

Albert's allowance under the civil list from being whittled down as the Radicals in parliament wanted, it was depressingly apparent to him from the start that his function was supposed to be decorative, supportive and generative, possibly in that order. He was her 'angel in the house'! But if Victoria tested their affection by her adamant assumption that her husband could have no part in matters of state, condemning Albert to a state of uselessness that he found humiliating and un-Christian, there were also times, early in the marriage, when she simply melted away in the amazed bliss of conjugal love. After their first night together, she wrote:

> When day dawned, for we did not sleep much and I beheld that beautiful angelic face by my side, it was more than I can express! He does look so beautiful in his shirt only with his beautiful throat seen ...
> ... Already the second day since our marriage; his love and gentleness is beyond everything and to kiss that dear soft cheek, to press my lips to his is heavenly bliss. I feel a purer, more unearthly feeling than I ever did. Oh! Was ever woman so blessed as I am ...
> ... My dearest Albert put on my stockings for me. I went in and saw him shave; a great delight for me ...

Albert and Victoria's passion for each other was, of course, a strictly private affair (only later revealed to us through her diaries, edited by her daughter Princess Beatrice). But very soon—and with an equal degree of innocence and calculation—it

186

became a public asset for the monarchy, especially as the economic climate deteriorated. At first sight, the Plantagenet Ball of 12 May 1842—at which Albert and Victoria appeared as the legendary happy royal couple, Edward III and Philippa of Hainault, with medieval dress and décor designed by the medieval antiquarian James Planché—looks like the most unconscionable extravagance, not to say appalling tactlessness, in a year of acute economic distress. While the queen's jewelled and brocaded stomacher was revealed as having cost £60,000, industrialists in Lancashire and Yorkshire, exploiting their power at a time of high unemployment, caused by mechanization, were imposing wage cuts of as much as 25 per cent. They were met by a wave of strikes. Teams of workers pulled plugs from the steam engines, so as to cut power to the factory floor. No wonder that Friedrich Engels, the future translator and collaborator of Karl Marx but now working for the family cotton firm in Manchester, assumed Britain would be the theatre of the first great class war between capital and proletariat. That same year there were two assassination attempts on the queen.

But the organizers of the ball were not suicidally obtuse. Since the proceeds would go to relieve the plight of distressed silk weavers in Spitalfields, they billed the event as an example of heartfelt royal philanthropy, Victoria's sympathy with the poor and unemployed. Thanks to the ball, the apologia ran, the Spitalfields weavers got some piecework and their charities received an inflow of funds. The weepy story—once known to all schoolchildren—of Queen Philippa interceding with her warrior husband in the Middle Ages to spare the lives of the burghers of Calais was now given a modern gloss as a philanthropic melodrama of the 19th century: a tender-hearted monarch moved by the plight not of hostages but of unemployed artisans. 'We have no doubt', declared the *Illustrated London News*, somewhat optimistically, 'that many thousands are this day grateful for the temporary aid which this right royal entertainment has been the means of affording them.'

Not everyone was persuaded, however, especially when it was revealed that half the proceeds from the ball were going to meet the expenses of the occasion. One newspaper printed lists of workers said to have starved to death in May 1842, and alongside it the expenses of the Plantagenet Ball. A minister preached a sermon warning that 'when Charity took to dancing it ceased to be charity and became wanton'. And for the seer of Ecclefechan, Craigenputtock and Chelsea, Thomas Carlyle, it was a monstrous case of medieval dilettantism, all the more offensive because medievalism was not, in his view, something to be toyed with as a fashion. It was the ideology of resistance to the despotism of the machine age.

In *Past and Present*, written in 1843, a year after the Plantagenet Ball, Carlyle reiterated his argument that the sacred relics of medieval Christian England were not just material for dressing up and dancing, much less bucolic reveries of 'Merrie England'. They were a reproach to the inhumane soullessness of an age in which everything was determined by material calculation;

in which the engineers of felicity greased the cogs of power and profit, and people got trapped between the flywheels. Travelling through East Anglia (where the young Victoria too had made a tour, wrinkling her nose at the sub-human specimens she found amidst the turnips and the brussels sprouts) while beginning research on his hero Oliver Cromwell, Carlyle visited the ruins of the great Cistercian monastery at Bury St Edmunds. The overpowering sense of another world, removed from the present not just by the passage of centuries but by a universe of morality, was what drove him to write *Past and Present*; part tract, part historical novel, it evoked the actual chronicle of the monk Jocelin of Brakelond. On the same trip Carlyle had visited the poorhouse at St Ives and had waxed wrathful at the inhumanity of systems that kept men either idle or, under the New Poor Law, in places designed to be like prison.

So Carlyle had the Plantagenet Ball squarely in his sights when he wrote, feelingly, of old Bury that

> these grim old walls are not a dilettantism and a dubiety; they are an earnest fact. It was a most real and serious purpose they were built for! Yes, another world it was, when these black ruins, white in their new mortar and fresh chiselling first saw the sun as walls long ago. Gauge not, with thy dilettante compasses, with that placid dilettante simper, the Heaven's Watchtower of our Fathers ...
>
> Their architecture, belfries, land-carucates? Yes,—and that is but a small item of the matter. Does it never give thee pause, this other strange item of it, that men then had a *soul*—not by

hearsay alone and as a figure of speech; but as a truth they practically *knew* and practically went upon! Verily it was another world then . . . Another world truly and this present poor distressed world might get some profit by looking wisely into it, instead of foolishly.

That world was dead and gone now, for sure. But Carlyle wanted to rescue its moral force, its lesson for the present, from the antiquarians and the fake medievalists; somehow to reinstate its spiritual power amidst a culture otherwise capitulated to godless machinery. He had grown up in southwest Scotland, one of the most intensely Calvinist corners of the country, listening to perfervid preachers call down the wrath of Providence on the vain and the profligate. To the summer thunder of their eloquence Carlyle had added German metaphysical philosophy, especially its musings on the historical Spirit of the Times, the *Zeitgeist*. Together they gave him his voice. And it was the voice of a modern Moses, exhorting the worshippers of the new Golden Calf to fall on their faces in front of the revealed light of truth before they were consumed in wicked self-destruction. In 1829, while still perching on his 'Hawk's Crag' at Craigenputtock, Carlyle had burst on the polite rationalist pages of the *Edinburgh Review* with a tirade against the tyranny of the machine and its destruction of the work of the hand. It was, in effect, a counter-blast to the jubilant mechanical triumphalism of the Brunels, the Cubitts and the Stephensons; and to the ethos that would produce the Great Exhibition.

Nothing is now done directly or by hand; all is by rule and calculated contrivance. For the simplest operation, some helps and accompaniments, some cunning abbreviating process is in readiness. . . . On every hand the living artisan is driven from his workshop to make room for a speedier, inanimate one. The shuttle drops from the fingers and falls into iron fingers that ply it faster. The sailor furls his sail and lays down his oar, and bids a strong unwearied servant, on vaporous wings [steamships] bear him through the waters. Men have crossed oceans by steam; the Birmingham Fire-King has visited the fabulous East. . . . There is no end to machinery. . . . We have machines and mechanic furtherances; for mincing our cabbages; for casting us into magnetic sleep. We remove mountains and make seas our smooth highway. Nothing can resist us. We war with rude Nature, and by our resistless engines, come off always victorious and loaded with spoils.

Machinery, for Carlyle and those increasing numbers who thought like him, was, moreover, not just moving metal parts. It was a state of mind: the utilitarian mentality that believed in a finely calibrated science of happiness. The scientists would detect a social or economic misfortune, an aberration from the mean of human felicity; then they would statistically measure its magnitude, devise the necessary correction, draft a report, lobby parliament to make it law and create the necessary administrative machinery (the word could not be avoided) to see it implemented and

191

inspected for efficiency. 'Has any man or society of men', wrote Carlyle in *Signs of the Times* (1882) in a pitilessly exact anatomy of the procedures of modern social benevolence, 'a truth to speak, but must first call a public meeting, appoint committees, issue prospectuses, eat a public dinner, in a word construct or borrow machinery, wherewith to speak it and to do it.'

It would be easy to write off Carlyle as a prophet crying in the wilderness, were it not for the fact that so much of his attack on materialism, on the government of the world through material satisfaction and the calculus of outward appearance, found an extraordinary response inside the Victorian world, ostensibly so frantic in the pursuit of speed, goods and power. To catalogue the very greatest, the most richly eloquent voices of the Victorian world—Charles Dickens, John Ruskin and, later, Matthew Arnold—is to enumerate the apostolic succession of Thomas Carlyle's preaching. And it was a gospel—voiced against the degradation of the division of labour, the reduction of humans to automata; against the stultifying captivity of mindlessly repeated tasks, all so that some manufacturer could reduce unit costs—that endured. Perhaps not enough people read John Ruskin today. But no one reads Samuel Smiles's runaway success, *Self-Help* (1859), and his paeans to the heroic age of the industrial engineers.

Whatever else might be said about the Victorians, it is impossible to accuse them (unlike later empires of material self-congratulation) of complacency. The more Carlyle berated them for preferring the physical over the spiritual, easy comfort over difficult beauty, social engineering over individual redemption, the practical over the profound, the more they lapped up the punishment and took it to heart. Whether they took the tongue-lashing in their stride, bowed their heads in a gesture of regret on Sundays and then got on with making more money is another matter. But at least their favoured architectural style—Gothic Revival—made a gesture towards this 'lost' world of medieval virtue, grace and hand-fashioned integrity that Carlyle and Ruskin lamented.

That the look of Victorian Britain went directly against the grain of its gung-ho lunge for profit was due to an extraordinary degree to the intense, proselytizing genius of Augustus Welby Northmore Pugin, the greatest of all the Gothic Revivalists. The son of a French immigrant stage-set designer and part-time architect, Pugin was a prodigy who, at the age of 15, had been summoned by George IV to design furniture for his Gothic Revival apartments. He shared Ruskin's rhetorical demand, voiced later, that when we look at a building and wish to judge its true value we should ask not how much or how little it cost to make or buy, but a quite different question: was the worker happy when he built it? Pugin devoutly believed that when the builders and craftsmen of the 14th century—in his book the last great age of English architecture—created their churches and guild halls, flooded them with the colour of tapestries and stained glass, sent buttresses flying and spires soaring, there was an instinctive communion between maker and user, bonded by shared Christian purpose. Those buildings, even the few that survived, were statements of a coherent community, not the expression of fatuous social grandeur seen in an aristocratic country house or a plutocratic mansion.

Contrasts (1836), with its systematic line-up of invidious comparisons between then and now—the beauty and coherence of the medieval town at the flowering of English Perpendicular against the chaotic mess of bastard Greek, bastard Roman and even bastard Egyptian town halls, cemeteries, workhouses and prisons—was Pugin's devastating visual correlate to Carlyle's *Past and Present.* Unlike Carlyle, however, Pugin did not despair that the lost Christian age was irrecoverable. He believed that some of the spirit, at least, survived in Britain, waiting to be given a new lease of life against the dead hand of classicism—the gaunt child of soulless geometry. Providence might always supply an opportunity for the work of revival. Just such an occasion delivered itself in 1834 when parliament burned down and a debate ensued about whether it should be rebuilt in the Gothic or neo-classical styles. The winner of the competition, Sir Charles Barry, had made drawings that amounted to an almost fantastic vision of a Gothic medieval palace; not, in truth, a structure that owed its precedent to anything truly medieval, but a decorated 'module' of pointed Gothic, extended indefinitely along the Thames as far as money and the needs of government dictated. It was a far cry, in fact, from Pugin's beautifully crafted fit between form and function.

But the arguments rehearsed to justify a Gothic Revival parliament must undoubtedly have appealed to the romantic historian in Pugin. For they were all about acknowledging that the distinctive characteristic of the 'ancient' British constitution—its liberty and the rule of common law—was a medieval inheritance. The pediments and columns, the dominant squatness of classicism, were thus made to seem, somehow, not only 'foreign' but also the expression of authority, in a way in which the pinnacles and pointed arches of Gothic building were not. Classicism was top down; Gothic was bottom up. Classical architecture was the visible declaration of hierarchy, built by slaves, in Ruskin's view; Gothic was about the community of craft, designed by free men. Inside a classical legislature, rulers would lay down the law; inside a Gothic parliament, they would make it accountable to the people. Such a building would not only be a dignified convenience for the law-makers; it would, by connecting them intuitively, with the world that had produced Magna Carta, also ensure that they would legislate in a spirit of freedom, justice and virtue.

This was indeed a work in which Pugin could rejoice, should he ever get the chance to participate in it. In 1836, at the age of 24, the same year that he published *Contrasts*, he joined Barry in the crucial role of designing much of the interior of the House of Lords and a good deal of the fabric of Big Ben. Here, his spiritual intoxication with colour, with the happy richness of ornament, was allowed full expression in the encaustic tiles, wallpaper, hangings, woodwork and furniture he designed and whose creation he supervised. And, already alert to the dangers of pastiche, Pugin avoided merely replicating medieval design in the rendering of flowers, for example. Instead he aimed at stylized, flattened, brilliantly coloured

195

forms that created almost mesmerizing patterns; a true evocation of the essence of what he thought was medieval decoration, rather than a dumbly literal repetition of it.

What Pugin wanted for secular building, he wanted even more urgently for Britain's churches. In 1819 a commission, responding to the evangelical tenor of the times and a burgeoning urban population, had recognized the crying need for a systematic rebuilding programme after decades of stagnation. But Pugin and other Gothic Revivalists were determined that new churches were not going to be constructed in the relentless Palladian idiom that they believed had sucked the spirit out of the houses of God in a vain, essentially secular preoccupation with light and proportion. Pugin wanted to dim the lights, the better to flood churches with stained-glass illuminations in which the worshipper could again feel himself in proper communion with the Saviour, a quality lost since the Reformation. And that, of course, was precisely the problem. Pugin's crusade to restore ornament was not theologically innocent. It was immediately and correctly seen as a campaign to drag Protestant faith, with its aversion to papist 'baubles', back to the idolatries it had left behind in the 16th century. And Pugin confirmed these suspicions when he himself converted to Catholicism in 1834.

The apostasy should have killed off his budding career. It certainly cramped it, but he was too obviously gifted to be left by the wayside. Brazening it out, Pugin went to live in Salisbury to be close as possible to the cathedral—glorified, of course, in the great, shimmering canvases of Constable—which more than any other embodied his vision of the pure and perfect Christian past. Later still he moved to Ramsgate, where Victoria had spent some of her childhood. Here he worked for high-minded, well-to-do Anglo-Catholic and Roman Catholic patrons, and continued to publish his manifestos against the debasement of contemporary taste. On the frontispiece of *The True Principles of Pointed or Christian Architecture* (1841), Pugin himself appears in the guise of a late medieval Christian builder, surrounded by altarpieces, lecterns and finely wrought crucifixes, wielding that ancient instrument the compass to craft his design. His last hurrah, before dying at the brutally early age of 40, was the creation of the Medieval Court for the Great Exhibition; an ensemble of some of the most perfect work produced by his own shop and his favoured craftsmen, brought right within enemy-occupied territory. But all the newspaper reports make it clear that, while the Medieval Court was treated with reverence and respect, the crowds were distinctly thin compared to the throngs who hurried past to gawk at the locomotives and the steam hammers.

Pugin did not despair, however, of making some impression on industrial Britain. At Cheadle in Staffordshire, a community of miners and textile workers, he was commissioned by the Roman Catholic Earl of Shrewsbury to restore and redecorate the parish church of St Giles. The result was arguably his greatest masterpiece and the only building, he said, about which he had no regrets: a glowing vault of intense, radiant colour.

Yet not many miles away in Manchester, Pugin's heaven-on-earth had been replaced, decisively, by what Sir Charles Napier described as 'the entrance to hell realised!' Napier was more used to fighting on the northwest frontier of India than on the northwest frontier of England, but had been commissioned in 1839 to keep order in what had come to be seen as an endemically violent and criminal city. Here, instead of heaven-reaching spires there was a mass of chimneys. Together they made the entire city one vast 'chimney of the world, rich rascals, poor rogues, drunken ragamuffins and prostitutes form the moral soot made into paste by rain . . . and the only view is a long chimney: what a place!' A succession of reports (beginning with Sir James Phillips Kay-Shuttleworth's *The Moral and Physical Conditions of the Working Classes Employed in the Cotton Manufacture in Manchester* (1832), had exhaustively documented Manchester's reputation as the 'shock city' of the industrial century, the very worst and the very best crammed into the 'Cottonopolis' of 150,000 souls. If the population of Britain had been multiplying at its fastest rate ever in the first decades of the 19th century, nowhere had this expansion been more spectacular (or terrifying) than in Manchester, where its numbers grew 600 per cent in less than 60 years, the vast majority by immigration from the countryside.

Not surprisingly, dwelling conditions were horrific. A government *Report on the Sanitary Conditions of the Labouring Population of Great Britain* published in the year of the costume ball, 1842, when between a quarter and a third of Manchester's male population was unemployed and when, according to a Salford newspaper, 'haggard and half-clothed men and women are

198

stalking through the streets, begging for bread', described a typical lodging house in the city:

> Six or eight beds . . . contained in a single room . . . it seems to be the invariable practice to cram as many beds into each room as it can possibly be made to hold . . . the scene which these places present at night is one of the most lamentable description; the crowded state of the beds filled promiscuously with men, women and children, the floor covered over with the filthy and ragged clothes they have just put off and with their various bundles and packages containing all the property they possess, mark the depraved and blunted state of their feelings . . . the suffocating stench and heat of the atmosphere are almost intolerable.

One result of this overcrowding and primitive sanitation was the lightning spread of infectious diseases like typhus, typhoid and cholera. Statistically, the average life expectancy, the report stated, for 'mechanics and labourers' in 1842 was 17 years. (For 'professional persons' in Manchester, it was 38.)

A long-term optimist might have supposed that the era of change ushered in by the Reform Act of 1832 would also have been more sensitive to the hardships of cotton spinners and handloom weavers—the latter beginning to feel the pinch as power looms replaced artisanal labour. If so, a bitter disappointment was in store, for arguably the 'new' political class empowered by the Act in fact took a tougher view of the plight of the unemployed. Kay-Shuttleworth's report on

Manchester, issued the same year, may have documented poverty but also made much of the 'moral degeneracy' of those who wallowed in dirt (especially, of course, the population of 'little Ireland'). The New Poor Law enacted by the Whig government in 1834 was designed expressly to deter these habitually slothful types, as they were perceived, from sponging off the rates by making the regime inside the workhouse so close to that of a prison that no one remotely capable of gaining any kind of legitimate work would submit themselves to it. Inmates of the 'Bastilles' (as they were popularly known) were brutally shorn, so that they were instantly recognizable on the 'outside', and dressed in uniform drab. Husbands were strictly separated from wives and both from their children—the most heartbreaking aspect of the institutions. In a society supposed to value the family as the school of social morality, it was the first casualty of misfortune. But of course, most of the Poor Law Guardians solemnly believed that that misfortune had been earned through some sort of moral failing. Weakness of backbone, then, had landed the reprobate in the workhouse. It would do him or her no favour to make the place flow with the milk of human kindness.

Likewise the Manchester oligarchs—cotton masters and bankers like the Gregs, Heywoods and Potters—who ran the city, who had cleared out its centre to build their swaggering neo-classical warehouses, made no bones about the fact that their first, in fact their supreme obligation was to the profitability of their business. It was from this, and only from this, that the welfare of the workers could be augmented. If the vagaries of the business cycle (like the collapse of foreign demand in the first five years of Victoria's reign) required wage cuts or lay-offs so that the firm might survive, who ever said capitalism was a funfair or a hand-out? If they thought the situation was dire now, let them see how much worse it could be if mills were to go under because of the 'blackmail' of high wages and demands for shorter hours! As far as the bosses were concerned, trade unions were nothing more than conspiratorial extortionists and saboteurs who would rather see legitimate business concerns fail than relinquish control over the gullible. Besides, they said, if the price of bread was too high it was undoubtedly the fault of the wicked Corn Laws, established to protect the 'landed interest' from the proper workings of the free market, which otherwise would have imported cheaper foreign grain. If the mill hands wanted to do something constructive about the earning power of their wages, they could do nothing better than join the great middle-class crusade of the Anti-Corn Law campaign, whose temple was the Manchester Free Trade Hall.

A few leaders of the working people of industrial Britain believed in self-improvement through education, temperance and religion, and for a while flirted with the possibility of some sort of broad middle- and working-class alliance. More of those leaders, however, remained deeply suspicious, believing that the abolition of the Corn Laws and the arrival of cheaper grain, flour and bread would just be a pretext for employers to lower wages further. Only if the mass of working men (women were only rarely an issue, despite the fact that they were very active in the movement, especially in Scotland and Lancashire) were granted the vote, only if a true democracy were created, could they be sure that 'reforms' would not be the means of even greater exploitation by the masters. James Bronterre O'Brien, the editor of the *Poor Man's Guardian*, put the matter succinctly: 'Knaves tell you that it is because you have no property that you are unrepresented. I tell you, on the contrary, it is because you are unrepresented that you have no property.' The answer was a Magna Carta for the modern age: a People's Charter, demanding universal manhood suffrage, no property qualifications for the vote, equal representation (each vote to count equally), annual parliaments, paid MPs and the secret ballot. Many of these issues, of course, had featured in the old radical gospel of the days of Major Cartwright, William Cobbett and 'Orator' Hunt, who were all now dead. But it was precisely the 'traditionalism' of the grievances that made them seem, in the eyes of activists who came together in torchlight meetings and processions in 1838 and the millions who signed the monster Chartist petitions in 1839, 1842 and 1848, their indisputably legitimate birthright as free-born Britons.

Inevitably the petitions, solemnly brought to parliament in hackney cabs or decorated farm wagons, and dragged on to the floor of the Commons, met with a dusty, not to say derisory, response. As economic conditions in the Midlands and north worsened, these repeated snubs divided the Chartists into those for whom only peaceful means of pressing their case were acceptable and those like John Frost, a draper from Newport in south Wales, and George Harney, a journalist from

London, for whom the rejections were a provocation to armed insurrection. Reginald Richardson, a Salford radical who had given up his trade as a carpenter to become an Anti-Poor Law campaigner, then a Chartist journalist (and whose wife distributed its tracts and pamphlets from their print shop), now concluded that 'there was no hope for the people of England but in hanging a sabre or some other offensive weapon' over his mantelpiece. Even so, the 'physical force' Chartists often liked to invoke the canon of British law—Sir William Blackstone—in justifying the right of resistance to 'tyrants'. According to the frightened local authorities, in April 1839 the London Chartist Henry Vincent told a crowd in Newport that 'when the time for resistance arrives, let your cry be, "To your tents, O Israel" and then with one heart, one voice and one blow, perish the privileged orders! Death to the aristocracy! Up with the people and the government they have established.' This turned out to be more than just incendiary hot air. In the autumn, while Albert and Victoria were billing and cooing, south Wales saw a dramatic armed uprising as small armies of thousands of Chartists marched on Newport and Ebbw Vale. At Newport on 3 November a battle took place between the Chartists and the authorities, resulting in at least 15 dead and at least 50 seriously wounded. It was the largest loss of life inflicted by a British government on its own people at any time in the 19th or 20th century.

The risings, which took place in Yorkshire as well as Wales, were crushed, but the resistance was certainly not over. As long as the brutal slump continued, so did the nocturnal meetings and processions on moors in Lancashire and Yorkshire; the 'conventions' of delegates from Chartist associations throughout the country; and, above all, the waves of local and regional strikes. A mass petition was mobilized to commute the death sentence passed on the rising's leader, John Frost. Crowds sang the variation of the national anthem they had once used for Tom Paine:

> God Save our Patriot Frost
> Let not his cause be lost
> God save John Frost.

And, prudently, preferring removal to martyrdom, the authorities commuted Frost's sentence to transportation to Australia. But governments, whether Whig or Tory, now began to see the Chartists as a vanguard of armed worker revolution. Richardson was one of many who were arrested, and spent nine months in prison (during which time he still managed to smuggle out newspaper articles) for 'incitement to tumult and insurrection and to use force to procure resistance to the law of the land'.

By 1842 the Chartists had an effective and charismatic leader in the lawyer Feargus O'Connor, nephew of the old United Irishman Arthur O'Connor, who was still alive but exiled in France. Inheriting Cobbett's parliamentary seat in Oldham, O'Connor founded the *Northern Star* (named after his uncle Arthur's Belfast broadsheet) as an Anti-Poor Law paper but turned it into the major organ of Chartist politics, edited by the fire-breathing socialist George Harney. O'Connor's task in holding the moderate and militant wings of the movement together was difficult and perhaps ultimately impossible, for he needed to steer a prudent course between alienating 'moral force' Chartists, scared off by the stockpiling of arms, and abandoning the strikers of 1842 who had responded to factory owners' wage cuts with the 'plug' strikes. But O'Connor managed to convert what had essentially been an uncoordinated scattering of regional insurrections into something like the shape of a modern political pressure-group campaign, with local units organized by, and answering to, a national coordinating office. The new strategy, partly borrowed from the phenomenally successful middle-class, Bible-quoting Anti-Corn Law campaign, worked well enough to produce a second monster petition in 1842 with over three million names on it. Needless to say, it was rejected out of hand once more on the floor of the Commons.

After 1842, with economic conditions improving, some of the steam went out of the Chartist campaign. But when the trade cycle took another dip in 1847–8 neither the grievances, nor the bitter memories of rejection had gone away. The most powerful account of the stinging humiliation felt by a Manchester Chartist appeared in a novel, *Mary Barton*, written by the bravest woman writer of the early Victorian age, Elizabeth Gaskell. Her tragic hero, the widower John Barton, struggling and failing to make a living for himself and his daughter Mary, politicized by unemployment, destitution and despair, goes to London with the Chartist petition of 1842. The marchers, in their clogs and ragged clothes, move

205

slowly through streets choked with fashionable traffic; they are prodded and beaten by truncheon-wielding policemen who, he tells his daughter and friends when he gets back, inform him,

> 'It's our business to keep you from molesting the ladies and gentlemen going to Her Majesty's Drawing Room.'
> 'And why are WE to be molested?' asked I, 'going decently about our business which is life and death to us and many a little one clemming [starving] at home in Lancashire. Which business is of most consequence i' the sight of God, think yo, ourn or them gran ladies and gentlemen as yo think so much on?' But I might as well ha held my peace for he only laughed.

When asked about the scene in parliament itself, John Barton is too angry to say anything at all except something deeply ominous, for himself and, so it seemed in 1848, the year *Mary Barton* appeared, for Britain.

> It's not to be forgotten or forgiven either, by me or by many another, but I canna tell of our down-casting just as a piece of London news. As long as I live our rejection that day will bide in my heart and as long *as I live I shall curse them as cruelly refused to hear us.*

Both Carlyle and Charles Dickens were admirers of Mrs Gaskell and *Mary Barton*. For although there had been 'social realist' novels before, there had been nothing quite like this one. Disraeli's *Sibyl* had purported to set the 'two nations' problem before the country, but told its story mostly through the eyes and mouths of the 'millocracy'. Although Elizabeth Gaskell was firmly middle class, as the wife of a Unitarian minister in Manchester, she had followed him into the most unsavoury and distressing areas of the city and its hovel-dotted outskirts, to places like Miles Platting, where children played in dark, filthy alleys with rats for their company. Nothing escapes her steely attentiveness: the gin palaces, the open sewers, even the sad little patches of wild flowers hanging on to scraps of dirt amidst the smoke and grime. For the first time, too, in the pages of *Mary Barton* the polite middle-class reader in Herne Hill or Bath could hear the voice of working-class Manchester, even its songs like 'The Oldham Weaver':

> Oi'm a poor cotton weyver, as moiny a one
>   knoowas
> Oi've nowt for 't yeat and oi've worn eawt my
>   cloos
> Yo'ad hardy gi tuppence for aw as oi've on
> My clogs are both brosten and stuckings oi've
>   none
> Yo'd think it wur hard
> To be browt into th'world
> To be clemmed an do th'best as you con.

'Clemmed'—starved—is the word that strikes like a hammer blow over and over again in *Mary Barton*. It is both reproach and battle cry: 'Theyn screwed us down to the lowest peg in order to makie their great big fortunes and build their great big houses and we, why we're just clemming many and many of us. Can you say there's naught wrong in this?' When John Barton visits a fellow-worker lying sick in a tenement cellar, where 'the smell was so fetid as almost to knock a man down', his eyes gradually become accustomed to the darkness and he makes out 'three or four little children rolling on the damp, nay wet, brick floor through which the stagnant filthy moisture of the street oozed'. The father tells the children to hold their noise as a 'chap' has got some bread for them. In the dimness, Barton feels the hunk of bread torn from him and gone in an instant.

Not surprisingly, Elizabeth Gaskell found herself cold-shouldered by the Manchester cotton barons and bankers, who thought she had given a grossly unjust account of their relations with their hands and had caricatured their own lifestyle without saying anything about their philanthropy and civic activism. They did, in fact, have a point. But the writer courageously stuck to her guns. There was something more important at stake than her own social popularity. 'My poor "Mary Barton" is stirring up all sorts of angry feelings against me in Manchester,' she wrote to her cousin Edward, 'but those best acquainted with the way of thinking and feeling among the poor acknowledge its truth; which is the acknowledgement I most desire because evils once recognized are half way towards their remedy.'

The Manchester cotton barons may have felt that 1848, the year of revolutions in Europe (there was already a republic in France by February), was the most tactless moment imaginable for a Unitarian minister's wife to unburden herself of her social conscience. But it was just *because*

Britain seemed to be on the threshold of another crisis that Elizabeth Gaskell felt duty-bound to tell the truth about the immense distance separating the fortunate and unfortunate classes. Only if she were able to make those who had the vote and a share of Britain's power and property fully aware of the anger, as well as the distress, of the millions who had neither might she be able to forestall a second civil war.

In the complacent light of hindsight, 1848 figures as the great anti-climax of the campaign for political and social democracy in Britain. The sense of a bogus panic was made much of in the sunny smugness of the Crystal Palace years, as if 'British Revolution' were itself an oxymoron. But that is certainly not how it appeared at the time, either to the foot soldiers of the People's Charter or to those who were determined to prevent them taking control of the capital. George Harney had no doubt at all about what was coming: 'From the hill tops of Lancashire, the voices of hundreds of thousands have ascended to Heaven the oath of Union and the rallying cry of conflict . . . Englishmen have sworn to have THE CHARTER and REPEAL [of the New Poor Law] or . . . "Vive la République".'

Feargus O'Connor, who, after being arrested, had come back to parliament as MP for Nottingham, held back the 'physical force' wing of Chartism only by promising a final attempt at moral persuasion. A Chartist Convention would meet in London at the beginning of April and present the latest monster petition—five million names, it was said, on a document so immense that it would have to be taken to parliament in great bales, loaded on to a farm wagon pulled by four big dray horses. Supporters, including a sizeable contingent of Irish nationalist 'confederates', would descend on the capital from the Midlands and the north, Wales and even Scotland; would meet in morning assemblies at Russell Square, Bethnal Green, Clerkenwell Green and Stepney Green; and move south in converging processions towards the Thames bridges, and thence to their mass meeting place at Kennington Common. After speeches had been made, the petition was then to be brought to Westminster. Whether the crowds would follow it and make their presence felt, if not irresistible, was, of course, the crucial question. Was this to be the final act of a peaceable demonstration, or the first of a revolution? A 'Charter', after all, as they were all well aware, had been the beginning of the end of the Bourbon monarchy in France in 1830. And now there had been another revolution there—this time, it seemed, one in which middle-class radicals, artisans and workers had all been united. With the traditional party of order, the Tories, broken by Peel's repeal of the Corn Laws two years earlier, O'Connor must have thought he had the best chance yet of gaining at the very least some concessions.

On an unseasonably warm spring morning, Monday, 10 April, the Chartist crowds gathered at their four London rallying points. The atmosphere was festive, rather than threatening. The Bloomsbury crowd (who picked up the enormous bales of paper) were beribboned and rosetted in green, red and white; the Bethnal Green marchers in pink and white; and the East Enders carried white flags. The spectators who looked at the marchers, and at the carts and cabs bearing

Chartist slogans—'Live and Let Live'; 'Liberty is Worth Living and Dying For'—and who saw a boatload of military pensioners, shipped in from Woolwich, join the parade over the bridges, seemed quiet or gently encouraging. This was despite the authorities' advance demonology that bloodthirsty British Jacobins were out on the streets.

Taking no chances, Lord John Russell's government certainly prepared as if they were expecting not just a rebellion, but an enemy invasion. With governments tumbling like skittles the previous month, there was a serious scare that French, Italian and German republicans, sworn to revolutionary internationalism, would take advantage of London's crowds to spread their subversive creed. Riding the panic, a Removal of Aliens Act was hastily sent through parliament, requiring foreigners to register with the authorities and alerting patriots to those with suspiciously insurrectionary facial hair.

And if there were a ghost of a chance that danger was approaching across the Channel, who better to repel it than the Duke of Wellington? With his Hyde Park mansion, Apsley House, boarded up, the white-haired old warrior, still quite trim if a little creaky at the joints, assumed command of his last army—now to be mobilized against the British working class, who were rumoured to have five cannon of their own! Some 85,000 men were sworn in as special constables to supplement the 4000 Peelers of Sir Robert Peel's Metropolitan Police and 8000 regular troops. Government offices were barricaded with crate-loads of official papers and copies of *Hansard*.

Guns and cannon were posted at critical sites: the Bank of England and the Tower of London. The Stock Exchange volunteered some 300 of its own employees as 'specials' to defend the bastion of capitalism. Defensive stations, complete with light artillery, were set up on the Mall to prevent access to Buckingham Palace. (The royal family had in any case, on the advice of the government, taken themselves off to the Isle of Wight to avoid anything disagreeable.) Orders went out to allow controlled access over the bridges to Kennington— but, if necessary, to bar the route back.

One ex-radical, John Cam Hobhouse, then an anxious government minister working at the India Office in the ghostly centre of the capital, mostly deserted except for green-ribboned demonstrators, was worried about being separated from his family at such a critical moment. The front door of his London house had been 'chalked' by the Chartists, identifying him as a declared Enemy of the People. 'I sat down to office business not expecting, but thinking it by no means improbable, that I should hear discharges of musketry or cannon from the other side of the river. Indeed the slamming of doors made me start twice.'

He need not have been quite so anxious. Given this overwhelming display of force, O'Connor had the same decision to make that faced all the leaders of European marches and demonstrations in the springtime of 1848: whether to force the issue by attacking the soldiers head-on and hoping for defections, or to opt for a tactical stand-off or even retreat. And here, perhaps as he knew, the geography of rebellion was not on the Chartists' side. In Paris, Berlin, Budapest, Prague and Vienna the foot soldiers of liberty were local artisans and workers who barricaded themselves in their quarters, hoisted the flags of revolution and defied government troops to come and get them. They could legitimately appear to be defending hearth and home. But Londoners *en masse* were not so unified in hatred of the government, still less of their rose-queen. It was the rank-and-file Chartists from the provinces, some with Irish, Scottish or Welsh leaders, who had been cast as the occupying army. Besides, O'Connor looked at the logistical odds should he choose to force a bloody confrontation and realized that his Chartists could never win. At Kennington, speaking through repeaters standing on platforms dispersed through the huge crowd, surrounded by his Irish praetorian guard gathered beneath a huge green flag decorated with the harp, O'Connor announced that his orders were not to provoke any kind of incident with the soldiers and police, however greatly the demonstrators were goaded. A pretext for slaughter was just what the authorities wanted. The trouble was that he himself, and certainly Harney, had raised the stakes very high. Some of the banners hanging from the petition wagon had rashly proclaimed that there would be 'No Surrender' or 'No Way Back'. Predictably, then, some of the younger men were not in the mood to hear the voice of the turtle dove. There were shouts and scuffles. On Blackfriars Bridge on the way back, faced with a solid wall of truncheon-wielding police, there was heaving and stone-throwing, charges and counter-charges. Arrests were made, and then the prisoners were rescued by the crowds. Heads bled along with disappointed hearts.

But O'Connor really had no choice. The bloody days of June in Paris, when the provisional government of the Second French Republic turned its guns on the workers' barricades, would show just how resolute the 'forces of order' could be when faced with ongoing popular strikes and insurrection. What good would a similarly futile and tragic scenario have done the cause of popular democracy in Britain? A glance at the photograph of the meeting at Kennington speaks volumes about the Chartist tradition handed down from the 17th and 18th centuries: it shows a disciplined, Sunday-best dressed 'respectable' protest by workers always anxious to give the lie to their demonization as a drunken, semi-criminal rabble.

After the immediate threat was over, not everyone was cackling with glee at the fake names said to have padded the numbers on the petition—all those 'Mr Punches' and 'Queen Victorias'. Those *canards*—faithfully repeated in the textbooks I grew up with, which treated a 19th-century revolution in Britain as though it were a biological impossibility—formed part of the self-congratulatory mythology of the governing class. At the time, opinion was often much more sober and uncertain. The *London Illustrated News*—certainly happy that 'the mountain has laboured: the mouse has been born'—still admonished those who had belittled the petition in parliament, or greeted it 'amidst great laughter', stating that it ill became those who derived 'their only real power from the people' to ridicule a document which, if 'a hundredth or even a five hundredth part of the signatures are bona fide . . . it is a petition which

214

the Legislature of England ought to receive with seriousness'.

The jitteriness with which he had handled 10 April spelled, indisputably, the end of Feargus O'Connor as a credible political leader of a mass movement. But it was certainly not the end of Chartism as a militant working-class crusade. Some of its stalwarts became early trade union leaders; others, like the fictional, traumatized John Barton, turned to desperate acts of terrorism. Just three months after Kennington, all the sniggering went suddenly silent when 50,000 demonstrators showed up at the newly built Trafalgar Square. On Whit Monday, at Bonners' Fields, London, another huge crowd appeared carrying tricolour republican flags and calling for 'More Pigs, Less Parsons' and 'England Free or a Desert' before colliding with a solid wall of police. Fitful rebellion still rumbled on in Lancashire, Cheshire and Yorkshire. The 'Wat Tyler of Bradford', Isaac Jefferson, organized more skirmishes, went on the run, was arrested (although his wrists were too big to be handcuffed), was sprung from captivity and managed to keep thousands of soldiers busy before the town finally calmed down at the end of the year.

If democratic agitation was not going to put bread on the table, perhaps quieter, less confrontational means might do better. A single cottage at Great Dodford in Worcestershire is all that survives of one of those peaceful schemes of working-class self-improvement, the Chartist Land Company. The company had been established by O'Connor in 1845 in fulfilment of a dream inherited from the 17th-century communes and more recently from Irish reformers. Its aim was to take back to the rural world from which they or their forebears had come those workers—often handloom weavers or stocking frame knitters made redundant by the new power machinery—who had been stranded in the slums of industrial Britain. (The vast majority of factory workers were still, in fact, first-generation immigrants from the countryside.) Those able to put down a little money would be given a plot of a few acres on which food could be grown and a few animals kept: this was the resurrection of the strips and back lots they had lost to enclosure and engrossment.

The Land Company was a classically British combination of dreamy utopianism and solid business sense. It tapped into the already active instincts of working men—and especially working women—to save. Enough money was raised to buy property including the land at Great Dodford. Subscribers were sold shares corresponding to their investment, and the first settlers chosen by lottery; then, when lotteries were made illegal, by auction or by the placing of direct deposits.

'Do or die' was the motto of the newcomers at Great Dodford, and their work was certainly no picnic. Boulder-strewn land had to be cleared, roads and paths laid out, hedges planted, all with no certain outcome. But some of the settlers did make a go of it. Ann Wood, for example, was an Edinburgh charlady who had had enough Scottish thrift to save £150, a sum impressive enough to give her the pick of the lots at Great Dodford. After settling at number 36, along with her two daughters, Ann did well enough to lead a long life in the village, dying at 86.

The conspicuous presence of women in the

Chartist Land Company village may be another indicator that, once the worst of the hard times were over, working families might be prepared to settle for a home rather than a revolution; a world in which the Great Exhibition, rather than Marx's *Communist Manifesto* (1848), pointed the way to the future. And although it is true that the propertied, political classes, having survived Chartism, would be in no mood to introduce a fuller democracy for another generation, it would be a patronizing mistake to write off the will to build domestic security as some sort of defeatist placebo. Arguably it was precisely the quieter, constructive strategies of the 1850s and early 1860s—cooperatives; friendly societies; peaceful unionism; the profile of a self-improving, responsible, labouring and lodging class—that made it possible for both Tories and Liberals to embrace household male suffrage in the second Reform Act of 1867, without fearing (although some inevitably did) that they were instigating a revolution by the back door.

The family may have been the great mid-Victorian fetish. But the boom economy of the decade and a half between 1848 and the 'Cotton Famine' of the mid-1860s did make it possible to stitch back together some of the fabric of domestic life that had been so badly ripped up in the first phase of the 19th-century Industrial Revolution. The militants of the 'hungry forties' had been, typically, surplus-to-requirement craftsmen and artisans, especially cotton spinners and handloom weavers, who had been put out of work while women and children (the 'tenters' of the mills, hired for menial but dangerous work like crawling

217

under moving machinery to clean cotton fluff) formed a disproportionately large part of the factory labour force. Elizabeth Gaskell's portrait in *Mary Barton* of despondent, demoralized and finally desperate men looking for some way to express their fury was based on a good deal of social truth. In 1851, for instance, 255,000 men and 272,000 women struggled for a living in cotton mills. But the 1850s did, in fact, make good on many of the promises made by the manufacturers and money men of Manchester, Salford, Bradford and Halifax. Rising export-led demand for manufactured cloth generated nearly full employment. The real value of wages rose. Savings were possible. And for the first time men became integrated in large numbers into the manufacturing labour force. Working the new steam-driven mules, they were given, as foremen, the right to hire and organize both men and women (and sometimes children), thus reinstating, in ways incalculably important for the restoration of morale, some of their lost domestic self-respect. Weaving—the last of the textile sectors to become mechanized—now developed its own technology, which could be manned by a male, as well as a female, labour force. In some other industries—especially coal mining—it was, on the other hand, the legislated removal of women and children from work in the pit (where sweltering conditions dictated virtual or actual nakedness as well as brutal physical labour) that, although taxing the domestic economy, actually restored to mining community homes a semblance of matriarchal domestic order.

The prosperous years of the mid-century made

for a less confrontational labour force. Women powerloom weavers in Lancashire and Clydeside formed their own unions. But they seldom needed to strike. In the 1860s legal trade unions became more like welfare associations and less like training camps for the class war. Union leaders themselves stressed that the strike would be the weapon of last resort. Dealing with a less confrontational labour force in turn allowed employers to rethink their paternalism. Where once, in return for compliance with wage cuts, they had offered what they claimed were benefits, like the provision of food, now they made room for unions, friendly societies and cooperatives to organize, collaboratively, more of their own independent culture. The 1850s were the decade when works brass bands appeared, sometimes with an initial investment by the owner; when annual works outings to the country, the seaside and the Crystal Palace, re-erected at Sydenham, south London, after the Great Exhibition closed, were organized. Of course, many of those occasions were custom-designed to show off the benevolence of the new industrial squirarchy: the summer tea party at the turreted rose-brick, Gothic Revival mansion on the hill where the full complement of servants (many of them from the same families as the factory hands) would be serving cakes and lemonade; the cricket match between owners (the sons just down from one of the 'new' public schools, such as Marlborough and Tonbridge) and the 'men'.

Reginald Richardson, ex-physical force Salford Chartist and gaolbird, was himself one of those working men who, in the less abrasively confrontational climate of the mid-Victorian boom, reserved his campaign energies for quite different battles. In the mid-1850s he took on the 'slink' trade, accused of slaughtering diseased cattle and 'dressing' them so they could be passed off as food. He campaigned for public rights of way on ancient footpaths in the countryside between Cheadle and Altrincham. In 1854 he waxed lyrical in the *Salford Evening Weekly*, while lamenting industrial pollution: 'How many thousands yet living remember the beautiful walk from Oldham Lane and down the Adelphi across Bank Mill Yard and along the southern side of the river, with its fine green bank shelving down to the pure stream overshadowed by tall poplars. . . . Along the river bank to Springfield . . . every inch of this has been absorbed—to use a mild term—by the rapacity of those who have built works along the river side.' The old warrior for working men's democracy had become—in advance of the invention of the term— an ecologist. The British revolution had been put out to grass.

CHAPTER 4

WIVES, DAUGHTERS, WIDOWS

Photographing Queen Victoria, the results make clear, was seldom an opportunity for a sunny grin. But then smiling seemed beside the point for most 19th-century photographers and their subjects. They were after grander things; in the case of the royal family, a fine balance between majesty and familiarity. Being summoned to take photographs of Albert, Victoria and the children must have been daunting for Roger Fenton and John Edwin Mayall; but also perhaps exhilarating. Who else got to tell a sovereign to sit perfectly still, even in the most respectful style of address? Lady Day, about whom little is known, went to Osborne House on the Isle of Wight in the summer of 1859 and managed to capture just the slight degree of informality that the prince and the queen had allowed themselves: a country bonnet and an easy lean against a creamy wall. It helped, of course, that the royals were such enthusiasts of the new art. A darkroom had been built and stocked at Windsor. Whenever painters came to do a portrait in oils, the first thing Victoria did was to press on them a photograph as a way of indicating her expectations. This put them on the spot. Were they really supposed to record, with the camera's unblinking faithfulness to the truth, the podgy cheeks, the rather alarming eyes and the excessively compact royal form?

Plainly, the queen was not vain. But the queen

221

was also not stupid. She and Albert knew precisely what they were doing when they commissioned photographs. The thousands of prints made between the late 1850s and the end of the reign transformed the relationship between crown and people more thoroughly than anything since the Civil War. Lady Day's photographs of the Osborne summer were engraved for public circulation; but 14 of the plates from a series made a year later by Mayall were specifically chosen for publication as cartes-de-visite. Invented by the French photographer André Disdéri, these were multiple (usually eight) exposures that could be taken from a single plate, and were originally meant, as their name implied, as trade or artistic advertisements to be exchanged between photographers themselves, either amateur or professional. In Britain, however, they were circulated—so the authority on royal photographs, Helmut Gernsheim, claims—in hundreds of thousands. Escaping from the rarefied circles of photography into the public domain of the middle class, the cards were prized, collected and traded as cherished objects. Family albums, specially designed with windows into which cartes-de-visite could be slipped without the need for gum, meant that for the first time the image of the royal family could appear on the drawing-room tables of the British middle classes.

That image, carefully designed by Albert and Victoria themselves, was itself an extraordinary departure from tradition. 'They say no Sovereign was ever more loved than I am (I am bold enough to say)', the queen had written to her uncle, King Leopold, in 1858 in a rush of pardonable self-congratulation. And she had no doubt why. It was 'because of our domestic home; the good example it sets'. So none of the Mayall, Day or Fenton photographs of the royal couple showed Albert and Victoria in anything remotely approaching a ceremonial role, or in military finery, swagged with the tiers of medals and ropes of epaulettes favoured by European autocrats. It would have been unthinkable, of course, for Victoria to have donned a uniform, and Albert had specifically declined the Duke of Wellington's proposal, in 1850, that he should serve as commander-in-chief of the army. So the prince filled his frock coat as majestically and martially as he could, while little Victoria, plumping out to the pudding shape that would be her enduring image, ballooned in satin crinoline. It was the rituals of the bourgeois calendar that were most on show—the holidays in the Highlands and on the Isle of Wight; the stroll with the dogs in the park; carol-singing around the Christmas tree; Albert playing Mendelssohn at the organ; Victoria adoringly cross-stitching. There was even a white-haired, bonneted granny to round out the scene since a chastened Duchess of Kent, far removed from her dynastic adventurism, had been welcomed back into the family fold. Never mind that the holiday homes were palatial; the park was Windsor and mostly off limits to the public; and that none of these activities was exactly comparable to the annual round of a Tunbridge Wells solicitor, much less a Solihull grocer; the artfully conveyed impression was of a reassuringly solid, unpretentious and, above all, Christian–patriotic way of life. Reciprocal visits in 1855 of the Emperor Napoleon III and the Empress Eugénie to Britain, and of Victoria and Albert to Paris, only reinforced the image of the queen as wholesomely innocent of glamour (although not of gaiety). Sniggering criticism of her fashion sense, or lack of it, was provoked not so much by dowdiness as by unfortunate gaudiness; typical (it was insinuated in Paris) of the bourgeoise trying a little too hard to be cheerful. The black and white collotypes of the 1850s do little to suggest the brilliant stripes and checks loved by Victoria, along with parasols of clashing colours. Parrot-green was apparently a favourite.

Especially when compared to modern royal photography, the albums from 1859, 1860 and 1861 seem startlingly candid in registering the strains and ambiguities of a relationship that had somehow to preserve the authority of a husband over a wife, while conceding the inferiority of the consort to the queen. Albert stands patriarchally lofty—but not so lofty as he would have been had the queen herself not been standing on steps concealed beneath the hooped crinoline. Victoria appears just as she must have been: weary of being a baby factory for dynastic posterity ('Vicky', the first of nine surviving, was born in 1840, 'Baby' Beatrice, the last, in 1857).

Serial pregnancies had taken their toll on the dewy-eyed romance with which Victoria had begun her marriage. When her eldest child, Vicky—who had been married at 18 to the Crown Prince of Prussia, 10 years her senior—became pregnant for the first time, making her a grandmother in her early 30s, she wrote gushingly of the Expected Event. The queen, however, responded with tactless earthiness: 'What you say of the pride of giving life to an immortal soul is very fine, dear, but

I own I cannot enter into that; I think much more of our being like a cow or a dog at such moments; when our poor nature becomes so very animal and unecstatic.' Inevitably, some of the royal children fell ill, sometimes dangerously. Fierce arguments erupted between Victoria and Albert as to which of the doctors to trust. It was then that the conflict between the dual role of the couple—on the one hand husband and wife, on the other sovereign and consort—became most aggravated. When Vicky was desperately sick, an unusually distraught Albert told Victoria that 'Dr Clark has mismanaged the child and poisoned her with calomel and you have starved her. I shall have nothing more to do with it! Take the child away and do as you like and if she dies you will have it on your conscience.' The queen shot back, operatically, 'You can *murder* the child if YOU want to!' No wonder that Albert thought, 'Victoria is too hasty and passionate for me to be able often to speak of my difficulties. She will fly into a rage and overwhelms me with reproaches of suspiciousness, want of trust, ambition, envy. '

But even these temporary estrangements were testimony to the fact that Albert and Victoria were both intensely engaged in the welfare of their family. Albert constructed an elaborate and exhaustive educational programme for the children and, although there were tutors to carry it out, supervised the instruction down to the last detail. When, to his growing anxiety and exasperation, Bertie, the Prince of Wales, showed no sign of applying himself to his lessons (quite the reverse, in fact), Albert bore down on him with relentless interrogations in an attempt to discover whether it

225

was intellectual or moral failing that was the problem. Equally, however, there were times when both the queen and the prince allowed themselves the luxury of cosiness. Victoria's journal recorded many such moments of bedroom happiness: 'Albert brought in dearest little Pussy [Vicky] in such a smart white merino dress trimmed with blue which Mamma had given her and a pretty cap, and placed her on my bed, seating himself next to her and she was very dear and good. And as my precious invaluable Albert sat there and our little Love between us I felt quite moved with happiness and gratitude to God.'

The bliss might not have been perfectly symmetrical. For many years in the late 1840s and 1850s, Albert chafed at the limitations placed on his part in public business. It did not help that they had been self-imposed, apparently willingly. Albert's German background in Coburg explains a lot about his mixed constitutional feelings. The smaller German states in the mid-19th century were on the cusp of making important decisions about how best to avoid the fate of the red republicanism that Karl Marx had confidently predicted for them (as well as for Britain). Would liberalism or authoritarianism be the best preventive against revolution? Albert was not so obtuse as to imagine Britain would even flirt with the latter possibility. In fact, after a period of innocence he had rather fallen in love with English (as distinct from British) constitutional history, swotting up on Sir William Blackstone's *Commentaries on the Laws of England* (1723–80) and, over-optimistic about Victoria's own eagerness to be enlightened about her monarchy, reading aloud to her passages from Henry Hallam's *The Constitution from the Accession of Henry VII to the Death of George II* (1827). But Albert's own mentor, Baron von Stockmar, had warned him that Britain was in danger of establishing, by political *fait accompli*, a mere 'ministerial government' in which the monarchy did no more than rubber stamp the decisions of parliament and the political parties. And to begin with—until put right by Sir Robert Peel's careful but firm guidance—Albert shared Victoria's uneducated instinct that the crown should reserve the possibility at least of withholding confirmation of ministerial appointments or policies of which it disapproved. What Stockmar wanted was that the sovereign be akin to a 'permanent Prime Minister'—above the fray of party—and therefore somehow entitled to the trust and respect of both politicians and the people.

It was to Albert's credit that he rapidly understood this to be an impossibly over-ambitious plan. Instead, the sketch of his duties written in 1843, and revised and extended in 1850 when he turned down the Duke of Wellington's invitation to command the army, described a subtler role. He would, he said, 'sink his own *individual* existence into that of his wife . . . assume no separate responsibility before the public but make his position entirely a part of hers'. This sounds like an act of almost perverse (and uncharacteristic) self-effacement—until, that is, one reads on in the Consort's job description and discovers that Albert also commanded himself to 'continually and anxiously watch every part of the public business, in order to be able to advise and assist her at any moment . . . . As the natural head of her family, superintendent of the royal household' (in which he had rapidly made swingeing cuts—no more wine allowance for the 'Red Chamber' at Windsor); 'manager of her private affairs, sole *confidential* adviser in politics, and her only assistant in her communications with the officers of the Government, he is, besides, the husband of the Queen, the tutor of the royal children, the private Secretary of the Sovereign and her permanent minister'.

The most extraordinary thing about this list was not its exhaustiveness, but its conversion of domestic authority into a substantive political equivalent. This was not the passive companionship exercised by the last 'Prince Consort', George of Denmark, husband to Queen Anne in the early 18th century, still less the nervously tentative presence of King Philip of Spain, the husband of Mary Tudor in the mid-16th. Albert was to be ubiquitous, watchful, omniscient; always there at the back of the chair, behind the desk; available for consultation even when not asked. What he had drafted was in some ways a throwback to the ancient privileges of the Groom of the Stool—the person, who, closest to the body of the monarch, made himself the indispensable medium through which politicians sought, and were granted, access to the sovereign. Whenever ministers were in the presence of the queen, so was Albert.

Exerting his authority by appearing not to, being a presence by confining himself to being a husband, father and secretary, was all very nice in theory but often tricky in practice. While it put little strain on

228

the constitution, paradoxically it put a lot of strain on the royal union. Early in the marriage he had complained that he was 'husband not master of my own house'; and he continued to fret that his necessarily inferior political standing somehow undermined his patriarchal role in the family, however ardently Victoria protested to the contrary. Neither of them would have disagreed with Carlyle's repetition of the truism that it was 'an eternal axiom [and] the law of nature that man should bear rule in the home and not the woman'. The queen, was, in fact, painfully conscious of the anomaly by which her public presence was supposed to convey, simultaneously, both wifely decorum and regal superiority. She was a conscientious and opinionated reader of state papers; but, as Albert came to have more outlets for his driven sense of civic responsibility, so Victoria came to feel that perhaps he had more of an appetite for this work than she did herself. Sometimes, especially in the chaotic years after the fall of Peel in 1846, with governments coming and going, she felt at sea politically. During these years Victoria leaned heavily on Albert's views, changing her opinion of Peel himself. Originally she had detested him as the common manufacturer who had usurped the rightful place of dearest Lord M; but, when seen through Albert's eyes, he turned into a figure of tragic rectitude. The terrier-like Lord John Russell had to be endured. Lord Henry Temple, Viscount Palmerston, whom they gigglingly nicknamed 'Pilgerstein' (from the German for 'palmer' or 'pilgrim'), with his dyed whiskers, languid manners and cynical jingoism, they could barely tolerate and wrote off as a suspicious adventurer—a staggering underestimate of the foreign secretary's dangerous talent. It was all very wearying. 'I love peace and quiet', Victoria wrote in her journal, 'in fact I hate politics and turmoil. . . . Albert grows daily fonder of politics and business and is so wonderfully fit for both—such perspicacity and courage—and I grow daily to dislike them both more and more. We women are not made for governing—and if we are good women, we must dislike these masculine occupations; but there are times which force one to take an interest in them.'

The place where the ideal of a family partnership came closest to realization was Osborne House. It was there, as at Balmoral in Aberdeenshire at the other end of the island, that the day would be divided into a governing morning and a family afternoon. And it was there that Victoria made the all-important symbolic gesture of providing Albert with his own desk, placed beside hers, so that incoming ministers would see the two of them, side by side, and get the message that this was indeed the Saxe-Coburg-Gotha monarchy. Albert had bought the 1000-acre estate on the Isle of Wight in 1845, on the advice of Peel, as a retreat for the queen; a resort where the cares of state could be balanced by the pleasures of family life. The prince claimed that the pine woods gently sloping down to the bay reminded him of the coast near Naples (as well as the forests near his birthplace at Rosenau), an impression made only a little less improbable by the brightly painted Italianate house with its yellow and white towers and formal gardens and fountains, whose every detail he either designed or supervised. By the time Albert had finished with the house it had cost a cool £200,000, an immense fortune by the standards of the mid-19th century; the 'retreat' had become, in effect, an alternative place of government, with ministers and dispatch boxes, to the queen's chagrin, constantly arriving. But the working routine of Osborne (and Balmoral) did indeed work: a walk before breakfast; newspapers with or after breakfast, followed by spirited discussion; the queen inspecting papers that Albert had already screened and prepared (in his capacity as private secretary) for her signature; *joint* meetings, if necessary, with ministers. And after luncheon, further informal discussion of the implications of the morning's business.

But afternoons were also the time when the family romance could be most fully indulged with picnics, fishing trips and pony rides. In Scotland there would be deer stalking; heavily unannounced 'visits' to local crofters; reels and flings in the evening, with the queen got up in the freshly invented Balmoral red and grey tartan. In both places Albert set his mind to all kinds of Improving Projects, which would provide, at the same time, physical exercise, moral instruction and even a little harmless play for the children. The *pièce de résistance* was the Swiss Cottage at Osborne, with its own kitchen garden, built in the park by the prince acting as foreman to his four eldest children—Vicky, Bertie, Affie and Alice—who provided the labour. It featured furniture and even working cooking stoves, all scaled down to child size, so that they could play house.

The idea was that the royal children should inherit from their parents the idyll of the happy family. (Predictably the boys, and most notoriously

231

Bertie, the Prince of Wales, who felt most put upon by their father, spurned the role as soon as they were of an age to escape.) But although she never stopped believing she had been uniquely blessed in her husband and (between tantrums) confiding professions of her love to her diary, Victoria was also capable of statements of startling disenchantment, especially when her daughters were contemplating their own dynastic marriages. Marriages were all very nice, she let it be known, assuming they were *happy* marriages. But many were anything but happy, and then a heaven could indeed turn into a hell. Single people were, she thought, much better off than partners who were doomed to inflict unrelenting daily misery on each other. Moreover, the chances of happiness were much slimmer than poor naïve girls, groomed for the altar, were made to believe by their ambitious parents. Keenly feeling the burdens of continuous childbirth, she declared, 'All marriage is a lottery, the happiness is always an exchange—though it may be a poor one. Still, the poor woman is bodily and morally the husband's slave—that always sticks in my throat.'

Victoria, of course, was no feminist, but at times like this she certainly sounded like one. The chances are that she knew about a number of notorious court cases highlighting the plight of unhappily married wives. The best known had been that of Lord Melbourne's intimate friend Caroline Norton, whose brutal husband, George, had then deserted her, denying her custody or even access to their children and leaving her without any means of support. The reason was that, as Blackstone had laid down (and therefore Victoria and Albert, both

232

assiduous Blackstone students, knew), 'by marriage, the husband and wife are one person in law, that is the very being or existence of the woman is suspended during the marriage, or at least is incorporated . . . into that of the husband under whose wing, protection and cover she performs anything'. In practice, this meant that, until reforms in the last quarter of the century, married women were incapable of owning property or of being party to any kind of contract, much less suing for divorce. It meant that Elizabeth Gaskell, for example, was not entitled to any of the earnings from her own novels, but had to satisfy herself with an allowance from her husband. Vindictively, George Norton had used his conjugal power to prevent Caroline from receiving any income after they were separated. The publicity given to the case had resulted in an act of parliament in 1839 that gave abandoned mothers custody of children under seven—but not thereafter.

Since Victoria was always inclined to give Lord M the benefit of the doubt, it is likely that she accepted his insistence, when Norton named him as co-respondent in the divorce, that his relationship with Caroline had been perfectly above board; so she would have been able to see Caroline as a victim, and her battle for custody and support as heroic as it genuinely was. But, 20 years on, could the queen conceivably have been reading the *Englishwoman's Journal*, published by the Victoria Press from 1860, which contained articles forcefully arguing the right of married women to their own property and, exactly like the queen, routinely compared bad marriages either to a lottery or to slavery? Perhaps Victoria had noticed or read

Barbara Leigh Smith's *Brief Summary in Plain Language of the Most Important Laws Concerning Women* (1854), and even sympathized with its mission of educating young women in what to expect from marriage.

The possibility of Victoria's familiarity with early feminist writing is not quite as staggering as it might seem. The founder of the Victoria Press (which employed women compositors) was the remarkable Emily Faithfull, of whom the queen thought well enough to appoint her as her own Printer and Publisher in Ordinary in 1862—not a position she would have given to someone who had incurred her disapproval. As a friend and colleague of Barbara Leigh Smith, Faithfull was a member of the Langham Place Circle—writers, social activists and critics who, at 19 Langham Place, just off London's Regent Street, spurred by Jessie Boucherett's Society for Promoting the Employment of Women, had established a register (in fact an employment agency) for women seeking work as teachers and governesses. The aim was to extend the list to the enormous category of domestic service, as had been done in Bristol. There, a similar office sent out inspectors to ensure that places of employment were physically and morally sound, and that working conditions and pay were decent. The Langham Place Circle's office included a reading room where women could peruse newspapers (including the *Englishwoman's Journal*) while they were looking at job opportunities, sign petitions for the campaign for married women's property, and read essays by Barbara Leigh Smith, Isa Craig and Bessie Rayner Parkes, editor of the *Englishwoman's Review* from

1858. These writers argued for the importance of women's work, and believed that it should extend to watchmaking, journalism, medicine, prison and workhouse inspection and custodial work, the arts and, of course, teaching in schools and colleges set up for girls.

These women were, admittedly, an exceptional, but middle-class vanguard. They had little in common with the Edinburgh Maidservants' Union, which in 1825 had had the temerity to threaten a strike. On the contrary, they depended on the 1.3 million women domestic servants to give them the freedom to agitate. Barbara Leigh Smith was a cousin of Florence Nightingale and the illegitimate daughter of the Radical Unitarian MP for Norwich, Benjamin Smith, who had deliberately refused to marry her mother, and who had settled an annual income on his golden-haired daughter precisely so that she might lead an independent life. But the 26,000 signatures that she and her colleagues secured for a petition to urge a Married Women's Property Bill on parliament in 1855 is evidence enough that the Langhamites were neither tiny in number nor insignificant. Among those who actively joined the cause were some of the best-known and most widely read and admired of all Victorian women writers—Elizabeth Gaskell, of course; but also Elizabeth Barrett Browning, Mary Ann Evans a.k.a. George Eliot, Harriet Martineau and Harriet Taylor. It is ironic that Taylor's part in the Victorian battle for women's rights (itself undeservedly less well known than the later militant suffragettes) is often best remembered as the recruitment of her husband, John Stuart Mill, the 'saint of rationalism' and the greatest pillar of mid-Victorian liberalism, to the feminist cause. Mill himself was at pains, especially in his *Autobiography* (1873), to insist that it was Taylor who had educated him in the outrageous anomalies of women's position in marriage, in the labour force and in political society; who had been his true partner in works like *Principles of Political Economy* (1848), where the absence of women as a subject for the discussions of social science was first explicitly addressed; and that the work for which he would be best remembered, *On Liberty* (1859), formally dedicated to his wife, was the result of their joint authorship.

Some of the urgency and passion that Mill (whose prose, as he endearingly knew, seldom smoulders with either) evinces here was due precisely to his dismay at Harriet's part in all this, being reduced to that of Supporting Wife. The ideal helpmeet as sketched in John Ruskin's *Sesame and Lilies* (1865) was permitted to cultivate only the kind of knowledge already acquired by her husband, and was expected to act as permanently indentured proof-reader, inkwell-filler and—when the reviews came in—up-cheerer. That, insisted Mill, had not been the case with him and Harriet at all. Theirs had been a meeting of minds long before a mating of bodies. Mill may have been stronger in the technical science of ideas, especially economic theories, but Taylor had understood and passed on two sorts of knowledge in which he was decidedly the weaker party—grand metaphysical ideas as well as practical human applications (the spiritual and the social). All that he, Mill, was left with was the 'intermediate' realm, which in his *Autobiography* he implied, disingenuously, any old pedant could master as best he could. The psychological subtext of this elaborately formal apologia was in fact powerful, even sensational. For what John Stuart Mill really meant was that when he had met Harriet, he found someone who emancipated *him*—from thralldom to his father.

It was 1830; he was 24. She was a year younger, married, with three children to John Taylor, a City trader in medical drugs, whose Scottish family was well known to the originally Scottish Mills. Harriet had already published poems, book reviews and essays. Mill was working as a clerk in the Examiners' Office of the East India Company, drafting dispatches to be sent out to the company's legal and fiscal councillors. His father, who also worked for the Company, had found him the job. But then James Mill had done everything he possibly could to make John Stuart, the eldest of nine children, in his own image. Mill senior had committed himself, as thoroughly as he knew how, to furthering the utilitarian creed of his friend and mentor Jeremy Bentham, which was to increase the 'greatest happiness of the greatest number' of mankind. Beginning with the presumption that man was a bundle of sense-receptors, responding to either pleasure or pain, the enlightened legislator would aim to maximize the former and minimize the latter. For the first time the ills, material and moral, that plagued humanity were to be systematically and scientifically analysed: their magnitude measured, the causes diagnosed and the remedies prescribed. A report would be issued and recommendations made for legislation; a salaried inspectorate would be recruited to see to its execution and enforcement. Hitherto, empires had been run by power. The British Empire would be run by knowledge. James Mill had become a candidate for the position in the Examiners' Office after publishing an immense, not to say unreadably exhaustive, *The History of British India* (1817).

John Stuart Mill was just 11 when his father's *magnum opus* was laid before the world. But his training to be one of the propagators of felicity had begun much earlier. Since a child's mind was a sheet of smooth, soft wax, perfectly empty but perfectly receptive, the impress of instruction could not be made too early. Three was just about the right age, James decided, to begin teaching his son Greek. Initiation was Aesop's *Fables* (in the original), swiftly followed by Plato, Herodotus (all of it) and Xenophon. Arithmetic was a lot less fun, but by eight there was always Latin, Nathaniel Hooke's *The Roman History from the Building of Rome to the Commonwealth* (1738–71) and John Millar's *An Historical View of the English Government from the Settlement of the Saxons to the Accession of the House of Stewart* (1787) for light relief. The Mills lived in the favourite suburb of radical Improvers and feminists, Dr Price's Stoke Newington Green. And it was while striding around the Green and on longer walks into what was still countryside that Mill senior drilled his 10-year-old in differential calculus, Roman agrarian laws and the analysis of Greek rhetoric. When his father was appointed to his post with the East India Company, it was John Stuart's turn to teach his younger siblings. In his spare time between reading the proofs of his father's *The History of British India* and being put through political economy and logic, he managed to smuggle in a little literature—

238

mostly Shakespeare. At 14 he was allowed a trip to the Château Pompignon near Toulouse; but when he returned, his father's relentlessly intensive instruction continued.

James Mill had been breathtakingly successful in turning John Stuart into a thinking machine crammed full of every conceivable kind of knowledge, his powers of calculation and computation perfectly calibrated. But he had also made a creature already cowed by the burden of his assigned mission to Know Everything That Mattered; fearful of his unyieldingly stern father; racked by a terror of his own inadequacy. But at least, he supposed, he had been given the foundation of wisdom and the vocation of virtue. That supposition was profoundly shaken by a series of attacks made in the middle and late 1820s on Jeremy Bentham and James Mill by some of the brightest and sharpest essayists writing in the *Reviews*, not least Thomas Carlyle and (in a different spirit) the young Thomas Babington Macaulay. Carlyle attacked utilitarianism for assuming that human beings and the cultures into which they were gathered were akin to machines that might be retooled as and when they showed signs of malfunction. Only the victims of a higher naivety could remain impervious to the manifest truth that it was spirit, not base matter, that made the difference between the happiness and the misery of societies. Macaulay attacked utilitarianism for its refusal to concede that there might be a direct conflict between the imposition of scientifically optimized reforms and the protection of liberty.

The rest of Mill's life was to be spent working

out exactly those conflicts—between freedom and amelioration, but also between the competing claims of logic and feeling. So when his father's Unitarian minister, William Johnson Fox, brought Mr and Mrs Taylor to the Mills' house, and Mill drank in the huge eyes, the swan neck and the confident, eloquent speech, he knew instinctively that he had found an altogether new kind of instruction. Within a short time he learned that Harriet, who had been married very young, was now bitterly unhappy. Her husband had committed no cruelty. By the standards of the day he might even have been judged a good spouse. It was simply that, measured by the exalted sense of what a properly companionate marriage might be, she saw the depths of their incompatibility; his imperviousness to everything she most cherished: art, poetry, philosophy. Tied to him, she would be no more than a dutiful helpmeet. John Stuart Mill, on the other hand, plainly admired her for precisely the qualities of spirit and independent thought that had made her feel her marriage was a prison. Within a few more weeks they were writing to each other as 'dearest'. In the summer of 1833 Mill wrote, 'O my own love, whatever it may or may not be to you, you need never regret for a moment what has already brought such increase of happiness and can in no possible way increase evil. . . . I am taking as much care of your robin [her bird] as if it were your own sweet self.'

Although, over the next 20 years of a tortured romance, Harriet Taylor and John Stuart Mill would spend as much time as they could in each other's company and achieve an extraordinary intimacy, it seems certain that Mill was telling the truth in his *Autobiography* when he insisted that no boundaries of physical propriety had ever been breached. Sexual consummation would only happen once they were married. But their predicament certainly made the two of them turn their attention to the obstacles in the way of divorce in Victorian Britain.

Given that, legally (as another of the Langham Place feminists, Frances Power Cobbe, put it), married women were in the same category as 'criminals, idiots and minors', they were disqualified from suing for divorce, although they themselves could be divorced by their husbands for adultery. A Divorce and Matrimonial Causes Bill was passed in parliament in 1857, but it was not what it seemed. Enacted specifically to pre-empt a measure that would have given married women property rights, this piece of legislation perpetuated, rather than corrected, the inequities between the sexes. Husbands could divorce their wives for adultery, but wives could only return the favour if that adultery took the form of rape, sodomy, bestiality or some indeterminate act of cruelty. And, needless to say, so long as injured wives still had no title to their own property or income, the heavy costs involved in bringing a suit all but precluded it ever being brought. The notion that a divorce action might be brought (as Harriet would have done) for mere incompatibility remained the most fantastic prospect.

By the time the Divorce Act was passed, Harriet and John Stuart Mill had been married for six years. During most of the 20 years that preceded it Harriet had lived apart from Taylor, who, after Mill and his wife had gone off to Paris together for six months, was sufficiently humiliated to ask for a separation. But the peculiar arrangement somehow persisted. Mill would call on the Taylors (reunited for a while) for dinner, whereupon the husband would obligingly make himself scarce at his club. John and Harriet seemed armoured by the certainty of their love against the discomfort and distaste they provoked even in people whom they had thought of as friends, like the Carlyles. When one night John Stuart abruptly drove up in the company of Mrs Taylor, Carlyle professed himself relieved to discover that a distraught Mill was confessing that a maidservant at his house had burned the entire first draft of Carlyle's *French Revolution*. Bad as that was, Carlyle thought, it was actually better than the expected announcement—that Taylor and Mill had run off together! (Jane Welsh Carlyle, who never liked Harriet, persisted in suspecting that somehow she had been responsible for the destruction of the manuscript.)

All these vexations were endured for the sake of an ideal union founded on mutual respect and love. The clarity and steadfastness of the conviction led the couple to submit the conventions of Victorian marriage to unsparing criticism, much of which was incorporated in *The Subjection of Women*, published by Mill in 1869. The entire institution, they argued, was gift-wrapped in a tissue of falsehood and hypocrisy. Young girls were indoctrinated with the fallacy that 'marriage was the true profession of women', and that it would be an abode of perfect contentment thereafter. By a conspiracy of silence and expediency, the sacrificial victims of the arrangement were kept in ignorance, not just of the physical but also of the social reality of what really lay in store for them as wives. Marriage among the propertied classes was overwhelmingly a business transaction, rationally calculated to accumulate wealth, status and power. Bargains of mutual profit were made between the contracting parties. A family of high rank but depleted fortune would be allied to one that was its complementary opposite. The driving force, always, was hard interest, not soft sentiment. While marriage was ostensibly ordained for the containment of lust, the practical circumstances in which many unions were entered into more or less guaranteed the opposite, once the partners who had been brought together by the spurious claims of romance became inevitably disillusioned. The women then found themselves corrupted and ensnared in a diabolical bargain. They kept their fashionable clothes, their fine carriage, their servants, their children and their social position (and even, if they were very discreet, their lovers); their husbands got to keep their mistresses. It was, Mill and Harriet supposed, a sort of cohabitation, but 'if this be all that human life has for women, it is little enough, and any woman who feels herself capable of great happiness and whose aspirations have not been artificially checked will claim to be set free from this, to seek more'.

It was only John Taylor's death, in 1849, that set Harriet free. The couple married two years later at Melcombe Regis register office, a month before the opening of the Great Exhibition, ostracized by Mill's family and many of their old friends. Before they tied the knot, Mill insisted on signing a formal renunciation of the conventional legal rights of the

Victorian husband. It is, perhaps, the most high-minded pre-nuptial declaration ever made:

> Being about, if I am so happy, as to obtain her consent, to enter into the marriage relations with the only woman I have ever known with whom I would have entered into that state, and the whole marriage relation as constituted by law being such as she and I entirely disapprove . . . I, having no means of legally disinvesting myself of those odious powers (as I most assuredly would do if an engagement to that effect could be made legally binding on me) feel it my duty to put on record a formal protest against the existing law of marriage. . . . And in the event of marriage between Mrs Taylor and me I declare it to be my will and intention and the condition of any engagement between us that she retains in all respects whatever, the same absolute freedom of action and freedom of disposal of herself and of all that does or may at any time belong to her, as if no marriage had taken place and I absolutely disclaim and repudiate all pretension to have acquired any rights whatsoever by virtue of such a marriage.

Their domestic happiness was short-lived. Both of them were suffering from what developed into fatal tuberculosis. As Harriet's more advanced condition grew worse, they separated for months at a time while she tried to slow the progression of the disease by stays at Swiss sanatoria, or in the warmer, drier air of Provence. Conscious that he himself had a limited time, Mill busied himself with what he called 'the sacred duty' of transcribing

Harriet's thoughts on the equality of the sexes. The doctors, who were not altogether candid with them about the galloping deterioration of Harriet's condition in particular, insisted on separate rest cures, even though the separation was agony for Mill. Trapped inside a railway carriage in France, his route back to Harriet and England blocked by impassable snow, Mill brooded poignantly on their shared plight, and on the sense of warmth and security 'given by the consciousness of being loved [and] by being near the one by whom one is . . . loved the best. . . . I have experience at present of both these things for I feel as if no really dangerous illness could actually happen to me when I have her to care for me . . . yet I feel by coming away from her I have parted with a kind of talisman and was more open to the attacks of the enemy than when I was with her.'

Harriet died in November 1858 at Avignon, *en route* to the Mediterranean. Mill bought a house close to her grave and lived there for much of the rest of his life, while he finished the treatise *On Liberty* that immortalized him as the strongest pillar of Victorian liberal thought, and that he dedicated to his wife. Although he faithfully reproduced Harriet's opinions, he did not wholeheartedly agree with all of them. Whilst he made no bones about the right of women to seek and gain 'useful' work outside the home, he was not at all convinced that doing so would necessarily make them happier. But if that were their choice, or their necessity—and the census of 1851 showed that fully half the six million adult women of Britain were in fact employed—then, it went without saying, Mill believed, that they should have equal pay for equal work. To those, like psychiatric researcher Dr Henry Maudsley, who argued that their 'biology' (a euphemism for the menstrual cycle) precluded them from working for as much as eight days a month, Mill responded bluntly: 'What is now called the "nature of women" is an eminently artificial thing. . . . I believe that their disabilities are only clung to, to maintain their subordination in domestic life because the generality of the male sex cannot yet tolerate the idea of living with an equal.'

In 1865 Mill, now a nationally known figure, was approached by a group of Westminster electors and asked if he would stand for parliament. It was a critical moment. Prodded by its radical wing, the leadership of the Liberal party, Lord John Russell and William Gladstone, had decided to embrace a measure of parliamentary reform that, for all its circumspection and caution, would still end up extending the franchise to almost all householders. Mill's voice would be powerful in support not so much in spite of, but because of, the fact that he was actually against universal suffrage and the secret ballot. The crucial qualification, as far as he was concerned, was education (indeed he actually wanted votes weighted to reflect the amount of education, rather than rateable property, possessed by the voter). He was well aware of the eccentricity of his views. 'I was convinced that no numerous or influential portion of any electoral body really wished to be represented by a person of my opinions.' As if that was not enough, he refused to stand as the candidate of any party, to campaign or canvass or spend a single penny on his own behalf.

And there was another issue that he thought

would make his election even more improbable. Following an article published by Harriet in 1851 in the *Englishwoman's Journal*, Mill insisted that if household suffrage were granted in the boroughs it must include women as well as men. For although married women could not own houses in their own right, there was nothing to stop single women or widows; and there were, almost certainly, tens of thousands of women who fell into that category. For that matter, 'householder' in 1866 included rate-paying tenants, and that would have multiplied the eligible female franchise even more.

Mill's stepdaughter, Helen Taylor, with whom he shared much of his life after Harriet's death, was determined to keep this flame lit. It was she who encouraged Barbara Leigh Smith (now legally Madame Bodichon, having married a French-Algerian sculptor—from whom, needless to say, she lived apart half the year) to approach Mill about presenting a petition to parliament. Some 1200 women had signed their names, asking for the franchise. Mill was constitutionally shy about stirring up noisy publicity on the streets, but he got the vocal support of the Langhamites whether he wanted it or not. One of their number, Emily Davies (later the founder of Girton College, Cambridge, the first Oxbridge college for women, set up in 1874, some 25 years after the first London colleges, Queen's and Bedford), remembered that during the campaign 'Madame Bodichon hired a carriage, occupied by herself, Isa Craig, Bessie Parkes and myself, with placards upon it, to drive about Westminster. We called it "giving Mr Mill our moral support" but there was some suspicion that we might rather be doing him harm as one of our friends told us he had heard him described as "the man who wants to have girls in Parliament".'

Mill was not, of course, arguing for women members of parliament (although he saw no reason why, one day, that too should not come to pass). But he believed it both absurd and manifestly unjust that half the otherwise qualified suffrage should be barred from exercising their right to vote solely on grounds of their sex. What was already an uphill battle was made more difficult when the Liberals fell from power in August 1866. When, under a Conservative government in February 1867, Disraeli presented his version of the bill, Mill stuck to his guns, if anything even more adamant than the Langham Place campaigners in his demand that women (not just single women) be admitted to the franchise. In March he presented another petition (one of three that arrived in the Commons), bearing over 3000 signatures from Manchester. On 20 May 1867, in an eloquent and moving speech, Mill formally submitted his amendment to the Representation of the People Bill, proposing to substitute the word 'person' for 'man' in the clause dealing with criteria for extending the franchise to householders in the counties (not achieved until 1884). The surprise was not that the amendment went down to defeat, but that Mill actually managed to persuade no fewer than 73 members to vote for it (81 including pairs). His supporters included some eminent Mancunians—the Radical Thomas Bayley Potter and Sir Thomas Bazley, manufacturer and self-styled workers' friend.

In a Manchester by-election in November 1867 (when John Bright's more radical brother Jacob stood on a platform that included women's household suffrage), a widowed shopkeeper, Lily Maxwell, became the first woman to cast a vote in a British election. She was only on the register as the result of a clerical error; but once she was discovered by Jacob Bright and the suffrage campaigner Lydia Becker, they were determined that she should go through with it. Escorted to the poll, she cast her vote to a round of loud applause. An obviously disconcerted pioneer, Lily must none the less have had a great deal of gumption, not to mention sympathy with the aim of the suffragists (who had been campaigning peacefully for the vote since 1866), to play her part in what became an elaborately staged event. A surviving photograph certainly suggests a woman with a good deal of flinty determination. As far as Bright and Becker were concerned, she was a gift to the cause. Like the Chartist Land Company settler Ann Wood, Lily Maxwell was a classic example of gritty Scottish thrift: an ex-domestic servant who had saved enough to become a shopkeeper, and who paid the respectable weekly rent of 6 shillings and 2 pence for her place in Ludlow Street, a mix of artisan and lower middle-class, two-up, two-down brick dwellings. When her case became famous—or, to the conservative press, shocking—Lydia Becker wrote a dignified letter to *The Times* on 3 December 1867, describing her as a model voter of the kind intended to be emancipated by the Reform Act, 'a widow who keeps a small shop in a quiet street in Manchester. She supports herself and pays her own rates and taxes out of her own earnings. She has no man to influence or be influenced by, and she has very decided political

249

principles, which determined her vote for Mr Jacob Bright at the recent election.' As a result of the publicity around Lily Maxwell's vote, Lydia Becker was able to open a register to enrol qualified women householders. By the end of 1868, her list numbered 13,000.

All this appalled Queen Victoria. She may have occasionally voiced her own reservations (at least privately) about the distance between the sentimental dream and the harder realities of marriage. She may even have sympathized with measures designed to restrain physically violent and flagrantly licentious husbands, or to take care of cruelly abandoned wives. But addressing injustices and cruelties was, to her mind, emphatically not a licence for any degree of political emancipation. In October 1867 she had been surprisingly liberal on the need to expand the suffrage to the 'lower classes' since they had become 'so well informed and are so intelligent and earn their bread and riches so deservedly' in contrast to 'the wretched, ignorant high-born beings who live only to kill time'. But any discussion of women's fitness to exercise political rights made her apopleptic. 'It is a subject,' she wrote, referring to herself as usual in the third person, 'which makes the Queen so furious she cannot contain herself.' And again she vituperated against 'this mad wicked folly of "Womens' Rights" with all its attendant horrors on which her poor feeble sex is bent, forgetting every sense of womanly feeling and propriety'.

How did the queen feel about the other great feminist cause: work for middle-class women? She continued to be a dutiful reader of dispatches and

250

papers. But, after marriage and motherhood, she never felt that it was more than a painful chore imposed on her by her constitutional obligations, and (until it started to kill him) that Albert was in every way much better suited to the work. For the most part, too, she subscribed to the middle-class truism that marriage was woman's profession. So it is extremely unlikely that Victoria would have given much thought to another revelation of the census of 1851, that there were (and, according to the demographic statisticians, there seemed always likely to be) around half to three-quarters of a million more women of marriageable age than men. This 'spinster surplus', thought the Manchester political economist and manufacturer William Rathbone Greg, might be reduced by projects of emigration to the colonies. But that would none the less leave around half a million single women who were to be either condemned to a permanent sense of their own redundancy, or trapped in notoriously underpaid and little-respected jobs such as governesses. In the late 1850s the *Englishwoman's Journal* and its editor, Bessie Rayner Parkes, had taken up the call of middle-class women to be employed, as paid professionals rather than genteel volunteers, in a broader variety of fulfilling professions: teaching in girls' schools and colleges; prison and reformatory work; 'deaconess' visits to the homes of the poor in country and town; and the one profession that had been officially declared a 'noble' field for women: nursing.

Nursing was the one single-woman's profession that the queen felt perfectly fitted with the feminine qualities of tenderness, solace and healing. And the carnage of the Crimean War, of

251

course, had everything to do with this. The genuinely epic history of Florence Nightingale, the single woman *par excellence* who had spurned marriage for the sake of a higher calling; who had brought her band of 38 young women to the hell of the barracks hospital at Scutari; who had taken on the mutton-chop whiskered medical corps and the army bureaucrats to wring from them the barest necessities: bandages, splints, soap; who had made the washtub her personal escutcheon—all this had stirred the nation, not least the queen herself. Many times Victoria had expressed her bitter regret that she was not the right sex to be able to join the soldiers in their heroic privations and combat. She knitted mufflers, socks and mittens; and sent letters to the front, and visited returning soldiers in hospital, so that the troops should know that no one grieved more deeply for their suffering or felt more warmly for their sacrifices. The heavy losses suffered at Balaclava and Inkerman kept her and Albert awake at night. And as the news, reported in October 1854 by one of *The Times*'s war correspondents, Thomas Chenery, of incompetent management and command, and of shortages of basic supplies became more and more appalling, so Victoria's sense of maternal concern grew more acute.

The nurses at Scutari were surrogates for her own presence. When Florence Nightingale returned to Britain after the armistice in 1856, Victoria invited her to Balmoral to hear, first-hand, her account of the ordeal. But there was another heroine of the Crimea whose work was unknown to the queen (until her own step-nephew Captain Count Victor Gleichen told her) but who was the

252

soldiers' own favourite pseudo-mother. In the same year that Nightingale met the queen, a gala banquet and concert, with 11 military bands, was held by guards regiments at the Royal Surrey Gardens to benefit Mary Seacole, who had been declared bankrupt. There was a good reason why the returning soldiers so admired Mary. If you had been sick or wounded and managed to get taken to her 'British Hotel', you stood a decent chance of surviving. It was not so at Scutari.

But Mary Seacole was the wrong colour to be an officially canonized Victorian heroine. Born Mary Grant, she was the mulatto child of a Scotsman and his Jamaican wife. After marrying one of Nelson's godsons, Edwin Horatio Seacole, she had run an establishment in Jamaica that was part hotel, part convalescent home; during both the cholera epidemic of 1831 and the even more serious yellow-fever outbreak of 1853 she had acquired a reputation for working miracles of recuperation among the critically sick. Her antidotes for dysenteric diseases and the associated dehydration, which almost always proved fatal, were all drawn from the Caribbean botanical pharmacopeia. This origin guaranteed that they would be ridiculed as 'barbarous' potions by the medical establishment and that Mary's application to go to the Crimea to treat the cholera and typhoid victims (which accounted for the vast majority of fatalities) would be dismissed out of hand, not least by Florence Nightingale herself.

Unlike Nightingale, Seacole had no Baron Sidney Herbert at the War Department to argue her case. But, using her own funds, she somehow got herself to the eastern Mediterranean along with two of her most trusted Jamaican cooks. Once there she made, not for the barracks hospital in Turkey where it was clear she was unwelcome, but for the Crimea—the theatre of war itself. About two miles from Balaclava, Mary spent £800 of her own money building—presumably in imitation of her Jamaican establishment—the British Hotel: a combination of supply depot, refectory for soldiers about to go into action, and nursing and recovery station for the sick and wounded. Unlike the Scutari wards, the British Hotel was kept warm and dry. The best thing that could happen to a soldier laid low with cholera or typhoid was to be cared for on the spot, rather than endure the excruciating, sometimes three-week passage across the Black Sea to the deathtrap hospital at Scutari.

There were rats, of course, at the British Hotel too—caught in legions by 'Aunty Seacole's' exterminators at first light. Once they were dealt with, she would begin the morning routine. Coffee and tea by 7 a.m.; then chickens plucked and cooked, hams and tongues (where did she get them?), broth, stewed rhubarb, pies and Welsh rarebits prepared, and the *pièce de résistance*— her patented milkless (and therefore safely transportable) rice pudding. Even without the milk there was something especially maternal about that pudding: comfort food spooned out to soldiers who, amidst all the terrors of war, were allowed to become small boys again, fed by their big mulatto nanny. 'Had you been fortunate enough to have visited the British Hotel upon rice pudding days,' wrote one returning soldier, 'I warrant you would have ridden back to your hut with kind thoughts of Mother's Seacole's endeavours to give you a taste

254

of home.'

Alexis Soyer, the celebrity chef of the Reform Club who in 1855 had come out to provide his own brand of stews for the soldiers (Mary watched him ladle it out with his fleshy, bejewelled hands), approved her fare as wholesome and her courage as heroic. Once the convalescents had been taken care of, she would saddle up two mules and load a wagon with hot and cold food and basic surgical supplies—bandages, blankets, splints, needles, thread and alcohol. She would then set off straight into the thunder of the siege and, guided by a Greek Jew who knew the lines of the trenches and the positions of the camps, would disappear into the smoke, looking for wounded men—sometimes enemy Russians as well as British and French—who needed rescuing along with a mug of tea, a word of consolation and, as she instinctively understood, the touch of a clean handkerchief. Mortars whizzed past the old lady and her mules plodding through the fire. More than once, when she heard shouts of, 'Lie down mother! Lie down', 'with very undignified and unladylike haste I had to embrace the earth'. She became inured to horror. One soldier whom she found had been shot in his lower jaw. Mary put her finger in his mouth to try to open it enough to get some fluid down, but the teeth clamped down on her finger, cutting through it, and she needed help to prise them open.

Those who did manage to survive the nightmare of sickness and slaughter seldom forgot Mary Seacole. When she came back from the Crimea to London there were no invitations to Balmoral; only a press of creditors. But the fundraising events—at Covent Garden and Her

Majesty's Theatre, as well as the Royal Surrey Gardens—saved her from bankruptcy. Alexis Soyer and William Russell both made sure her work would be given public recognition. And Queen Victoria's half-nephew, Prince Victor of Hohenlohe-Langenburg, who had served in the war and was an amateur sculptor, made a bust of the woman he knew as 'Mami'. It was probably through him that she eventually became known to Victoria, who in 1857 wrote to Seacole officially recognizing her work. Seacole lived on until 1881, and left an estate worth £2000—all subscriptions from those whom she had cared for. But her memories were still haunted by the casualties: the frostbitten and the hopelessly mutilated; young men she thought should have been playing cricket, but who died in the mud, their eyes 'half-opened with a quiet smile' or 'arrested in the heat of passion and frozen on their pallid faces, a glare of hatred and defiance that made your warm blood turn cold'.

The Victorians—especially leathery old nurses like Mary Seacole—ought to have been hardened to death. It was all around them: in the typhus-riddled barracks of soldiers; in the cholera-infested slums of the poor; in the sputum-stained handkerchiefs of the tubercular middle classes. The high-minded salons would be reduced to silence by sudden, terrifying fits of uncontrollable coughing while well-dressed guests stood suspended between compassion and terrified self-preservation as the mucus droplets misted the aspidistras.

The omnipresence of death seemed disproportionately chastening to a generation breezy with not entirely undeserved confidence that they had done more than any of their predecessors to master their physical environment. A civilization that had made steam-driven ships float on the oceans, that had thrown great iron spans across broad rivers, and that had shrunk the world by electric telegraph must soon, surely, conquer disease. It was indeed at this moment that advances in lensed microscopy were revealing, for the first time, the existence and culture of pathogens; although not (other than by the use of the scrubbing brush) how their multiplication might be checked.

In this tantalizingly slight gap between knowledge and mastery, mortality entered to mock the Victorian sense of control over life. Perhaps the shock of translation from apparently omnipotent physical presence to the dumb inertia of death— the *grievance* of mortality—explains the extreme peculiarity of their rites of mourning; their determination to make the dead commandingly visible amidst the living. The immense scale and grandeur of Victorian tombs, with their passionate, hyperbolic masonry—so much more flamboyant than anything allowed for the living—are all attempts to postpone oblivion and absence. With every ton of alabaster and porphyry, every weeping cherub and crepe-draped portrait, the lost one seems evermore available, waiting in some recoverable world just around the corner.

No one wanted this more desperately than Queen Victoria, vexed with God for reneging on what she felt sure had been his promise never to have Albert abandon her to the woeful burden of her constitutional toil. To see our pure happy, quiet, domestic life which *alone* enabled me to bear my *much* disliked position CUT OFF at forty-two—when I had hoped with such instinctive certainty that God never *would* part us, and would let us grow old together—is too *awful*, too cruel!' Part of her anguish was precisely because the manner of Prince Albert's decline and death seemed to testify to the indispensability of partnership as the only way to make the duties of both family and sovereignty supportable. By doing more than his share—for their family, for the country and for (she would not hesitate to say) humanity—he had worked and worried himself to death. Nor did it help that he had been under-appreciated in Britain. Instead of being granted the 'King Consort' title she had wanted, he had had to make do, in 1857, with 'Prince Consort' (as Wellington and the Tories, fearing foreign, even papal interference had blocked 'King Albert'). Nor, for all the town halls and model factories he had visited, the innumerable hospital foundation stones he had laid, was Albert the Good and Great ever regarded as other than a foreigner; the very seriousness with which he took his duties being further proof of that for the drawling aristocracy, who still, to Victoria's chagrin, seemed to set the tone for Society.

Not all of this was the widow's fantasy. Albert's obsession with the 'Eastern Question' and the Crimean War did seem to age him. Just because he had been suspected in the Russophobic years before the war of being soft on the Tsar, he over-compensated by throwing himself into a madness of statistical investigations, plans, inquiries. His comments on the state of the army (not good); on the need for a proper training camp; on the horrors of military medicine; on the pitfalls of logistics; on the condition of the Ottoman government; on naval issues at the Bosphorus, and so on and so on, fill 50 folio volumes. By the time Victoria arrived at her desk each morning there was a neat tower of pre-sorted, pre-screened papers for her to peruse, approve, sign. After the war was over Albert turned his attention to the complications of the Peace of Paris and relations between the two allies; the implications for Britain's economy of the likely civil war in the United States; not to mention plans for the improvement of native cattle; schemes to use urban sewage for agrarian manure; and his work for the British Association for the Advancement of Science. Always an early riser, Albert now took to getting up in deep darkness to work in the green glow of his desk lamp. Even in more easy times he 'enjoyed himself on schedule', according to one court commentator, noting that it was at lunch and only at lunch at Balmoral or Osborne that heavy puns were allowed. By the late 1850s, although Albert stalked the deer at Balmoral with unrelenting devotion, even the plodding jokes seemed fewer and further between. More and more time was spent by himself or lost in his own anxieties. They were turning into the royal Jack Spratt and his wife. Albert, ever more sallow and gaunt and on a hair-trigger of anger; Victoria, the perpetual mother, her wrists now disappearing into bracelets of flesh, sitting solidly by his side. He worried for Britain and she worried for him.

Both of them worried for Bertie, the Prince of Wales. Vicky, their eldest, so sweet and so sensible, had gone to the Prussian court as the Crown Princess, at just 17, amidst much unhelpful wailing on the part of her mother that she was sending her 'lamb' to be 'sacrificed' on some Teutonic marriage bed. Albert, too, missed her badly. Her departure threw her eldest brother's chronic inability to conform to his parents' expectations into even sharper relief. 'Bertie's propensity is indescribable laziness,' his father fumed. 'I never in my life met such a thorough and cunning lazybones.' Away from the suffocation of the court Bertie was, in fact, a cheerful, open-faced young man who was not quite as allergic to his duties as his father thought. He did not disgrace himself academically at Christ Church, Oxford, and a tour of Canada was an out-and-out personal triumph. A spell at the Irish military camp at the Curragh, however, was less of a success. For there, as everywhere else, there was no getting away from the fact that Bertie liked his pleasures, especially when they came voluptuously corseted. It was the notoriety of his philandering that seemed, to his father and mother, calculated to wound their own publicly promoted sense of the decencies of domestic morality. His irresponsibility threatened to undo all their hard-won achievement in making the British monarchy respectable again.

Plans to marry Bertie to Princess Alexandra of Denmark were accelerated. Alix's ravishing beauty of face and figure, as well as her genuine sweetness of character, would surely be enough to satisfy the Prince's yen for lechery within the marriage bed. But even as the negotiations with the Danish court were under way, late in 1861, Albert and Victoria learned that Bertie was having an affair with a notorious 'actress'. Horrified by this latest act of almost treasonable sabotage, they wrote brutally candid letters to the prince warning him of the wanton self-destruction that this latest dalliance could bring—disease, pregnancy, blackmail, the republicanism of the boudoir and the bordello! At the same time, Albert was in the throes of dealing with a diplomatic crisis when Captain Charles Wilkes of the USS *San Jacinto* stopped the British mail steamer *Trent* and removed Confederate agents, in violation of the laws of neutrality during the American Civil War. Palmerston's Whig government, sympathetic to the South, was prepared to take the issue to the very edge of belligerence against Lincoln's government in Washington. Albert was doing everything he could, constitutionally, to soften that response and avoid another futile war.

In late November the Prince, already 'feeling out of sorts' from a 'chill' caught during a recent visit to Sandhurst, went to see Bertie near Cambridge and read him the riot act. The weather was that of a classic East Anglian Michaelmas, with driving rain and slicing winds. On his return to Windsor, Albert's chill worsened and refused to abate. He had once mused morbidly, when planting a sapling at Osborne, that he would not survive to see it mature. Now, to the acute distress of Victoria, he seemed to be measuring himself for his shroud: 'I am sure if I had a fatal illness, I should give up at once, I should not struggle for life. I have no tenacity of life.' His physician, Dr James Clark, was the same man whose diagnosis and treatment of the children had driven Albert to raging despair many years before. Now Clark disposed of his critic by failing to realize that what the Prince Consort was actually suffering from was typhoid fever. By the time Palmerston-Pilgerstein had managed to

261

summon a different doctor, it was too late.

Albert wandered in and out of clarity and from room to room in Windsor Castle, finally settling down in the Blue Room and not moving. Princess Alice played some hymns from an adjoining chamber. The queen came to read him Sir Walter Scott's *Peveril of the Peak* (1823). The copy survives in the Royal Library, the flyleaf inscribed in Victoria's hand, 'this book read up to the mark on page 81 during his last illness and within three days of its terrible termination'. The relevant paragraph on page 81 reads, incredibly, 'He heard the sound of voices but they ceased to convey any impression to his understanding and within a few minutes he was faster asleep than he had ever been in the whole . . . of his life.'

Was this truly coincidence? Or had the point she had reached in her reading of Scott's novel been chosen by Victoria as a literary valediction— especially since it describes, in fact, not a death at all but a deep healing slumber? For a moment on the afternoon of 14 December, Albert stirred, seemingly better, began to arrange his hair as if he were about to dress for dinner, and murmured, '*Es ist nichts, kleines Frauchen* (It's nothing, little wife).' Victoria left the bedside for a moment or two. When she came back he was gone, and out from that plump little face there came a howl of unutterable misery.

The sovereign of the greatest empire on earth had been vanquished by the one power against whom there was no defence. She spent so many hours collapsed in great, ragged, half-choking spells of sobbing that her secretaries and ministers thought she would go mad. 'You are right dear

262

child,' the queen wrote to her almost equally distracted eldest daughter, 'I do not wish to feel better . . . the relief of tears is great and though since last Wednesday I have had no very violent outburst—they come again and again every day and are soothing to the bruised heart and soul.' When she came to visit in 1862, Vicky saw her mother crying herself to sleep with Albert's coat thrown over her, hugging his red dressing gown. 'What a dreadful going to bed,' Victoria had written in her diary. 'What a contrast to that tender lover's love! All alone!'

If Victoria did ever seriously contemplate suicide, duty and memory held it at bay. 'If I live on', she confided to the diary, 'it is henceforth for our poor fatherless children—for my unhappy country which has lost all in losing him and in doing only what I know and feel he would wish for he is now near me—his spirit will guide and inspire me.' As it turned out, this was an understatement. Denying death the cruel victory of separation, sustaining the illusion of the prince's proximity, became a compulsion. Victoria spent £200,000, the same cost as the whole of Osborne, on the elaborate Italianate mausoleum at Frogmore for their tombs (which also accommodated her mother, the Duchess of Kent, who had died earlier that year) by Carlo Marochetti and the extraordinary statue by William Theed III of the two of them in Anglo-Saxon dress—the costume that defined the union of the Saxe-Coburg dynasty with what lingering historical mythology believed to be the ancient English constitution. But cold marble was not allowed to declare finis. Everything in Victoria's world—other than the widow's black and white cap that she would wear for the rest of her life—was designed to maintain the fantasy of Albert's continued presence, turning court life into one long séance. The Blue Room in which he died was preserved not as a German death-chamber, a *Sterbezimmer*, but exactly and for ever as it was when he was still alive. Should the upholstery wear out, it had to be replaced with its precise replica. Every day, hot water, blade and shaving soap were laid out along with fresh clothes. His other clothes remained untouched except those on which, in her distraction, Victoria insisted on sleeping. Even when she became somewhat more composed, she continued to take his nightshirt to bed along with a plaster cast of his hand. On Albert's side of the bed was a large photograph of the prince and a sprig of evergreen, symbolizing in the Germanic Christian tradition not just immortality but resurrection.

Widowhood became the queen's full-time job. What was left of Victoria's life (and, as it turned out, there was a lot) would be committed to the supreme vocation of perpetuating Albert's memory amongst her under-appreciative subjects. If there must be merriment, it had better not be in her presence, not even during the weddings of Bertie to Alix and of Alice to Prince Louis IV, Grand Duke of Hesse-Darmstadt—both of which seemed to the guests more like funerals, and were obviously torture for Victoria. At Alice's nuptials she confessed to her journal that 'I say "God bless her" though a dagger is plunged in my bleeding desolate heart when I hear from her that she is "proud and happy" to be Louis's wife.' The only tolerable literature consisted of requiem poems like the Poet Laureate Tennyson's *In Memoriam* (1850). A new edition was dedicated of course to the late Prince. Victoria herself resolved to create a memorial bookshelf, commissioning an anthology of Albert's speeches; a biography of his early life; and another five-volume biography of the complete career and works. Memorial stones went up everywhere. Granite cairns were put up along the Highland trails where Albert had stalked deer, the most imposing bearing the inscription 'Albert the Great and Good, raised by his broken-hearted widow'. Statues were erected in 25 cities of Britain and the empire. Victoria left her seclusion in November 1866 to travel to Wolverhampton to unveil yet another, alighting from the train with 'sinking heart and trembling knees' to the noise of military bands and cheering, flag-waving crowds. The queen was so moved by the occasion that she called for a sword to knight the Lord Mayor, who was momentarily terrified that he was about to be beheaded. An epidemic of civic monuments broke out, to the point where Charles Dickens wrote to a friend in 1864 that 'If you should meet with an inaccessible cave anywhere to which a hermit could retire from the memory of Prince Albert and testimonials to same, pray let me know of it. We have nothing solitary or deep enough in this part of England.'

Other signs of restiveness began to register. A fund was launched to build a memorial hall at Kensington, as close as possible to the site of Albert's triumph, the Great Exhibition, with yet another monumental statue facing it. But only £60,000 was subscribed of the £120,000 needed, leaving the memorial committee no option but to commission the statue alone in Kensington

Gardens. Sir George Gilbert Scott's Gothic Revival design was to make the massively enthroned figure of the prince, sculpted by Marochetti, the centrepiece of a shrine, with Albert as the gilded relic in a pinnacled ciborium or reliquary, set above a monumental base unhappily compared by its critics to a giant cruet or sugar sifter. The canopied shrine was flanked by the four colossal greater Christian Virtues. Another four statues personified the moral virtues, and eight bronzes the Arts and Sciences whose qualities he had personified and patronized. At the base were emblems of the Four Continents to which the blessings of the Albertian empire had flowed, and above them was a 200-foot frieze featuring 170 of the geniuses of European civilization, so that Albert would keep company with fellow-immortals such as Aristotle, Dante, Shakespeare, Hogarth and Mozart. As the biographer Lytton Strachey perceptively remarked in *Queen Victoria* (1921), this massive embalming of the sainted prince did some disservice to the complicated, open-minded and unquestionably gifted man who had acted, in effect, as the first presidential figure of modern British society.

But for Victoria he had become not the entrepreneur of modern knowledge so much as the Perfect Christian Chevalier. Devotion to His Way of Doing Things bade her rise every morning, punctually at 7.30, then tunnel her way through state papers and dispatches (as He had done). When a prime minister like Lord Derby or Lord John Russell presumed to suggest an end to the official period of mourning, or even that the queen might perhaps consider resuming her constitutional duty to open parliament, Victoria responded with a mixture of self-pity and outrage that anyone could be so heartless as to inflict further stab-wounds on 'a poor weak woman shattered by grief and anxiety'. After a decent interval, Victoria's total disappearance from the public eye began to provoke irreverent comment in the press and to nourish the most sustained British flirtation with republicanism since the Civil War of the 17th century. It was especially serious during the passage of the Reform Bills of 1866 and 1867, when radicalism had its head of wind, and the Tory leader Benjamin Disraeli, in particular, needed the solidity of the monarchy to assuage fears that he was going down a road whose outcome no one could predict. In 1866, despite protesting to the prime minister Lord Russell her abhorrence of being subjected to a spectacle whereby people could witness 'a poor broken-hearted widow, nervous and shrinking, dragged from deep mourning', Victoria did finally consent to open parliament, but so grudgingly that the occasion probably alienated more of her subjects than it won over. As a condition of her appearance the queen had stipulated no state coach, no procession, no robes and especially no speech from the throne. Instead, the Lord Chancellor read the address while Victoria sat in deep gloom in her widow's cap and mourning black. She was not eager to repeat even this gesture. The next June, when Victoria again failed to open parliament, a famous cartoon appeared in the satirical journal *The Tomahawk*, showing a throne draped by an enormous shroud bearing the legend: 'Where is Britannia?' Earlier, someone had put a satirical poster against the railings of Buckingham Palace announcing: 'These commanding premises . . . to be let or sold in consequence of the late occupant's declining business.'

Any attempts to persuade Victoria to emerge from this politically damaging seclusion bounced off the immovable guardianship of the one man whom the queen seemed to be able to lean on in her unrelenting grief: the Balmoral ghillie John Brown. The fact that he had been Albert's personal favourite naturally recommended him to Victoria, for whom he became an indispensable and ubiquitous presence, and to whom she allowed liberties unthinkable in her secretaries, children or ministers. To their horror and embarrassment Brown would address her as 'wummun', comment on her dress, tell her what was the best plan for the day and always protect her against the importunate demands of the rest of the world. In return she created the special position of 'Her Majesty's Servant'. Brown organized her daily pony-trap rides and the Scottish dances at Balmoral, and was not always sober when he did so.

It would take the near fatal illness of the Prince of Wales in 1871, combined with another narrow escape from assassination (Brown personally caught the culprit), to shock Victoria out of this deep, self-willed isolation. When Disraeli proposed a day of national thanksgiving for Bertie's recovery, complete with a service in St Paul's Cathedral (not least because the republican movement was at its height), Victoria relented. She was rewarded with huge crowds. In the same year, the completed Albert Memorial was finally unveiled in Kensington Gardens. (A joint-stock company would later build the Royal Albert Hall.) Three years later, in 1874, Disraeli finally managed to give Victoria a renewed sense of her own independent authority with the passing of the Royal Titles Bill that made her Queen–Empress of India.

But as far as the queen herself was concerned, she never swerved from the vow she had taken after Albert's death that '*his* wishes, *his* plans, *his* views about *every*thing are to be my law'. This, indeed, was what she supposed was the right and proper duty of widows, just as during the life of a marriage the whole duty of wives was to dissolve their own wills into that of the domestic household. Widows like Margaret Oliphant, who of necessity turned to popular novel-writing (she published a hundred of them before she died), were objects of pity rather than admiration. For how could a commercial career ever be thought compatible with the ordained role of women to preserve the sanctity of the home from the beastly masculine jungle of the capitalist marketplace? This, at any rate, was the message delivered by the holy trinity of works dedicated to the destiny of womanhood, and all published at the time of Victoria's bereavement: Coventry Patmore's long verse effusion 'The Angel in the House' (1854); Ruskin's 'Of Queen's Gardens', one of the two lectures delivered in Manchester in 1865, and subsequently published as *Sesame and Lilies*; and not least Mrs Isabella Beeton's *Book of Household Management* (1861). All three were extraordinary best-sellers. *Sesame and Lilies* sold 160,000 in its first edition, not least because it became a standard fixture on prizegiving days at girls' schools, but it was overshadowed by Mrs Beeton's book, which sold two million copies before 1870. None of these books, however, portrayed domestic women in a state of perpetual submission. Ruskin especially was at pains to reject the 'foolish error' that woman was only 'the shadow and attendant image of her lord'. In fact the popularity of these works owed a lot to the delivery of messages that credited women with a great deal of power—and power of a more concrete kind than that attributable to romantic seduction.

Coventry Patmore and Mrs Beeton were the complementary bookends of the cult of hearth and home, the poet lyricizing the transcendent mystery of wifeliness, the *Book of Household Management* providing over 1000 pages of instruction on how the 'shrine' was actually to be kept spotless. If one was a kind of liturgy for the high priestesses of the home, the other was an exhaustive manual for domestic command and control. The very first paragraph of Isabella Beeton's truly astonishing book says it all: 'As with the commander of an army or the leader of any enterprise, so is it with the mistress of a house.' Ruskin's stance was more complicated. As his title implied, his essay–lecture added to the metaphors of priestess and general that of the 'queen'. Her sovereignty was not just a matter of making sure the pillows were plumped and the roast cooked on time. To her fell the exalted responsibility of protecting society against the corrosions of acquisitive capitalism. The illiberalism of the home was its defence against the vulgar battering ram of the marketplace; the guarantee that inside the front door, at least, values other than those of competitive individualism would prevail—those of a 'Place of Peace, the shelter not only from all injury, but from all terror,

270

doubt and division'.

Ruskin's personal qualifications for making these prescriptions, had they been known, would not have done much for his credibility. His marriage, to Effie Gray, had been an unconsummated fiasco. He had written *Sesame and Lilies* while hypnotically spellbound by his own spotless lily, the adolescent Rose La Touche, to whom he acted as tutor and mentor before deluding himself that she ought to be his wife. Rose fled in horror from the proposal, triggering first in her, and then in the spurned Ruskin, an almost equally violent mental collapse. The crisis had been brought about by Ruskin's apparently reckless change of role from trusted tutor, moral and intellectual guardian to would-be lover and husband. Ruskin failed to see this disaster in the making precisely because, as 'Of Queen's Gardens' made clear, he imagined that through intense reading women would actually be liberated from unattractively vapid servility to their husbands (and from the worthless chatter of fashion) and would instead be converted into their equals. Art, philosophy and morals would be ventilated over the breakfast marmalade.

But unlike some of the more conventional Victorian legislators of domestic virtue, Ruskin did not, in fact, insist that women belonged *only* at home. 'A man has a personal work or duty, which is the expansion of the other, relating to his home and a public work or duty relating to the state. So a woman has a personal work or duty relating to her own home and a public work or duty which is also the expansion of that.' What had he in mind by that? Anything, in fact, that would help *others* out

271

in the world, especially out in the world of the poor, make their own homes: 'what the woman is to be within her gates as the centre of order, the balm of distress and the mirror of beauty; that she is also to be without her gates where order is more difficult, distress more imminent, loveliness more rare.' The commercial success of *Sesame and Lilies* enabled Ruskin to help young women philanthropists and reformers like Octavia Hill to be 'angels *outside* the house' in just this way. Hill was the granddaughter of the social reformer Rowland Hill, and Ruskin had met her when she was just 15. Although she was single and obviously committed to a career other than that of wife and mother (at least until she was 40), Ruskin saw Octavia as a home-maker for others, if not for herself. It was his money that enabled her Charity Organisation Society to buy up its first London tenements and convert them into 'improved' lodgings for working-class families. But Octavia's aim was to remodel the tenants as well as their buildings. When her volunteers came to collect the rent they arrived bearing a stack of forms on which the residents were required to make a report of their weekly conduct. 'Persons of drunken, immoral or idle habits cannot expect to be assisted' [with a charity allowance] unless they can satisfy the committee that they are really trying to reform.' Incorrigible delinquents and recidivists would be removed as morally infectious. For Ruskin, this was a perfect instance of the benevolent exercise of 'queenly' power to make domestic peace where before there had been only dirt and clamour. A den of beasts would be turned into the abode of beauty and faith.

Suppose, however, that a happily married middle-class Victorian woman would actually dare to import into her home some business that more properly belonged to the world? Could that enterprise, especially if it came with the trappings of art, be reconciled with domesticity, or would it inevitably pollute the sanctity of what Ruskin had called 'the vestal temple'? All that Victoria had to do to test the issue would have been to drive her pony trap a few miles down the Freshwater road on the Isle of Wight, past the house of her Poet Laureate, Alfred, Lord Tennyson, to 'Dimbola', the enlarged pair of cottages that, from 1863, were the studio as well as the residence of the greatest of all the Victorian photo-portraitists, Julia Margaret Cameron.

The case was complicated by the fact that photography in the 1860s was very much divided between genteel amateurs practising their art, and professionals turning out travel views, pictures of literary and military celebrities, police and medical documentation, and, for a more arcane but lucrative market, pornography. The considerable expenses of equipment and processing (not least the chemically reduced silver nitrate needed to sensitize glass plates and gold bullion for toning) confined the hobby to the upper middle class and Victorian gentry, who often worked out of studios and darkrooms in their own houses. The greatest of Cameron's immediate predecessors, Clementina, Lady Hawarden (whose startlingly unconventional and sensually loaded talent was cut brutally short at the age of 42), was herself from an Irish aristocratic family. She used her house at Dundram as one of her first studios, but when she and her husband moved to South Kensington, a stone's throw from the site of the Great Exhibition, she was able to annex part of the apartment for her photography—and use her own daughters, each of them on the verge (or over it) of sexual maturity—as models. In other words, for all her dazzling originality Lady Hawarden presented no problem and no challenge to the authority of the lords of the new art, the award of the Photographic Society. She exhibited—just three times, in 1865–6 at the London print sellers P. & D. Colnaghi's, in 1866–7 at the French Gallery, London, and in 1867–8 at the German Gallery, London—and was awarded a silver medal for her work and showered with richly merited praise.

Julia Margaret Cameron was an altogether different kettle of fish. Her background was respectably, even reassuringly, colonial. As Julia Pattle she was one of seven children born to a French mother and British-Indian father. The Pattle girls, however, became famous in India as eccentric beauties, who favoured brilliant Indian silks and shawls rather than the decently demure Victorian dress expected of the memsahibs. 'To see one of this sisterhood float into a room with sweeping robes and falling folds', wrote one of their admirers, 'was almost an event in itelf and not to be forgotten. They did not in the least trouble themselves about public opinion.' In 1838, at the age of 23, Julia made a serious marriage—to Charles Hay Cameron, a classical scholar (Eton and Oxford) who had aspired to be professor of moral philosophy at London University but had been turned down for not being in holy orders. Cameron had gone on to an eminent career as a member of the Governor-General's Council and law commissioner for Ceylon (Sri Lanka), where he had extensive plantations.

In 1848 Charles Cameron suddenly gave all this up and retired with Julia to Britain, where he evidently meant to devote himself again to the Higher Things and write a treatise on the Sublime and the Beautiful. Through the Prinsep family—a dynasty of orientalist scholars in India and painters and poets in London—the Camerons mixed in salon society that included Tennyson and the great astronomer Sir John Herschel. While visiting Tennyson at Freshwater, Julia saw the pair of cottages that, remodelled, became 'Dimbola'. There they established themselves along with their children, and Charles Cameron became, if not exactly a recluse amidst his books, then certainly the retiring philosopher whom Tennyson once glimpsed asleep in his bedroom, 'his beard dipped in moonlight'.

At some point, probably early in 1863 when she was 48 years old, Julia was given a camera—the hefty wooden-box apparatus of the time. She swiftly converted her coalhouse at 'Dimbola' into a darkroom and the henhouse into what she called 'my glass house'—the studio. Most accounts of her career make this departure seem like the enthusiasm of an amateur who needed a hobby to fill in time between the polite rituals of middle-class life on the Isle of Wight and the rounds of Pre-Raphaelite visitors. In fact, it is evident from family papers that from the outset Julia was up to something much more serious, both artistically and commercially. With coffee harvest after coffee harvest failing in Ceylon the Camerons were becoming seriously hard-up. There was no sign of Charles, buried ever more deeply in his library, being willing or able to recover their fortunes. In September 1866 her son-in-law, Charles Norman, asking one of Julia's patrons for a loan of £1000, wrote that 'my father-in-law for the last two months has been utterly penniless so that his debts are increased by butchers' bills'. So whether or not Julia had always meant to be a professional, now she felt bound to succeed for the sake of the family. Clementina Hawarden could afford to sell her work at a fête to benefit the 'Female School of Art'; Julia had to sell hers to benefit herself. But her professionalism was not going to compromise her aesthetic standards. One of her models believed that Mrs Cameron 'had a notion that she was going to revolutionise photography and make money'. Making money cost money. Charles, who evidently worried about his mother-in-law as well as his father-in-law, reported to a creditor that he had 'told my mother for positively the last time that any assistance of this kind can be given her and that her future happiness or discomfort and misery rests entirely with herself'.

But then this was exactly the opportunity Julia Margaret Cameron was looking for—to make her own way. And she had the toughness to persevere. Although some of her Tennysonian images of luminous madonnas and gauzy damozels reinforced, rather than undermined, the more fantastic stereotypes of women as embodiments of the pure and the passionate, there was not much of the angel about Julia herself. Unable to afford assistants, she did all the mucky work of the wet collodion process herself: staining her fingers and dresses with silver-nitrate sensitizer, making sure the glass plates were exposed while still wet, washing and fixing images, and developing the prints. Since she depended on natural light, in the not invariably sunny Freshwater, to obtain the intensely expressive effects of light and shade that characterized both her portraits and her 'poetic' studies, she needed extraordinarily long exposures, sometimes of 10 minutes or more. Not only her own children, and domestic servants who obediently posed, but also the good and great—the artists George Frederic Watts and William Holman Hunt; Carlyle, Sir John Herschel and Tennyson—all were bullied into keeping stock-still for unendurable periods of time. Herschel—one of the most distinguished men in Britain—was told to wash his hair so that Julia could fluff it up with her blackened fingers to get just the right look of back-lit electrified genius. As is evident from the famous portraits—some of the most mesmerizing face-images in the history of art—Carlyle did fidget. But the photographer turned this to advantage. His head, she had thought, was a 'rough block of Michelangelo sculpture'. But Carlyle's personality was also notoriously edgy and mercurial. So she gives us a head that is both monumental and energized—the authentic hot tremble of the Carlylean volcano, the burning 'light in the dark lantern'.

Predictably, the extreme manipulation of focus and exposure did not meet with the approval of the eminences of the Photographic Society, who sneered at Julia's 'series of out of focus portraits of celebrities' as tawdry vulgarities in which technical incompetence masqueraded as poetic feeling. ('We must give this lady credit for daring originality,' a typically snide review in the *Photographic Journal* commented, 'but at the expense of all other photographic qualities.') The more popular she became, the nastier they got: 'The Committee much regrets that they cannot concur in the lavish praise which has been bestowed on her productions by the non-photographic press, feeling convinced that she herself will adopt an entirely different mode of reproduction of her poetic ideas when she has made herself acquainted with the capabilities of the art.' The subtext of this was, of course, that women, with the rare exceptions of noble amateurs such as Clementina Hawarden, had no business prematurely parading their work without mastering the one quality by which photographic excellence was properly judged: crispness of definition. Crispness, of course, like the heavy lifting and chemically saturated processes of photography, was a matter of self-effacing mechanics; a stiff-upper-lip kind of art, definitely not the flouncy, dreamy, mushy thing that they believed Julia Margaret Cameron executed.

But crispness repelled Julia. She had no interest in making dumbly literal facsimiles of nature. Her aim was to make a poet out of a lensed machine. The great 'heads' that so disconcerted the Photographic Society were meant to take Romanticism's exploration of the external signs of interior emotions (anger, sorrow, elation, ecstatic vision) a step further—to create expressive images of the thinker/artist-as-hero. Although she also bathed children, servants and obedient friends in the more diffused light she needed for her poetic costume dramas, Cameron was capable, on

278

occasions, of deliberately, even cruelly, playing with the self-consciousness of sitters in their allotted roles. Her sublimely beautiful portrait of the 16-year-old actress Ellen Terry (who had gone on the boards at nine) as 'Sadness' is as poignant as it is precisely because her marriage to the much older Watts was evidently already falling apart on their honeymoon in Freshwater. At the opposite end of the emotional spectrum are the photographs of Cyllene Wilson, the daughter of a repent-or-be-damned evangelical preacher who had been adopted by the Camerons. To get just the right look of despair on Cyllene's powerful face, Julia was not above locking her in a cupboard for a few hours until the expression came naturally. Perhaps this was, in the end, too much for Cyllene, who ended up running off to sea, marrying an engineer on an Atlantic steamship line and dying in her 30s of yellow fever in Argentina.

Julia was successful but not, it seems, quite successful enough. Held at arm's length by the photographic establishment, she had secured crucial patronage from one of her husband's old Etonian friends, the banker Samuel Jones Loyd, Baron Overstone, to whom she assigned some of her most extraordinary albums in return for his investment. She showed and sold at Paul Colnaghi's gallery and entered into a contractual arrangement with the Autotype Company to publish carbon reproductions. To ensure herself against piracy, Julia registered 505 of her photographs under the recent Copyright Act (1869), giving the impression that she meant to profit as much as she could from her originality and popularity. Thanks to the efforts of dealer and publisher, her work became famous. But it never held ruin at bay. In 1875 she and her husband, with their fortunes evaporating, returned to Ceylon, where she died in 1879. Although there was a flourishing Indian-Oriental photo-industry under way, views of temples and tea parties were not Julia Margaret Cameron's line. The images petered out and then stopped altogether. But the power of her accomplishment was already enough to have wiped the sneer from the face of those who condescended to 'lady artists'.

It is almost certain that, through Cameron's photographs to illustrate Tennyson's 'Idylls of the King' (1874–5), a poem associated in the queen's mind with the memory of Albert, Victoria knew of her work and would not have disapproved of a woman photographer. A woman doctor, on the other hand, was a great deal more shocking. The very idea of girls familiarizing themselves with the gross details of human anatomy, much less dissecting corpses in the company of men, was, needless to say, perceived by the queen as a revolting indecency. And those who took the first courageous steps in this direction could only do so while pretending to study for the acceptable work of nursing—paradoxically regarded as less shocking despite nurses' equal familiarity with living anatomy. In the year of Prince Albert's death, 1861, Elizabeth Garrett was—to the consternation of the examiners at the Middlesex Hospital, who had not realized that 'E. Garrett' was a woman—placed first in the teaching hospital's qualifying examinations. The daughter of a rich Suffolk businessman, Garrett had left school at 15. But instead of grooming herself (perhaps through a

Ruskinian education in reading and drawing) for the altar and parlour, she had quite other ideas. A speech by Elizabeth Blackwell changed Garrett's life. Blackwell, born in Bristol, had been transplanted to the United States where in 1849, at the age of 28, she had become that country's first accredited woman doctor. After losing the sight of an eye while working at the obstetric hospital of La Maternité in Paris (where women were welcomed, according to her, as 'half-educated supplements' to the male physicians), Blackwell had returned to America, set up a one-room dispensary in 1853 in the New York tenements, and eventually, in 1857, opened the New York Infirmary and College for Women. She was, in short, a living inspiration.

Elizabeth Garrett was determined to do for Britain what Blackwell had done for the United States. Initially horrified by her bone-headed temerity and obstinacy, her rich father was eventually won round—enough, at any rate, to subsidize her ostensible education as a nurse, which included her attendance at medical college lectures. Despite being ostracized by the male students and prevented from full participation in dissections, Elizabeth was undeterred, buying body parts and dissecting them in her bedroom.

Begged to keep quiet about the result of her examination in 1861, Garrett (possibly egged on by a number of articles in the *Englishwoman's Journal* that advocated the creation of a corps of women doctors specializing in female and paediatric medicine), chose instead to publicize it, scandalizing the profession. Her application to matriculate at London University was denied—but only after a divided 10:10 vote in the Senate, with the Chancellor, Lord Granville, voting explicitly against the recommendation of his Liberal party colleague Gladstone, an early admirer of Garrett's. In 1865 she took and passed the examination of the Society of Apothecaries, who, horrified at their oversight, passed a statute retroactively excluding women from the profession. In 1870, after performing two successful surgeries and passing written and oral examinations in French, the University of Paris awarded her their medical degree. But this was by no means the end of the battle for women's medical aspirations. In the year that Garrett achieved her French licence a group of five women, led by Sophia Jex-Blake, were subjected to the physical intimidation of a near riot when they attempted to take the Edinburgh University medical examination. When a path was cut through the jeering crowd to the examination room, a flock of sheep was pushed in after the women. Whether it rankled or not, it was, inevitably, often a supportive marriage that gave these women power. When Elizabeth Garrett became Elizabeth Garrett Anderson, as the result of marrying a steamship owner, she was finally in a position to open her New Hospital for Women.

Her refusal of what had been the accepted confines of proper women's work was becoming less of a rarity by the 1870s, a decade when the Victorian litany of the Great Exhibition—Peace, Prosperity, Free Trade—was starting to sound off-key. The great pillars of commerce had been shaken by a series of bank upheavals and mergers in the late 1860s. In Europe, the Pax Britannica seemed helpless to stop the wars of national aggression by which new nation states and empires were being roughly forged. Irish violence and Balkan massacres were beginning to supply the sensation-hungry popular press with headlines. But something even more explosive had been set off in the libraries and debating circles of the Victorians and that something was Darwin's *Descent of Man* (1871).

In their mothers' and grandmothers' generation, the urgent longing to be, above all, useful—beyond the duties set out by Mrs Beeton—had been filled by Christian works of healing and charity. But although Darwin himself often protested that the implications of his theory were no threat to faith (starting with his own), there was at least an element of disingenuousness in the protest. The fact was that the great sheltering dome of faith—authority based on direct revelation —had been shattered by Darwin's vision of a morally indifferent, self-evolving universe. Once it was read, digested and believed, it was hard, if not impossible, for at least some young women born around the time of the Great Exhibition to surrender themselves to the male-governed kingdom of prayer. In place of the old gospels of Church and Home, they now needed the new gospels of Education and Work. And since competition, the struggle for survival, seemed to be the truth of the way in which the world worked, why should they themselves flinch from the fray? Against Ruskin's appeal that the 'queens' stand above and against the noisy, frantic shove and bustle of the world, the champions of women's higher education and more ambitious fields for women's work argued that, on the contrary, it was direct experience of the wider world that would make them better wives and mothers, and at the very least better women. The queen needed to get out of the garden and into the urban jungle.

Ruskin, of course, had been a sponsor, not a critic, of women's education. But he had made it very clear that the content of that education was never to extend beyond subjects deemed fit by males; and that its function in the end was to make young women more interesting wives and companions. Better a dinner table at which the Angel of the House could talk about Tennyson or Tintoretto rather than crinolines and curtain lengths. Whilst Emily Davies, a friend and contemporary of Elizabeth Garrett, certainly agreed that marriages would be the better for educated, rather than uneducated, wives, she wanted more out of that education than the training of amusing partners. 'All that we claim', she wrote when arguing, unsuccessfully, for women to be awarded degrees at the University of London, 'is that the intelligence of women . . . shall have full and free development.' And for that to happen required not just schooling but higher education. Of those men who insisted that women were somehow biologically unsuited to mathematics or science, Davies inquired how they would know when so many men could be accused of precisely the same failing. What she hated most of all was the acceptance by so many women themselves of the degrading assumption of 'mental blankness'.

Since London University was evidently not going to countenance the award of full degrees to women students at Bedford and Queen's (at least not until 1878), Davies herself, the daughter of an evangelical minister, began in 1866 to raise funds for the creation of a women's college. In 1869, Hitchin College opened its doors to the first six undergraduates, and four years later reopened as Girton College, a few miles north of Cambridge. Fired by her battles to prove that women's intellect was indistinguishable from that of men, Davies insisted on a curriculum identical to that offered by the Cambridge faculties. A fellow-enthusiast, the moral philosopher and economics don Henry Sidgwick (who founded a residence for women students in 1871, which evolved into Newnham College in 1880), disagreed with Davies on what kind of education would best advance the learning and professional skills of women students. Let the ancient disciplines decay in their male seminaries, he thought, while women would be the vanguard of those embracing the new sciences—economics, history, modern philosophy and politics—and be all the better fitted to become full citizens of the world. Davies, however, was not convinced by arguments that only a 'soft' education was suitable for women. If making the point of their intellectual equality meant compulsory examinations in Greek, so be it.

At least as important—and revolutionary in its implications for the fate of women—was the fact that colleges like Girton now provided young women with an alternative home, a community of the like-minded. Among the most precious gifts bestowed on each Girtonian was a scuttle of coal every day, so that she might be as independent as she wished in her own study. Sometimes, however, the elation of the child became (as parents of college-age offspring have known ever since) the transparent unhappiness of a mother or father. As one young Girtonian, Helena Swanwick, later the author of *The Future of the Women's Movement* (1913), wrote:

> When the door of my study was opened and I saw my own fire, my own desk, my own easy chair and reading lamp—nay my own kettle—I was speechless with delight. Imagine my dismay when my mother turned to me with open arms and tears in her eyes saying, "You can come home again with me, Nell, if you like!" It was horrible . . . I hardly knew how decently to disguise my real feelings. To have a study of my own and to be told that, if I chose to put 'Engaged' on the door, no-one would so much as knock was in itself so great a privilege as to hinder me from sleep.

Whether it meant the first break with a life of idle grooming for the marriage market, or the makings of a new professional career, college represented freedom, self-discovery, the beginnings of independence. Another Girtonian, Constance Maynard, who recalled that she and her sister had been 'shut up like eagles in a henhouse' at home, now could exult, 'At last, at LAST, we were afloat on a stream that had a real destination, even though we hardly knew what that destination was.' For some of them, that destination might be other schools or colleges so that they might produce further cohorts of ambitious, independently minded young women. Constance Maynard, for instance, went on to found Westfield College, London University. Others—like Elizabeth Garrett's sister the suffrage leader Millicent

Garrett Fawcett—might re-create the Mill–Taylor equal intellectual partnership in their marriage. Millicent married the blind political economist and Radical politician Henry Fawcett, Postmaster-General in Gladstone's second government, and, after he died in 1884, instead of shrinking into the shell of the devoted widow embarked on an outspoken career of promoting public causes. But almost 30 per cent of the first generation of Oxbridge women graduates (from the colleges of Somerville, St Hugh's, Newnham and Girton) did not marry at all. And, faced with a barrage of evidence about the immense and increasing distance between rich and poor Britain, many of them decided to abandon not just domesticity, but the whole world of liberal, Victorian middle-class comfort, and take their hard-won independence into the factories and the slums. In 1887 the Women's University Settlement opened its first lodgings in Southwark, where young women from Oxbridge colleges went to live alongside some of the poorest people in London.

Many of the women who came of age in the 1880s looked around and saw that, if you were middle class, there was much to celebrate. By 1882 married women finally got control over their own property. Nine years later, legislation was passed making it unlawful for husbands to lock up their wives for refusing sexual relations and to beat them 'so long as the cane was no thicker than his thumb'. By the mid-1880s it was possible for women to vote in some local elections and for school boards, and in 1885 no fewer than 50 of them, including Helen Taylor, Harriet's daughter, were elected to the London School Board. And there were other subtler but no less subversive agencies at work—the latch key, the cheque book and the bicycle—all of which would render obsolete the Patmore fantasy of the hermetically isolated priestess of the domestic shrine.

If, on the other hand, you happened to be a 15-year-old East End girl and needed a pound or two to make the difference between food and famishing, fancy talk about repossessing the integrity of your body would not mean much. Middle-class women reformers had first become involved in the life of street girls in the 1850s. Led by Josephine Butler, they had campaigned more vocally against the double standard of the Contagious Diseases Act (1864), which required brutal physical inspection of prostitutes while doing nothing about diseased male clients. The Act was repealed in 1883, and in the same year the age of consent raised from 13 to 16, thanks to the efforts of the muckraking editor of the *Pall Mall Gazette*, W.T. Stead, who, to prove that his allegations about the trade in virgins were not a figment of his overheated imagination, went to the East End, bought one for himself, got her story and then turned the girl over to the Salvation Army.

Stead was one of the most eloquent of a generation bent on doing constructive damage to the complacency of late Victorian Britain as it moved towards the Queen's Golden Jubilee year of 1887. Instead of the middle classes reading the queen's sequel to her massive best-selling *Leaves from a Journal of Our Life in the Highlands*, with its picture of the royal couple taking tea with adoring crofters, Stead wanted them to wake up to the destitution of outcast London, and read George

Sims' *How the Poor Live* (1883). As far as Stead was concerned, the steady drumbeat of imperial self-congratulation, the histrionic wailing and weeping over the martyrdom of poor General Charles Gordon at Khartoum, and the elaborate fanfares tuning up for the queen were just so many charades masking a society divided between the swells and the slums. His pessimism was contagious. One day, warned the young George Bernard Shaw, sheer force of demographics would force a reckoning: 'Your slaves breed like rabbits, their poverty breeds filth, ugliness, dishonesty, disease, obscenity, drunkenness and murder. In the midst of the riches which they pile up for you their misery rises up and stifles you. You withdraw in disgust to the other end of town and yet they swarm about you still.'

It was, in fact, the apparent correlation between 'breeding' and poverty that moved one of the most daring young women of her generation, Annie Besant, to try to do something about it. In 1877, Besant, the estranged wife of a Lincolnshire clergyman, was tried alongside the atheist republican MP Charles Bradlaugh on a charge of obscenity. Their crime was to have reprinted a treatise, the 'Knowlton Pamphlet', originally published in 1830, euphemistically called *The Fruits of Philosophy* but actually full of practical advice on contraception. It was all very well, Besant and Bradlaugh believed, for the fashionable classes to have—and increasingly make use of—this knowledge, but until it had become part of working-class life there would be no possibility (especially in the hard times of the 1880s) of their ever being able to budget for survival, much less savings. All the high-minded lecturing that philanthropists such as Octavia Hill inflicted on her tenants in the Dwellings would be pointless hypocrisy unless poor families were given some control over their size. Bradlaugh and Besant went out of their way to make sure they would get prosecuted—and so attract the necessary publicity—by actually delivering copies of the book to the magistrates' clerks at the Guildhall.

During their trial—in which the Solicitor-General himself handled the prosecution—the two shamelessly used the proceedings to proselytize for sex education and birth control. They were eloquent enough for the judge to declare that he thought the case absurd. The jury was less enlightened, finding that, although the book was indeed obscene, the defendants had not meant to corrupt public morals. The order to desist from publishing was, of course, just what the accused were waiting for. They duly refused to abide by the judgement. Bradlaugh went to jail, but *The Fruits of Philosophy*, with its graphic description of pessaries, condoms and sponges, enjoyed brisk undercover sales for months.

Annie Besant suffered a harsher penalty for her temerity than prison. Her husband, who already had custody of their son, now brought a suit to remove their young daughter, Mabel, from her mother on the grounds that consorting with atheists and purveyors of filth proved beyond a shadow of a doubt that Annie was unfit to be a parent. The loss of her child threw Annie into a deep depression. What pulled her out of it was socialism. 'Modern civilisation,' she wrote in 1883, 'is a whited sepulchre . . . with its outer coating of princes and lords, of bankers and squires and within filled with men's bones, the bones of the poor who built it.' Two years later she joined the Fabians, who worked for a peaceful and democratic revolution.

The attraction of socialism to young, altruistically minded women of Annie's generation was an inadvertent payback for years of being told that their sex was supposed to be the softer, humane face of capitalism. Even John Stuart Mill had written of Harriet Taylor's governing impulses as social and humane while his were theoretical and mechanical. Now women could do something in keeping with this unasked-for assignment as nurses to the wounded of liberal capitalism—they could try to change it. This was what moved another young founding Fabian, Beatrice Potter (later Webb), to leave Octavia Hill's organization of philanthropical snoopers and go to live among the Lancashire mill girls of Bacup; she ended up editing the 17 volumes of Booth's *Life and Labour of the People in London* (1892-7).

Annie Besant found her workers' cause in the plight of the teenage match girls who worked for Bryant and May's at their Fairfield Works in the East End. The match girls had a history of conspicuous public action: they had participated in a mass demonstration at Victoria Park in 1871 against Gladstone's government's proposal to impose a tax on matches. The publicity was such that it moved even the queen to write indignantly to Gladstone that it would punish the poor much more heavily than the well-off and 'seriously affect the manufacture and sale of matches which is said to be the sole means of support for a vast number of the poorest people and LITTLE CHILDREN!'

The mass meeting and the march down the Mile End Road were shamelessly exploited by Bryant and May themselves, who had no interest at all in seeing their product penally taxed. When the measure was dropped, the company paid for a victory celebration and the construction of a drinking fountain in Bow Road.

The factory-feudal mobilization of their young workforce, however, backfired against Bryant and May a decade and a half later, when *The Link*, the crusading investigative halfpenny weekly founded by Stead and Annie Besant, published an article exposing the conditions under which the match girls worked. Wages were between 4 and 12 shillings a week, at least half of which went on rent for a single room, often shared with brothers and sisters. The girls were subject to a managerial regime of draconian severity. If they were judged to have dirty feet (few could afford shoes) or an untidy bench, fines would be deducted from their already meagre wages. Many of them suffered from the disfiguring condition of 'phossy jaw' caused by the phosphorus fumes they inhaled, at a time when other matchmaking companies had abandoned the chemical. Whilst the company claimed that narrow profit margins made it impossible for them to be more generous, it was paying hefty dividends to its shareholders, a disproportionate number of whom seemed to be Church of England clergymen. For the muckrakers this was pure gold. 'Do you know,' Annie asked rhetorically in *The Link*, piling on both the agony and the irony, 'that girls are used to carry boxes on their heads until the hair is rubbed off and their heads are bald at fifteen years of age? Country clergymen with shares in Bryant and May, draw down on your knee your fifteen year old daughter, pass your hand tenderly over the silky clustering curls, rejoice in the dainty beauty of the thick, shiny tresses.'

To crank up the publicity machine further, Besant stood outside the gates of the Fairfield Works along with her socialist colleague Herbert Burrows, handing out specially printed copies of the article to the match girls. A few days later a delegation of the girls came to their Fleet Street office to tell Besant and Burrows that they had been threatened with dismissal unless they signed a document repudiating the information contained in the article. Instead, they had gone straight to *The Link* with their story. 'You had spoken up', one of them told Annie. 'We weren't going back on you.' A strike committee was formed to resist the threats of the company. Photographs of the plucky, photogenically salt-of-the-earth girls were taken. In another brilliant and shaming stunt, Besant and Burrows solemnly promised to pay the wages of any girls dismissed for their action. George Bernard Shaw volunteered to be treasurer and cashier of the strike fund. Some 1400 of the girls came out. Hugely embarrassed and economically damaged by both the publicity and the stoppage, Bryant and May eventually settled, and the match girls won a rise in July 1888. Annie Besant was hailed as the champion of London working women and was immediately sought after by many other constituencies in need of a campaign—boot-finishers and the rabbit-fur pullers who worked for the felt trade in even more horrible conditions than the match girls. In 1888 Annie entered the political fray through the same route used by many of her generation of 'platform women': election to a school board, in this case Tower Hamlets. She campaigned from a dog cart festooned with red ribbons. Incredibly, 15,296 votes were cast for her.

Could the queen—just entering her 70s—comprehend, much less sympathize with, any of this? The answer is less straightforward than one might imagine. Her chosen role, now that she was a little more in the public eye again, was that of matriarch, and her motherliness or grand-motherliness extended to utterances and even acts of sympathy for the victims of an increasingly plutocratic Britain. She was much more likely to erupt in rage against the immorality, idleness and general worthlessness of the upper classes than the lower classes and took special exception to those who defamed the working families of Britain by painting a portrait of them soaked in beer and beastliness. She too read *The Bitter Cry of Outcast London* (1883), by the Congregationalist minister Andrew Mearns, and was so shaken by its revelations of the one million East Enders living in horrifyingly overcrowded and insanitary conditions that she pressed Gladstone's government to spend more of its time on the problem of housing for the poor. Her indignant pestering paid off with the setting up of a royal commission.

The last of Victoria's many roles—after English rose, model wife and grief-stricken widow—was that of imperial matriarch. As such, she genuinely felt herself to be mother or grandmother to all her people. But in the ever expanding household of her empire there were more and more orphans; millions kept shivering on its doorstep. And, lest the queen become unduly distressed at the spectacle in the streets, there were always servants who Knew What Was Best—to close the carriage blinds until cheerful, loyal throngs could be guaranteed. It is unlikely, for example, that Victoria would have known that on 19 March 1887, in her Jubilee year, fully 27 per cent of the 29,000 working men, when asked about their last job, replied that they were unemployed. A third of those had not worked in over three months. The previous year, in February 1886, she would certainly have noticed that something was unsettled. A mass meeting of unemployed dock and building workers in Trafalgar Square had listened to radical and socialist orators denounce the heartlessness of the rich and the unscrupulousness of capitalists. On their way to Parliament Square, the processing demonstrators were assaulted by missiles thrown from the open windows of Pall Mall clubs where the well-heeled members were jeering. The procession turned into a riot. Gangs looted shops; windows were smashed and carriages overturned.

Victoria gave Gladstone, whom she thought had no idea how to keep order, a piece of her mind: 'The Queen cannot sufficiently express her indignation at the monstrous riot which took place in London the other day and which risked people's lives and was a momentary triumph of socialism and a disgrace to the capital.' She consoled herself with the certainty (not entirely misplaced) that the vast majority of working people in Britain were of an unrevolutionary temper. When she went to Liverpool and Birmingham as a warm-up for the Jubilee celebrations, she saw nothing but adoring crowds cheering themselves hoarse, even though in

Birmingham she had been warned that she would be moving among the 'roughest' kind of people. During the summer festivities, tens of thousands of the unemployed who were sleeping in the parks of central London were turfed out and moved on to more remote heaths away from the royal gaze. Some used the open coffins that lay around in undertakers' yards as improvised beds. When she got to Hyde Park all Victoria saw were 30,000 poor schoolchildren, their faces well scrubbed, who each got a meat pie, a piece of cake and an orange to celebrate the great day. 'The children sang "God Save the Queen" ', she wrote, 'somewhat out of tune.'

All the people whom she really cared about expressed their devotion, starting with her own extended family, which had by now expanded to a small army. Exactly 50 years to the day after she had been woken, an 18-year-old in a nightdress, to be told she was queen, she rode in an open carriage from Buckingham Palace to Westminster, wearing not the state robes that she had been implored to don but her usual black and widow's cap. In front of the carriage were 12 Indian officers, and in front of them her posterity: 'My three sons, five sons-in-law, nine grandsons and grandsons-in-law. Then came the carriages containing my three other daughters, three daughters-in-law, granddaughters, one granddaughter-in-law.' The evening before, she had been surrounded by this enormous troop of royals, 'the Princes all in uniform and the Princesses . . . all beautifully dressed'. Two days later a deputation from 'The Women of England' presented her with a gift on behalf of millions of their sex. At Eton, as Victoria was *en route* to

Windsor Castle, it was the boys' turn. 'There was a beautiful triumphal arch, made to look exactly like part of the old College and boys dressed like Templars stood on top of it. The whole effect was beautiful, lit up by the sun of a summer evening.' On the Isle of Wight, the general good cheer was so heartwarming that a toothy smile broke out between the plump cheeks. Her private secretary's wife, Lady Ponsonby, claimed it happened more often than people imagined, coming 'very suddenly in the form of a mild radiance over the whole face, a softening, a raising of the lines of the lips, a flash of kindly light beaming from the eyes'.

It would be like this for the rest of her life, through another Jubilee a decade later: the country bathed in summer evening light; the throngs on the street, much flag-waving; brass bands from barracks and collieries; a great Handel–Harty coda on the opening night of the big round Albert Hall, finished at last. But *that* reminded her that there was someone missing from the family photographs. In Westminster Abbey, in June 1887, she felt the sudden pang and wrote that 'I sat alone (OH!) without my beloved husband for whom this would have been such a proud day.' It would be another 14 years before she would be reunited with 'him to whom I and the nation owe so much'. Sir Henry Frederick Ponsonby, her private secretary, said that there was nothing Victoria enjoyed so much as arranging funerals, and her own was no exception. This would be the one occasion when, in anticipation of her reunion, she would doff the widow's black. When she had taken Tennyson into the mausoleum at Frogmore, 'I observed that it was light and bright, which he thought a great point.' So

Victoria ordered an all white funeral. The queen was robed in white, her body covered with cheerful sprays of spring flowers like some bedecked virgin bride. Some of them, however, had to be tactfully placed since, along with the locks of hair, rings and many other keepsakes she had ordered to be placed in the coffin with her, there was also, embarrassingly, in her *left* hand, a photograph of John Brown; it was carefully concealed by lilies and freesias.

There was another problem, too, that Victoria had left for the managers of the obsequies. For, when Albert's memorial effigy had been ordered from the sculptor Carlo Marochetti in 1862, Victoria had insisted on hers being made at the same time, and in the likeness of her at exactly the time the prince had been taken from her. (If anything Marochetti followed his orders too well, and made Victoria seem more like she had been when they were first married.) They were supposed to be reunited, at least in marble, at the same age they had been in the glowing prime of their union. The trouble was that this had been so long ago that no one could seem to remember where the Victoria sculpture was. It was finally discovered behind one of the walls of a renovated room in Windsor Castle. The image of a young, medieval princess lies next to her *preux chevalier* as if the clocks had stopped along with the heart of the Prince Consort.

But Albert, above all others, knew that they had not; that progress had indeed been the mainspring of his modern century. By 1900 that progress had extended beyond anything he could have imagined—and not just to science, technology and commerce, but to the lives of Britain's women.

Education and politics had begun to give the angels in the house an altogether earthier set of ambitions. And those subtle but powerful revolutionaries, the latch key, the cheque book and the bicycle, would go a long way to realizing them.

Young ladies would never be quite the same. Riding with the body of Queen Victoria from London to Windsor was Lady Lytton, the widow of one of her viceroys of India, the Earl of Lytton. Seven years later her daughter Lady Constance, in prison as a militant suffragette, hunger-striker and compulsive cell-scrubber, would make *her* statement about the future of women in Britain by desecrating the 'temple of purity' so slavishly adored by the fetishists of domestic life. Her idea was to carve the slogan of her movement on her upper body all the way up to her face. She chose a piece of broken enamel from a hatpin as her tool of mutilation, but it took her 20 minutes to carve a great 'V' on her breast before the prison officers caught her in the act. Never mind. 'Con' had made her statement. It was 'V' not for Victoria, but for Votes.